Which "Real" Jesus?

Which "Real" Jesus?

Jonathan Edwards, Benjamin Franklin,
and the Early American Roots of the Current Debate

STEVE BATEMAN

WIPF & STOCK · Eugene, Oregon

WHICH "REAL" JESUS?
Jonathan Edwards, Benjamin Franklin, and the Early American Roots
of the Current Debate

Wipf & Stock
A Division of Wipf and Stock Publishers
199 W. 8th Ave., Suite 3
Eugene, OR 97401

www.wipfandstock.com

ISBN 13: 978-1-55635-931-6

Manufactured in the U.S.A.

All Scripture quotations, unless otherwise indicated, are taken from the *Holy Bible:
New International Version*, Copyright 1973, 1978, 1984 by the International Bible
Society.

Contents

Acknowledgments

I HAVE BEEN UNCOMMONLY blessed with mentors marked by character and competence. From Dr. Johnny Miller, I learned to love teaching the Bible. From Dr. Robertson McQuilkin, I learned to love missions. From Dr. Bob Livesay, I learned to love the pastorate. From Dr. Ken Horton, I learned to love (some parts) of church administration. From Dr. Darrell Bock, I learned to love the Gospels. From Dr. Timothy George, I learned to love Reformation history. From Dr. John Hannah, I learned to love Jonathan Edwards.

Dr. Hannah in particular encouraged me that I had something here worth writing about and that he actually thought I could write it. I am especially indebted to Dr. Bock, Dr. George, and Dr. Hannah for their review of a manuscript written by a rookie author. Once again, Cynthia McPherson rescued me, as she did with my dissertation a few years ago, from the painstaking process of copy-editing.

Dr. Kenneth Minkema was exceptionally generous with his time in fielding my questions and getting me oriented at the Beineke Rare Book and Manuscript Library at Yale University. Dr. Adriaan C. Neele at Yale's Jonathan Edwards Center was also very helpful during my research visit there, helping me edit some of Edwards's unpublished sermon manuscripts. I also received gracious treatment from the library staff at Samford University in Birmingham, Alabama.

I have been exceedingly blessed with an understanding and supportive church family. I have served the members of First Bible Church of Decatur for over sixteen years, and they have served me right back! Many of them through the years have told me, "You ought to write a book." What pastor is not encouraged by that? Well, here it is! The Elders not only allowed, but insisted, that I take a sabbatical to finish the manuscript.

My children, Josh and Joy, could not have been more supportive and helpful, and will never know how grateful I am to God for their love and worship of the real Jesus.

Above all, I would have never written this book without the constant, faithful, and reassuring encouragement of my wife, Lori.

Introduction

*And he is the head of the body, the church; he is the beginning
and the firstborn from among the dead, so that in everything
he might have the supremacy.*

—Paul the Apostle[1]

*With apologies to the ladies, one is inclined to paraphrase an old saying:
'There are only three things not worth running for—a bus, a woman,
and a reported disclosure of the real Jesus; if you wait a little while,
another will come along.'*

—Richard John Neuhaus[2]

THE COVERS OF THE bestselling magazines in America routinely announce the breathtaking news of a revised Jesus. Recent discoveries and groundbreaking scholarship threaten to set aside traditional, orthodox[3] Christianity and give us a new and improved view of its founder. Competing groups claim to have found the "real Jesus," and because they are all so different, they cannot all be right. Which "real Jesus" shall we choose?

Jesus knew that his followers would encounter innumerable cases of identity theft. "Many will come in my name," he warned them, "claiming, 'I am he,' and will deceive many."[4] Jesus's questions to his disciples still

---

1. Colossians 1:18.

2. Neuhaus, "While We're At It," 65.

3. In this book, I will use the word *orthodox* in its common sense of something established or traditional, thus referring to the historic, traditional, apostolic Christian faith. It should not be confused with the word *Orthodox*, referring to the eastern branch of the Christian family.

4. Mark 13:6.

ring with relevance: "But what about you?" he asked. "Who do you say I am?"[5] Jesus did not want his disciples to get their Jesuses confused. From the beginning, they preached Jesus in a way to avoid confusion. Someone might ask them, "Which Jesus are you talking about?" "God has raised *this* Jesus to life," Peter proclaimed at Pentecost, "God has made *this* Jesus, whom you crucified, both Lord and Christ."[6] Paul was equally clear in Thessalonica where he was "explaining and proving that the Christ had to suffer and rise from the dead. '*This* Jesus I am proclaiming to you is the Christ.'"[7] Which Jesus? *This* Jesus!

The apostles warned the early church about religious leaders who would replace the original with an alternative. When the Corinthian church took pride in their uncritical, man-pleasing tolerance, the Apostle Paul was not favorably impressed. "For if someone comes to you and preaches a Jesus other than the Jesus we preached," exhorted Paul, "or if you receive a different spirit from the one you received, or a different Gospel from the one you accepted, you put up with it easily enough."[8]

Across America, even in many churches that once held the line on orthodoxy, Jesus is being dethroned, deconstructed, revised, and replaced with alternative Jesuses. Of course, each rival group claims to have in their possession the "real Jesus." As a result, many Christians are losing confidence in the uniqueness and supremacy of Jesus Christ.

But we should not be alarmed. Every generation tries to improve Jesus by making him less than he claimed to be and more like they want him to be. This impulse folds neatly into the growing popularity of religious pluralism and the rather old idea that "all the religions are basically the same." The more we can make Jesus like the rest of us, the less demands he can make on our lives. What makes Jesus so different, after all? And what is so distinctive about Christianity that sets it apart from other religions? These are fair questions and Christians ought to be prepared to answer them.

As it turns out, we are not in new territory. The new views of the real Jesus are old news. Christians in America have faced these challenges before. In the years immediately before and after the founding of the

5. Luke 9:18–20.

6. Acts 2:32, 36. Italics mine.

7. Acts 17:3. Italics mine.

8. 2 Corinthians 11:4.

United States, the possibility of a new and improved Jesus was a hot issue. Jonathan Edwards and Benjamin Franklin contemplated the real identity of Jesus decades before the signing of the Declaration of Independence. And several influential Founding Fathers gave serious thought to the question, Which Jesus is the real Jesus? This is a book about the early American roots of the current debate on the real Jesus. The questions being raised in the eighteenth century are startlingly relevant today:

- Are the Gospels reliable accounts of Jesus?
- Did Jesus claim to be God?
- Was Jesus bodily raised from the dead?
- Is Jesus the only way to heaven?
- Are Christianity and Islam basically the same?
- Were the Founding Fathers orthodox Christians?
- What did Jesus say about faith and politics?

You may be curious about Jesus, and find yourself drawn to him, but you also stumble over legitimate questions like these. I have struggled with these questions myself through the years, and this book is largely the product of my own quest for some answers. If my answers do not satisfy you, that does not mean there are no answers. Throughout this book, I will refer you to many people who are authorities in this field if you want more information.

If this book helps any reader know, love, obey, and exalt Jesus Christ, my purpose in writing will have been accomplished. Secondarily, but importantly, if any reader grows in appreciation for the remarkable contribution of Jonathan Edwards, not only to our understanding of the real Jesus but to the history of America, I will be a happier man. Jonathan Edwards is widely viewed as America's greatest theologian and philosopher. But he was a local pastor, not a college or seminary professor, and he took seriously his duty to prepare his congregation—people who spent their weekdays running businesses, selling products, building houses, teaching school, growing crops, administering government, and raising children—to "contend for the faith that was once for all entrusted to the saints."[9] He had high expectations of lay people to understand the issues and engage the culture for Jesus's sake. Today's pastors can do no less, and this book is my earnest attempt to follow the example of Jonathan Edwards.

9. Jude 3.

2

Jesus in America, 1758

*Our willingness to hear the voices of Franklin and Edwards, and to edit
their work and celebrate their achievement two centuries after their death,
pays tribute to their genius and to the power of their representativeness in
our conception of culture.*

—David Levin[1]

*It was Edwards who attempted to induce New England to lead a godly, not
sober life; it was Franklin who succeeded in teaching Americans to lead a
sober and not a godly life.*

—Herbert Schneider[2]

*The world of the founding grandfathers shaped the attitudes of the
Founding Fathers.*

—Steven Waldman[3]

CHRISTOPHER HITCHENS IS A smart man. It says so right on the dust
cover of his best-selling 2007 book, *God Is Not Great: How Religion
Poisons Everything.* "To his own amusement," we are told, Hitchens was
named "number five on a list of the 'Top 100 Public Intellectuals' by
Foreign Policy and Britain's *Prospect.*" [4] And now Christopher Hitchens is
on a mission. With the religious zeal of an itinerant evangelist, he travels the
world declaring his gospel. What is the good news? God did not create us.

1. Levin, "Reason, Rhythm, and Style," 184.

2. From a broadside for an exhibition, "Preaching and Printing: Jonathan Edwards,
Benjamin Franklin, and the Popular Mind," held between January 19 and March 30, 1990,
at the Beineke Rare Book and Manuscript Library, Yale University.

3. Waldman, *Founding Faith*, 17.

4. Hitchens, *God is Not Great*, dustcover.

Rather we created God. God does not exist, and the sooner we instill this in our children, the sooner we will eliminate the single greatest cause of war, cruelty, mayhem, and disease in our world today. Religion kills. In an effort to save the world, Christopher Hitchens is a missionary for atheism.

Since September 11, 2001, we have come to expect these kinds of books to climb up the best-selling list each year. Religion is what killed people in the Twin Towers of New York and the Pentagon in Washington, D.C. Religion kills people in Afghanistan and Iraq, Lebanon and Syria, Israel and Gaza, Somalia and Sudan. To eliminate the killing, we must eliminate religion. To eliminate religion, we must eliminate God.

That has been a hard sell in the United States, the most religious techno-industrial nation on the planet. "In God We Trust" is right there on our coins. To be an atheist, even to suggest the improbability of the Christian God, is just un-American. But an important strategy of evangelistic atheists like Christopher Hitchens is showing Americans just how American it is to distrust God. To do that, they often appeal to the founders of the United States. Hitchens does not disappoint, and one of his favorite founders is Benjamin Franklin.

Franklin, Hitchens tells us, was a brilliant thinker who had to keep his thoughts to himself. As a political figure, revealing his true thoughts concerning God would have wreaked havoc on what we would call today a "high approval rating." Even though Franklin publicly credited God with leading him to the invention of the lightning rod, Franklin privately believed, according to Hitchens, that God did not intervene in our lives much at all.[5] Why the duplicity? Franklin was fearful of the social and political fallout in eighteenth century America if he did not credit God with the invention. How does Hitchens know this about Franklin's private beliefs? He just knows it.[6]

It has never been more important for American Christians to understand American history. On one extreme, many in the church hold a naïve understanding of a Christian Nation, reading more into the public expressions of faith by some of our founders than is actually there, misunderstanding the religious language of the eighteenth century. To talk

---

5. Ibid., 266.

6. Ibid., 266. "You may choose to believe, of course, that Franklin sincerely meant every word of it . . ." but Hitchens does not. For more on Hitchens's penetrating insight, see page 3: "I simply knew it, almost as if I had privileged access to a higher authority, that my teacher had managed to get everything wrong in just two sentences."

of God, even a God of fatherly benevolence and kingly providence, is not necessarily to talk of the God of orthodox Christianity. There really were political motives for leaders to speak openly about God, fasting, praying, and humbling oneself before the Almighty. But to talk about Jesus Christ is quite another thing, and several founders were averse to it. Reacting to the threat of militant atheists like Christopher Hitchens, some Christians unwisely gloss over America's founders, making Christ-followers of those who were not. In reality, we have much to learn about the founders from people like Hitchens, if we will but listen.

On the other extreme we find those Christians who not only listen, but are also persuaded. Perhaps reacting against their naïve brethren, and seeking to be associated with smart people who make the top 100 lists of intellectuals, they buy what Hitchens sells. Often, that very appeal to intellectual snobbery is the draw. Magazine covers routinely announce, just in time for Christmas and Easter, another remarkable new discovery concerning the historical Jesus. "Evidence" is produced. "Experts" are interviewed. "Scholars" weigh in. The debate is framed in a way that puts orthodox Christians at a disadvantage from the start. Either you can believe the Bible or you can become a scholar, but you cannot do both.

What is surprising is how often the Founding Fathers are summoned to testify in this court of religious opinion. Why? I propose that the answer comes in two parts. In the first part, producing a founder (or two or more) who held to an alternative Christianity (a religion that shows some respect for Jesus but denies his uniqueness, deity, and supremacy)[7] demonstrates that it is not at all un-American to be unorthodox. Jesus can be improved, conveniently reshaped, to accommodate a new generation and advance an updated agenda. In the process, orthodox Christianity is discredited. In the second part, once alternative Christianities gain legitimacy by connecting with a Founding Father, anti-religionists like Hitchens can use the same arguments used by these early American advocates of alternative Christianities to do even more damage to the credibility of orthodox Christianity. And orthodox Christianity, having exerted a potent cultural influence in America since before 1776, is a strategic target.

In the end, strident atheists, intoxicated with their own intelligence and braced by a stunning confidence in human reason, leverage alternative

7. I credit New Testament scholar Darrell Bock for the term "alternative Christianities" from his book *The Missing Gospels: Unearthing the Truth Behind Alternative Christianities* (2006).

Christianities to serve their own agenda. That agenda certainly includes the removal of Christian influence from the public square.[8] In short, advocates of alternative Christianities want to *improve* Jesus, while advocates of aggressive atheism (like Hitchens) take the next logical step, which is to *remove* Jesus. It seems to me that we can go a long way toward defusing the challenge of atheism if we strongly meet the arguments of alternative Christianities. The process of improving Jesus actually results in removing Jesus, and that is just alright for people like Christopher Hitchens.

This very public, and often nasty, debate did not first arise after 9/11. In the years leading up to the founding of the United States, Benjamin Franklin had to deal with the enduring influence of Jonathan Edwards, and in numerous ways, Edwards guides us in confronting alternative Christianities. If we understand some significant things that happened in America three hundred years ago, a half-century before the infamous year of 1776, we might gain a better understanding of what is happening in our nation today.

EDWARDS AND FRANKLIN AS "REPRESENTATIVE MEN"

Jonathan Edwards was born in East Windsor, Connecticut, in 1703, and Benjamin Franklin was born in Boston in 1706, three years and one hundred miles apart. Though their paths would often cross, we have no record that they ever met.[9] Edwards is considered by many historians to be "the most acute early American philosopher and the most brilliant of all American theologians,"[10] not to mention the "greatest systematic thinker of the day."[11] Benjamin Franklin was "America's best scientist, inventor, diplomat, writer, and business strategist and he was also one of its most

---

8. Hitchens is not covert about his intentions. His mind is made up that science and reason have proven the non-existence of God. He does not care what believers do, "now that their faith is optional ... as long as they make no further attempt to inculcate religion by any form of coercion," (96) stop "imposing [their religious beliefs] on all other citizens," and are "kept out of" diplomatic negotiations (24). It would be naïve to assume that Hitchens does not have an agenda, especially when he states that he does. To be fair, I have no reason not to take him at his word that he really believes that the removal of a Christian presence from the public square would improve the quality of life for all people.

9. George Marsden says that if they ever met, it was during Edwards's trip to Philadelphia in 1755. Marsden, *Jonathan Edwards*, 419.

10. Marsden, *Jonathan Edwards*, 1

11. May, *Enlightenment in America*, 54.

practical, though not most profound, political thinkers."[12] Admittedly, the closest rival that Franklin had for the title of "best writer" at that time would be Jonathan Edwards, "who was certainly more intense and literary, though far less felicitous and amusing."[13] It is hard to imagine American history without either man.

The intriguing parallels and staggered intersections of their lives have not gone unnoticed by historians. Because their significant careers overlapped and intersected, they are considered by many to be "arch-symbols"[14] of the eighteenth century. As early as 1840, historians viewed them as "representative men"[15] at the head of two opposing worldviews in American history that exist to this day. Princeton scholar Barbara Oberg and Yale historian Harry Stout cannot think of "two more widely studied colonial figures"[16] than Franklin and Edwards. Drew University professor Leonard Sweet insists they "have embodied for historians the contrary tendencies of their age."[17]

Franklin has certainly received more positive attention by published historians and teachers instructing children in American history. He is, after all, a grown man who flies kites, "the founding father who winks at us,"[18] not high-born, but a common man who pulled himself up by his own bootstraps, extolling the virtue of hard work, exuding practical ingenuity, achieving financial security, and all the while doing good to others. What could be more American? He is an irreverent, affable, flirtatious, approachable prankster. When we read his works, he points us to ourselves, and makes us laugh.

Edwards, on the other hand, is often caricaturized as a stern, judgmental moral policeman, a stereotype based largely on what one biographer calls "the best-known and least-read sermon in American history—'Sinners in the Hands of an Angry God.'"[19] I would add that even when it is read in this generation, it is the least understood. In truth, those

---

12. Isaacson, *Benjamin Franklin*, 2.

13. Ibid., 61.

14. Leonard Sweet attributes this term to Harvard University professor Perry Miller (1905-1963). Sweet, "Laughter," 114, 127.

15. Oberg and Stout, *Benjamin Franklin, Jonathan Edwards*, 3.

16. Ibid.

17. Sweet, "Laughter," 115.

18. Isaacson, *Benjamin Franklin*, 2.

19. Sweet, "Laughter," 115.

who care to dig beneath the stereotype will find a beer-drinking,[20] pipe-smoking Puritan, bristling with brilliance. Uncommonly self-disciplined, he was deadly serious in his disparagement of replacing God-dependence with self-reliance. When we read his works, he points us to God and makes us think. Already, Edwards is at a disadvantage in America's feel-good culture.

In the main, the tendencies represented by Franklin have been victorious in America, dominating the culture, especially in the elite institutions of government, education, arts, entertainment, and media. But Notre Dame historian George Marsden has wisely noted "a good case can be made that stories of America are deficient if they do not at least temper emphasis on the Franklins of the heritage with a serious reckoning with its Edwardses." Marsden continues, "Most strikingly, the standard narratives fail to account for why levels of religious practice came to be much higher in the United States than in other modernized nations."[21]

Scholars have compared and contrasted Edwards and Franklin for over a hundred and fifty years on numerous topics such as personality, humor, rhetoric, philosophy, virtue, morality, views of human nature, and politics. But my focus will be on what I believe to be the central and defining difference between the two men, and the two cultures that have co-existed in America since the eighteenth century: their views of Jesus Christ.

Jonathan Edwards represents a view of Jesus that is orthodox, historical, and apostolic. He presented Jesus to the world as the New Testament presents him: sovereign God in the flesh, creator, redeemer, risen savior of the world, supreme judge of the universe, worthy of worship and deserving of praise. Benjamin Franklin is respectful but restrained as he represents a new and revised Jesus. To Franklin, Jesus was good but not

---

20. We have his family's beer mug and clay pipes (See Sweet, 119). Many readers may be surprised that Puritans were not wholly averse to all alcoholic beverages. In the long age of human history prior to refrigeration and access to large amounts of pure drinking water, this liquid nourishment sustained many a metabolism. In its most famous transatlantic journey, the Mayflower held much more beer (11,000 gallons) than drinking water (1500 gallons) (Hodgson, *Great and Godly Adventure,* 65). Samuel Adams, sometimes referred to as the Last Puritan, inherited the family brewery in Boston. However, Edwards, like all Puritan pastors, never advocated drinking in excess and throughout his life consistently warned against the abuse of alcohol. Benjamin Franklin joined Edwards in criticizing "tavern-haunting" but for different reasons.

21. Marsden, *Jonathan Edwards,* 9.

God, powerful but not sovereign, admirable but not the object of worship. Franklin intended to improve Jesus and, in his mind, make him more useful for the civic and social purposes of a new nation. In short, Benjamin Franklin was not only one of the founders of the United States, but also one of the founders of alternative Christianities in America.

TEENAGERS IN NEW YORK, 1723

The orbits of Edwards and Franklin came tantalizingly close for half a century. At the age of nineteen, Jonathan Edwards, freshly graduated with an M.A. from Yale, took his first pastorate in New York City, population about eight thousand. The Presbyterian Church at Wall Street and Broadway had experienced a sad division, and a group withdrew to form another church a few blocks away. The newly formed congregation invited the young Edwards to serve as a supply pastor. New York was the most bustling and cosmopolitan city Edwards would ever see, and he would often retreat "to a solitary place, on the banks of the Hudson River, at some distance from the city" for prayer and Bible study, spending "many sweet hours there."[22] Minister and church family grew to love one another deeply in the brief time they had together, but after eight months, Edwards reluctantly left New York City. His departure in May of 1723 was probably at the urging of his father, who wanted him to return to Connecticut to serve as minister of a small church in Bolton. As he left New York Harbor, Edwards gazed with a heavy heart, on the city where, as he would later write, "I had enjoyed so many sweet and pleasant days."[23]

When he was seventeen, Benjamin Franklin knew he had no future in Boston. As a printer apprentice to his brother, James, he could no longer tolerate what he considered an unfair arrangement. Breaking the bonds of an apprenticeship was a serious matter in 1723, and when young Benjamin abandoned his brother, James made sure that no other printer in Boston would hire him. Because his father and brother would have prevented him from leaving Boston, Franklin secretly enlisted the help of a friend. "He agreed," wrote Franklin, "with the Captain of a New York Sloop for my Passage, under the Notion of my being a young Acquaintance of his

---

22. Edwards, *Works*, 16:797. Unless otherwise indicated, "Edwards, *Works*," refers to the Yale Edition of Edwards's works, while "Edwards, *The Works of Jonathan Edwards*" refers to the Hickman Edition of Edwards's works.

23. Ibid., 16:797–78.

that had got a naughty Girl with Child, whose Friends would compel me to marry her, and therefore I could not appear or come away publickly."[24] Franklin sold a few precious books from his small library to pay for the stealthy voyage, and the captain hid Franklin on board until they reached New York three days later. It was September of 1723. Four months after Jonathan Edwards left New York with honor, Benjamin Franklin arrived in disgrace.

THE PREACHER AND THE PRINTER, 1742

Franklin, among other things, was a shrewd businessman. As a publisher in Philadelphia, he knew that controversy sells books. He did not agree with George Whitefield, the famous evangelist of the Great Awakening, on many important points, but that did not keep Franklin from publishing some of his writings.[25] Franklin also had profound differences with the Calvinist and Father of English Hymnody, Isaac Watts, but it was Franklin, the Printer, who introduced the first American edition of Watts's hymns in 1724.[26]

Likewise, when Jonathan Edwards delivered a rather controversial sermon at his alma mater, Yale College, challenging Yale's president and trustees, Benjamin Franklin did not hesitate to publish Edwards's address.[27] We also know that Franklin read Edwards's work. In July 1744, Franklin wrote to his sister, Jane, who had expressed concern, spurred by Franklin's sporadic church attendance, that he was against worshipping God and relying too heavily on his good works to merit heaven. "Both are fancies of your own," he wrote, "I think, without foundation." To make his point that good works cannot be uncoupled from a God-pleasing life, Franklin appeals to a theologian that Jane respected: "Read the pages of Mr. Edwards's late book entitled *Some Thoughts concerning the present Revival of Religion in N. E.* [New England] from 367 to 375."[28] Surely "Jenny," as he referred to her, being an orthodox Christian, could not have

---

24. Franklin, *Autobiography*, 71.

25. Marsden, *Jonathan Edwards*, 203.

26. Sweet, "Laughter," 115. And speaking of firsts, Franklin printed *The Constitution of the Free-Masons* (1734), "the first Masonic book printed in America." Ibid.

27. This was "Distinguishing Marks of a Work of the Spirit of God." See also Marsden, *Jonathan Edwards*, 235, 552.

28. Franklin, *Works*, 7:8, 9.

disagreed with the great Jonathan Edwards. So throughout their days on this earth, the lives of these two fascinating men continued to intersect. Edwards and Franklin, as representative men, were, in the words of one historian, "The Preacher and the Printer."[29]

A MUTUAL PHYSICIAN FRIEND, 1758

The diverse competencies of Benjamin Franklin are stunning: printer, author, scientist, inventor, politician, philosopher, and diplomat. But Franklin was a practical man, and his interests did not remain theoretical. Understanding electricity, for example, was fascinating, but for Franklin, the ultimate quest was putting electricity to some practical use. And so, in the spring of 1749, he gathered with friends at the home of Dr. William Shippen in Philadelphia. Shippen, a physician who would later serve in the Continental Congress, was in the circle of Philadelphia's intellectual and social elite led by Benjamin Franklin. In fact, Shippen and Franklin were instrumental in founding what would become the University of Pennsylvania. It was at the Shippen House that Benjamin Franklin first put electricity to good use. He built a primitive battery and used it to shock a turkey to death, which, he later claimed, improved the flavor of the meat. Then, to the delight of the dinner guests, he used the battery to power the spit over the roasting fire.[30]

But Dr. Shippen had other famous friends. On February 16, 1758, Jonathan Edwards had just been installed as the third president of the College of New Jersey, now Princeton University, where Shippen was on the Board of Trustees. Edwards was an advocate of the controversial practice of smallpox inoculation and Shippen agreed to inoculate Edwards and his family. While the rest of the family recovered, Edwards's inoculation did not go well. He had experienced a serious fall from a horse several months earlier and was probably in a weakened state at the time of the inoculation. On March 22, after only one month of serving as its third president, Jonathan Edwards died in the President's House at Princeton. Writing to Edwards's wife Sarah, who had not yet moved to Princeton, Shippen assured her that "never did any mortal man more fully and clearly evidence the sincerity of all his professions, by one continued, uni-

---

29. Breitenbach, "Religious Affections and Religious Affectations," 14.
30. Isaacson, *Benjamin Franklin*, 136–37.

versal, calm, cheerful resignation, and patient submission to the divine will, through every stage of his disease, than he."[31]

Dr. Shippen's communication with Sarah Edwards would shortly become even more personal. In the fall of 1758, Sarah traveled to Philadelphia to pick up the two orphaned children of her daughter Esther Burr who had died in April. Sarah could not have known then that her grandson, Aaron Jr., would grow up to become the third vice-president of the United States and kill Alexander Hamilton in a famous duel in 1804. But in 1758, doubtless burdened with the brutal grief of losing a husband and a daughter in a two-month span, Sarah's body could endure no more. While in Philadelphia she was stricken with dysentery and was cared for by Dr. Shippen in his home where she died on October 2 at the age of forty-eight. In the cleverly caustic words of Leonard Sweet, the Shippen House, "the home where the beautiful wife of the man known for barbecuing sinners over the coal pits of hell died, is also the home where Franklin introduced his battery-operated spit, America's first rotisserie."[32]

THE GOSPEL ACCORDING TO JONATHAN EDWARDS

This book focuses on four main tenets of historic Christianity and how Edwards defended them against attack. Here is what Edwards, as well as the overwhelming majority of Christian denominations represented in America at the time, believed about Jesus Christ:

1. Gospels: The New Testament account of the life of Jesus is reliable and authoritative.

2. God: Jesus claimed to be God and those who knew him best presented him to the world as God.

3. Grave: After dying on the cross in the place of sinners, Jesus was bodily raised from the dead, validating his claim to be God.

4. Grace: All who are saved from eternal judgment and reconciled to God are saved by grace alone through faith alone in Jesus alone.

31. Marsden, *Jonathan Edwards*, 494.
32. Sweet, "Laughter," 114.

EXAMPLES OF EDWARDS PATRIOTS

Edwards scholars have often speculated about the position he would have taken on the Revolution, had he lived as long as Franklin. What we do know is that by 1776, virtually all of the congregational ministers in New England supported independence, fearing, among other things, the encroachment of the state-sponsored Church of England. History had demonstrated in Old England that Anglican dominance would not be favorable for the gospel. We also know that most of Edwards's followers and protégés favored independence. However, by calling these founders "Edwards Patriots," I do not mean I am confident about which way Edwards would have voted on American independence and armed revolution against the crown.[33] Neither do I mean that all of their political views and strategies were consistent with the teachings of Christ. They were not. My point is that these are Founding Fathers who shamelessly held to orthodox Christianity to the end of their lives. All were imperfect men, and much in need of grace.

Samuel Adams, hailed as early as his death announcement in Boston's *Independent Chronicle* as "The Father of the American Revolution,"[34] considered by some to be "the last of the Puritans,"[35] was born in 1722, the same year Jonathan Edwards moved to New York. Adams was instrumental in organizing and energizing the non-violent protests, boycotts, and redress of grievances against England that culminated in the Declaration of Independence. He, more than any single man, kept the American colonies united in those early years of protest. He served in the Massachusetts Legislature and the Continental Congress working closely with Franklin, Washington, and Jefferson. While a student at Harvard, he was influenced by the Great Awakening. His mother became an ardent follower of Edwards,[36] and his sister, Mary, a persuasive presence in Adams's life, carefully wrote down the sermons of visiting preachers in Boston, including Edwards, recording the Bible verses and studying the texts.

---

33. Evangelicals like John Wesley on the other side of the Atlantic scolded their American brethren harshly for their sin of rebellion against governing authorities in violation of Romans 13. See Wesley's *A Calm Address*.

34. Cited in Puls, *Samuel Adams*, 231.

35. Holmes, *Faiths of the Founding Fathers*, 143.

36. Ibid., 145.

In an age when public figures were inclined to use more deistic and generic references to God, Adams was unashamed to refer specifically to the authority of Scripture, the deity of Christ, salvation by grace alone, and the physical resurrection, even in state documents.[37] His commitment to orthodox Christianity, as received and taught by Jonathan Edwards, was "indisputable," writes David Holmes. "He opposed Freemasonry, led his family in grace before meals, read to them from the Bible, led morning and evening devotions in the household, and strictly observed the Lord's Day."[38] But Adams did not trust in these good works for eternal salvation. In his will, he entrusted "my soul to that Almighty Being who gave it, and my body I commit to the dust, relying on the merits of Jesus Christ for a pardon for all my sins."[39]

Other Edwards Patriots include Patrick Henry, the Voice of the American Revolution; John Jay, the first Chief Justice of the Supreme Court; John Witherspoon, sixth president of Princeton and the only clergy member to sign the Declaration of Independence; and Elias Boudinot, President of the Continental Congress (1782–1783). Because Boudinot was serving as President of the Continental Congress when the Treaty of Paris was concluded, he is considered by many to be the first president of the United States, rather than George Washington.

THE GOSPEL ACCORDING TO BENJAMIN FRANKLIN

Before we go further, I need to introduce you to deism, a belief system that had become fashionable during the lifetimes of Jonathan Edwards and Benjamin Franklin. There is no formal deist creed or confession of faith, but historians and philosophers have noted some major tenets of deism:

1. There is only one God.
2. God is morally and intellectually perfect.
3. God created, sustains, and orders the world through the laws of nature.
4. The events of the world are therefore governed by natural laws, or general providence.

---

37. Holmes, *Faiths of the Founding Fathers*, 146.
38. Ibid.
39. Ibid.

5. God does not interfere with these natural laws through miracles, or special providence.

6. God made men with the ability to discern truth and morality through their reason. (Therefore, there is no need for revelation such as the Bible, which would be a miracle anyway, and God does not do miracles.)

7. God holds men responsible to obey the natural law.

8. The highest worship of God is to lead a moral life and do good to others.

9. God has given men immortal souls.

10. After death, each person will be judged by his or her works. Those who lived moral lives are rewarded, those who did not are punished.[40]

It is often claimed that Benjamin Franklin was a deist. The veracity of the claim may depend on which season of Franklin's life is in question. In general, his younger years were marked by a defiant skepticism concerning Christianity, fed by an understandable revulsion to the hypocrisy he saw in the churches of New England. After seeking to satiate his youthful and carnal appetites, he experienced compelling guilt and came back around to seeing the usefulness of morality in making a man happy and prosperous. It is probable that he was a deist for a season of his life, enamored by deist authors, but later moderated his views, moving back toward orthodoxy. For example, the deistic idea of a clockmaker God who created the world, set it in motion, then withdrew, leaving creation to be governed by natural law seems to be countermanded by Franklin's famous motion for prayers in the Constitutional Convention, June 28, 1787:

> And have we now forgotten that powerful Friend? Or do we imagine we no longer need its assistance? I have lived, Sir, a long time; and the longer I live, the more convincing proofs I see of this Truth, that God governs in the Affairs of Men. And if a Sparrow cannot fall to the Ground without his Notice, is it probable that an Empire can rise without his Aid?[41]

While it looks like Franklin, in his eighties, turned back to a more biblical notion of God, it is likely that he never returned to an orthodox view

---

40. Novak and Novak, *Washington's God*, 110. I have paraphrased the Novaks's list.
41. Franklin, *Works*, 5:154. The motion failed to pass.

16

of Jesus. The influence of deism[42] on Benjamin Franklin never seems to have relented with regard to the four core tenets of historic, orthodox Christianity.

1. Gospels: Franklin believed the Scriptural account of the life of Christ was flawed and useful only in the moral system presented in the New Testament. The Old Testament, to Franklin and all deists, was brutal, backward, and nearly worthless.

2. God: Franklin successfully navigated controversial issues, avoided confrontation, and maintained his popularity by being discreet and subversive. He was, after all, a political animal, who manipulated and maneuvered his way into the highest echelons of American power. We have no formal statement by Franklin that assures us of his belief in the deity of Christ. All we have, as we will see, is a practiced ambiguity. To his dying day Franklin insisted that the deity of Christ was unknowable and unimportant.

3. Grace: Franklin misunderstood the doctrine of justification by faith alone (perhaps intentionally) and consistently highlighted the role of works as the basis for salvation, rather than faith in Christ. His most famous statement in this regard is solidly set in the American psyche: "God helps those who help themselves."

4. Grave: As with the deity of Christ, Franklin doubted the physical resurrection of Christ and did not see it as essential in his "alternative Christianity."

EXAMPLES OF FRANKLIN PATRIOTS

Thomas Jefferson, The Pen of the American Revolution, principal author of the Declaration of Independence, and third president of the United States, is Benjamin Franklin's best-known ally in the founding of alternative Christianities in America. Because his role in this is so pivotal, Jefferson has long been the darling of secularists, atheists, liberals, skeptics, and anyone who desires to see the Edwards wing of American culture marginalized. Though a "wall of separation" between church and state is not mentioned in the Declaration or the Constitution, Jefferson's influence has insured its permanent place in American culture. Franklin, being

---

42. Since deism has no formal dogmatic statement of faith, there are many versions. It is possible that Franklin can be claimed by deists for most of his life, though he adopted a milder form.

thirty-seven years older than Jefferson, likely had a fatherly influence on Jefferson as they worked together in Congress and in crafting (along with John Adams) the Declaration of Independence. Carl Van Doren, somewhat omnisciently, affirmed that Jefferson had "no doubt that Franklin was the greatest American, and felt no envy of him."[43] Walter Isaacson notes that "The last letter Franklin ever wrote was, fittingly, to Thomas Jefferson, his spiritual heir as the nation's foremost apostle of the Enlightenment's faith in reason, experiment, and tolerance."[44]

Other Franklin Patriots were John Adams, America's first vice-president and second president; James Madison, Father of the Constitution and fourth president of the United States; James Monroe, lieutenant, then colonel, in the Revolutionary War, injured at Trenton, mentored by Jefferson, and later the fifth president of the United States.[45]

GEORGE WASHINGTON:
FEET FIRMLY PLANTED ON BOTH SIDES

George Washington, the Sword of the American Revolution, commands such unparalleled respect, that everyone wants him on their side. The Franklins and the Edwardses are still battling for his endorsement. Washington was able to say enough things to sound like a deist for the secularists to claim him. On the other hand, he said enough things to sound like an orthodox Christian for evangelicals to enlist his services. Everyone wants to wrap themselves in Washington.[46]

In his public statements, even while holding office, Washington is quick to refer to God, most often in terms that would cause no concern for a deist. But he cannot seem to bring himself to speak the name of Jesus. In the view of Michael Novak, Washington's God sounds more like the God of the Hebrews than the God of deists, a pre-Christian God who

---

43. Van Doren, *Jane Mecom*, 726.

44. Isaacson, *Benjamin Franklin*, 469.

45. An amusing fact most American historians cannot resist mentioning: Jefferson and Adams died on the same day, July 4, 1826, exactly 50 years after the proclamation of the Declaration of Independence. Monroe died exactly five years later on July 4, 1831.

46. I credit this imagery to Richard Brookhiser, who comments that when Abraham Lincoln wanted to prove that the federal government had the authority to regulate slavery in the territories, he demonstrated how twenty-one of the signers of the Constitution, including George Washington, agreed with him. Says Brookhiser: "He wrapped himself in Washington." Brookhiser, *What Would the Founders Do?* 2.

is sovereign, providentially intervening in the affairs of individuals and states, determining the outcome of battles, raising up nations and setting them down. "If it was George Washington's intention," concludes the diplomatic Novak, "to maintain a studied ambiguity (and personal privacy) regarding his own deepest religious convictions, so that all Americans, both in his own time and for all time to come, might feel free to approach him on their own terms—and might also feel like full members of the new republic, equal with every other—that is an intention, if such it was, he abundantly fulfilled."[47] Washington's God seems to be rather generic and politically safe.

So I hesitate to place him in either category (the Franklins or the Edwardses, deist or orthodox) because, while he had many external marks consistent with a Christ-follower, there is little in his private letters or his will to make me think he was a true worshipper of Jesus Christ. Admirable as it is to be sensitive to the religious diversity of the people he governed, that should not have kept him from declaring his faith to friends and family. It is in his private correspondence that his profession of faith would come out (if it ever comes out) but that profession, if it exists, remains forthcoming. The worst we can say is that Washington was a closet deist who avoided alienating voting Americans, the majority of whom professed belief in an orthodox Jesus. The best we can say of George Washington is that he was a closet Christian who feared to publicly declare his ultimate allegiance to Jesus Christ. In the end, we are left with the troublesome possibility that George Washington, who faced down the greatest military superpower on the earth at the time, was a coward when it came to owning the gospel for which the Apostle Paul (and many others) died. Still, if I cannot claim him outright, I am not persuaded to concede him to the deists.

CHOOSE YOUR JESUS

By 1758, twenty years before George Washington would lead his troops out of Valley Forge to attack the British Army at the Battle of Monmouth, another skirmish line was clearly drawn. Americans had at least two Jesuses to choose from: orthodox or alternative. Orthodox Christianity held a dominant and defensive position but it was beginning to lose ground, especially among the cultural elites. A revised Jesus was being

47. Novak and Novak, *Washington's God,* 222–23.

imported from Europe, where generations of religious wars, the welding of the sword of the state to the mission of the church, widespread hypocrisy among church members, and deeply rooted corruption in the clergy had crippled the ability of Christ-followers to resist the onslaught.

Today in America, the religious options are unlimited. You can find a scholar to support almost any view of Jesus you prefer. You can have a political revolutionary Jesus, a social reformer Jesus, a white Jesus, a black Jesus, a feminist Jesus, a gay Jesus, a married Jesus, a sexually active Jesus, a health and wealth Jesus, a Buddhist Jesus, a Hindu Jesus, a self-deluded Jesus, a Democrat Jesus, or a Republican Jesus. And for people like Christopher Hitchens, you can have a Jesus whose very existence is "highly questionable."[48]

In 1758, the options were few. On one side was the orthodox Jesus, recorded in writing by those who knew him best, apostles who heard his audacious words and witnessed his authenticating works. On the other side, an assortment of warmed over heresies in the various forms of deism, selectively retaining the wisdom of Jesus while divesting him of his divine majesty. In 1758, Benjamin Franklin still had thirty-two years to live on the earth, and orthodox Christianity in America had just lost its greatest champion to physician-assisted smallpox.

---

48. Hitchens, *God Is Not Great*, 114.

3

Playing the Scholar Card

After God had carried us safe to New England, and wee had builded our houses, provided necessaries for our livelihood, rear'd convenient places for God's worship, and settled the civill government: One of the next things we longed for and looked after was to advance learning and perpetuate it to posterity; dreading to leave an illiterate ministery to the churches, when our present ministers shall lie in the dust.

—Tablet on the Johnston Gate into Harvard Yard[1]

Let every Student be plainly instructed, and earnestly pressed to consider well, the main end of his life and studies is, to know God and Jesus Christ which is eternal life. John 17:3.

— First College Laws, Harvard College[2]

ON JULY 8, 1731, Jonathan Edwards stood before the large crowd in Boston that had gathered to hear his public lecture. It was commencement week at Harvard College, and the town was filled with visitors from all over New England. At the age of twenty-seven, he had been invited to address the assembly of prominent and powerful people, seasoned pastors, Harvard students and faculty, and community leaders. And they were curious to hear the young Edwards. Less than two years earlier, Edwards's grandfather, Solomon Stoddard, a Harvard graduate, died and was succeeded by his grandson as pastor of the church in Northampton, Massachusetts. Stoddard, "the Pope of the Connecticut Valley," was a giant in New England life, and there had been much discussion about Edwards's ability to fill the void.

---

1. The quote is from *New England's First Fruits in respect . . . of the Progresse of Learning in the College at Cambridge in Massachusetts Bay*, September 26, 1642.

2. Marsden, *Soul of the American University*, 41.

Adding to the drama, Edwards, a graduate of Yale College, would be speaking to a crowd teeming with Harvard graduates. In 1731, Harvard was already ninety-five years old. The upstart Yale, only thirty years old, was established in response to a perceived shift in Harvard from its original mission. Although Jonathan Edwards's father was a Harvard graduate, Timothy Edwards sent his son to Yale. Founded by the Puritans, both schools were created to produce an educated clergy for New England and both originally held a firm commitment to the doctrinal standards of the Westminster Confession. To this day, Harvard's seal is dominated by the Latin word for truth, *Veritas*, an abbreviated version of an earlier motto of Harvard adopted in 1692: *Veritas Christo et Ecclesiae*—Truth For Christ and the Church.[3] By 1731, there were deep rumblings as Harvard drifted from a God-centered theology. The planners of the public lecture calculated the timing and the speaker with precision.

Edwards surely felt the weight of the event. He had delivered this lecture as a sermon to his church in the Fall of 1730, so he had invested much thought in the propositions he would advance. The manuscript of the lecture reveals that he worked on it as he had so many sermons, writing, revising, crossing out a word here, adding another there. With each revision, the point became sharper, the argument tighter, and the transitions smoother. On July 8, 1731, Jonathan Edwards was ready to stand and deliver.

VERITAS AT HARVARD

The controversial central thesis of Edwards's lecture at Harvard is that when someone who once professed a belief in the orthodox Jesus revises his or her position, it is due to human pride, not increased knowledge. The same is true for institutions, such as Harvard and Yale, which were

3. This earlier motto can still be viewed on several of the older entry gates into old Harvard Yard on the campus of Harvard University. Also, in an enduring affirmation of man's smallness before the greatness of God, the inscription over the entrance to Emerson Hall at Harvard is taken from Psalm 8:4: "What is man that Thou art mindful of him?" Similarly, the 1749 Yale diploma of Ezra Stiles displays "the oldest surviving and legible Yale seal" which states *In Christi Gloriam*—"For the Glory of Christ." The current seal of Yale sets forth the motto, *Lux et Veritas*—"Light and Truth" around an open book that is most likely a Bible. (Oren, "Stamp of Approval"). There is abundant evidence that no matter the current prevailing opinions of the faculty and students of both of these renowned universities, the founders of both schools were unashamed and unembarrassed of the orthodox Jesus.

originally established to exalt Jesus Christ. If Jesus is all he claimed to be, then all grounds for human boasting are demolished. The orthodox Jesus is incompatible with self-exaltation. As God speaks through Isaiah: "I will put an end to the arrogance of the haughty and will humble the pride of the ruthless."[4] Jesus was simple and direct: "For whoever exalts himself will be humbled, and whoever humbles himself will be exalted."[5] Edwards was as plain: "It is necessary in order to [have] saving faith, that man should be emptied of himself, be sensible that he is 'wretched and miserable, and poor, and blind, and naked.' Humility is an essential ingredient of true faith."[6]

Edwards crystallizes the premise of his lecture in this single, elegant sentence: "So much the more men exalt themselves so much the less will they surely be disposed to exalt God."[7] This is the guiding principle of Edwards's life and thinking, and by it, he evaluated every idea that was advanced in American culture. As Edwards would come to see, few ideas exalted men and demoted God more than deism.

STUMBLING IN LESSING'S DITCH

How did deism arrive in America? In the next few pages I want to follow a trail of history. It winds and turns across two continents. In between, it crosses an ocean and finally ends up at the feet of several of the men whose faces are etched on our money. It will be tedious, but it is, I think, an important trail to follow if we are to understand the challenge to Christianity in America today.

One of the more important deists who lived during the lifetimes of Edwards and Franklin was a man whose name most Americans have never heard—Gotthold Ephraim Lessing. Lessing had studied under Hermann Reimarus, a German philosopher, who wrote an analysis of the historical Jesus. After Reimarus's death, Lessing[8] published Reimarus's work be-

---

4. Isaiah 13:11.

5. Matthew 23:12.

6. Edwards, *Works*, 17:213.

7. Ibid., 17:211.

8. Lessing was also an influential playwright, his best-known play being *Nathan the Wise*, published in 1779, set in Jerusalem during the Third Crusade. It calls for tolerance between Jews, Christians, and Muslims and to live peacefully by laying aside religious distinctives. I am told by friends in Germany that *Nathan the Wise* remains a popular play there today.

tween 1774 and 1778 under the title *Fragments by an Anonymous Writer*. In *Fragments*, Reimarus argued that the Jesus of the Gospels was different from the Jesus the apostles present in their epistles, and that the historical Jesus was an ordinary Jewish man living in a Jewish culture. Since, as a pure deist, Reimarus was prejudiced against miracles, he concluded that Jesus was not raised from the dead and that the disciples stole his body and perpetrated a fraud. This began what New Testament scholar Darrell Bock calls "the first quest"[9] of the historical Jesus—the "real" Jesus—a quest that may have begun in Germany, but spread to America.

Lessing developed his mentor's ideas further by alleging that the real, historical Jesus was someone very different from the Jesus presented by the apostles. The real, historical Jesus was often called Jesus of Nazareth while the embellished Jesus described by the apostles became known as the Christ of faith. Between the two, the historical Jesus and the Christ of faith, there was what Lessing called an "ugly ditch" which could never be crossed.[10] Faith was unhinged from reason, religion separated from history. "This opened the door," writes Bock, "to the view popular among many critics today that the Gospel story was valuable as a lesson even if the events did not happen. This divorce between history and the Gospel was unprecedented for the church."[11]

Of course, Edwards could not have read Lessing's work, and Franklin probably did not. But these unorthodox concepts of Jesus were floating around continental Europe, bounding over the English Channel, and from England, across the Atlantic to America during the lifetimes of Edwards and Franklin.

While Lessing was busy publishing *Fragments*, Benjamin Franklin was living in London where, in 1774, he met Thomas Paine. Paine had a questionable past, but Franklin apparently detected some potential in him and assisted him in moving to America. In 1776, Paine wrote *Common Sense*, a tract printed by Franklin that forcefully argued for American independence and galvanized the colonies in that cause. On December 19, 1776, the *Pennsylvania Journal* printed Paine's essay *The American Crisis*, which opens with the famous lines "These are the times that try men's souls. The summer soldier and the sunshine patriot will, in this

9. Bock, *Studying the Historical Jesus*, 143.
10. Ibid., 157.
11. Ibid.

crisis, shrink from the service of his country; but he that stands it now, deserves the love and thanks of man and woman."[12] It was written during the retreat of Washington and his troops to the Delaware River, and Washington ordered that it be read to his demoralized army. Six days later, on Christmas Day, 1776, somewhat emboldened by Paine's stirring prose, Washington crossed the Delaware in a surprise attack at Trenton and won a stunning victory.

But Paine's writing accomplishments were not over. From 1794 to 1807, he published in three parts what would become a national bestseller, *The Age of Reason*. In this work, Paine successfully popularized many of the deistic arguments that had been influencing the educated elite for decades. He piles scathing criticism of the church upon criticism, using caustic ridicule and sarcasm to point out alleged discrepancies in the Bible one after the other. The intent is to rock the reader's confidence in Scripture, and especially, the New Testament. It was most probable to Paine that the Gospels were written by men who had ulterior motives. The New Testament writers created a religion "very contradictory to the character of the person whose name it bears. It has set up a religion of pomp and of revenue in pretended imitation of a person whose life was humility and poverty."[13] Paine viewed most priests and preachers as corrupt and in love with the money they received for holding an official position in the church.

The Gospels, in Paine's view, were fraudulent. "The disordered state of the history in these four books, the silence of one book upon matters related in the other, and the disagreement that is to be found among them, implies that they are the production of some unconnected individuals, many years after the things they pretend to relate, each of whom made his own legend."[14] They were not written by the apostles, or even under the supervision of the apostles, but "they have been manufactured, as the books of the Old Testament, by other persons than those names they bear." [15]

EDWARDS PATRIOTS ON THE GOSPELS

Americans have never really warmed up to Paine and many do not consider him one of our Founding Fathers. Some theorize that it was his vitri-

12. Paine, *Writings*, 1:170.

13. Ibid.

14. Ibid., 4:156.

15. Ibid.

olic *Age of Reason* that sealed the deal to make him forever an outsider. But his popularity seems to be reviving, and if he had a fan club, Christopher Hitchens might be the president. In *God is Not Great,* he quotes Paine at length. "The great Thomas Paine," writes Hitchens, "a friend to Franklin and Jefferson" was not afraid to "expose the crimes and horrors of the Old Testament, as well as the foolish myths of the New."[16]

Samuel Adams was unspeakably grieved by Paine's attack on Jesus. The last known letter he wrote before he died in 1803 was to Thomas Paine. Although Adams and Paine had worked together throughout the nation's founding, Adams never hesitated to confront his old friend when he believed Paine was in the wrong. Adams's rebuke might easily be directed to Christopher Hitchens today. "Do you think," asked Adams, "that your pen, or the pen of any other man, can un-Christianize the mass of our citizens? Or have you hopes of converting a few of them to assist you in so bad a cause?"[17]

Samuel Adams was not alone among the founders who trusted the Gospels. Unlike Thomas Paine, John Jay, who served as the President of the Continental Congress, an author of the Federalist Papers, and the first Supreme Court Chief Justice in our history, had a scholarly background in biblical studies. In order to be admitted as a student to the newly founded King's College in New York, Jay was required to translate the first ten chapters of the Gospel of John from the Greek into Latin.[18] Jay was unaffected by Paine's rants. "Jay believed the Bible," writes one biographer, "He knew every word of it to be completely and literally true."[19]

As Patrick Henry, another founder and accomplished lawyer, got older, and the ambitions of youth began to fade, the Bible became more important to him. He began to read it every morning and lamented to friends that he had not "found time to read it with the proper attention and feeling till lately. I trust in the mercy of Heaven that it is not yet too late." Like so many Christians before and after him, he regretted in his last years that "I find much cause to reproach myself that I have lived so long and given no decided proofs of my being a Christian."[20] Thomas Paine's

16. Hitchens, *God Is Not Great,* 268.

17. Samuel Adams, *Writings,* 4:412.

18. Monaghan, *John Jay,* 26.

19. Ibid., 428.

20. Mayer, *Son of Thunder,* 467–68.

subversive attacks on the veracity of the Bible notwithstanding, Patrick Henry only grew more confident in the Gospels as the years went by.

Even John Adams, Samuel's cousin, whose Unitarian belief led him to deny the deity of Jesus, saw the dangerous flaws in Paine's attack. Paine's writings, like *The Age of Reason*, which were "stolen from Blount's Oracles of Reason, from Bolingbroke, Voltaire, Berenger, &c., will never discredit Christianity, which will hold its ground in some degree as long as human nature shall have any thing moral or intellectual left in it." Christianity, wrote Adams, "will last as long as the world."[21]

HOW TO CREATE AN ALTERNATIVE CHRISTIANITY

While many of Thomas Paine's fans today want to totally remove theism from our culture, that was not Paine's intent. Disappointed with the Jesus he found in the New Testament, Paine gave him a total makeover. Like a customer at a salad bar, he chose the characteristics of Jesus he preferred and rejected those that would not fit into the church of his mind. Deists like Paine were not seeking to destroy Jesus but to replace the orthodox Jesus with an alternative Jesus who was more cooperative with the deist agenda. Paine, Franklin, and Jefferson were trying to *improve* Jesus. But in the process, they provided the groundwork for today's skeptics whose goal is to *remove* Jesus.

Of course, the main obstacle to the founding of an alternative Christianity is the New Testament. In particular, skeptics must demolish confidence in the reliability of the Gospels. The deists of the eighteenth century set a pattern of undermining trust in Scripture as a credible witness to history by staking a claim to the intellectual high ground. That is a tactic that is still common today.

Jonathan Edwards was not unaware of this intellectual snobbery. Deism, wrote Edwards, was a "medium between Christianity and atheism." Deists do not deny the existence of God but "ridicule the story about Jesus Christ, and deny the Scripture." The influence of deism had made it "fashionable to despise and laugh at religion and godliness and a fear of hell or future judgment." As a result, a man who accepts the orthodox Jesus, having a "serious regard to the holy Scriptures, or anything of religion, is looked upon as unworthy of a gentleman."[22]

21. John Adams, "Letter to Benjamin Rush, January 21, 1810."
22. Edwards, *Works*, 14:499.

Although Paine's bold attack on the orthodox Jesus came after Edwards's death, keep in mind that Edwards was defending the orthodox Jesus in America at the same time Hermann Reimarus was laying the groundwork in Germany for a massive attack on the reliability of the New Testament. However, the particular deist influence that Edwards addressed came mainly from England. For example, one of the most influential works by the English deists, or Freethinkers, of Edwards's day was *Christianity as Old as the Creation* by Matthew Tindal (1656–1733). Gerald McDermott calculates that because Edwards saw deism as "the gravest threat facing Christian faith," more than twenty-five percent of the entries in Edwards's private notebook (the *Miscellanies*) are dedicated to addressing the deist challenge that came from writers like Tindal.[23] In those entries, we find the framework of a solid response to critics of the New Testament today.

MEET SCHOLARSHIP WITH SCHOLARSHIP

Alternative Christianities normally claim to be intellectually, as well as morally, superior. Benjamin Franklin would not have abandoned the orthodox view of Jesus he inherited from his parents for the revised Jesus of the deists if he thought the deists were uneducated, unscientific, and unreasonable. After reading orthodox tracts defending Christianity against deism, Franklin wrote in his biography that "the Arguments of the Deists which were quoted to be refuted appeared to me much Stronger than the Refutations."[24] Franklin, who had not attended college or received any formal training in biblical studies, concluded that the deists had the stronger, more scholarly, argument. Like Franklin, countless Americans in the last two centuries have been swayed by "scholars" advocating alternative Christianities.

Playing the scholar card is a common and effective means of shaping public opinion. Every trial lawyer knows the importance of using an "expert witness" with scholarly credentials. The more prestigious the school from which he or she earned the degree, the more weight the jury puts on the testimony. Words like "Harvard" or "Yale" are uttered with unchallenged finality. "Well that's it then. He's from Harvard, so it must be true." Of all the schools Dan Brown could have picked for the employer

23. McDermott, *Jonathan Edwards Confronts the Gods*, 5.
24. Franklin, *Writings*, 1359.

of his alter-ego, Professor Robert Langdon, in the *DaVinci Code*, he did not pick his own alma mater, Amherst College. Instead, he chose Harvard. This fictional Harvard professor became the popular cultural vehicle of remarkable attacks on the veracity of the Gospels. Amherst is an excellent school, but it was founded to train young men for the ministry who did not have the connections to get into Harvard, and the perception is that it does not quite carry the scholarly weight of its cross-state rival. Of course, everybody likes to quote a scholar: liberals and conservatives; orthodox Christians and alternative Christians. In fact, I'll do it a few times in this book. But no one does it better than the Jesus Seminar.

What is the Jesus Seminar? I'll let them introduce themselves. Five times in their mission statement, the Jesus Seminar's parent group, Westar Institute, uses the word "scholar" or "scholarship." They aim to "communicate the results of the scholarship of religion to a broad, non-specialist public." The Jesus Seminar is "an exchange involving thousands of scholars." Furthermore, "scholarship of religion should be collaborative" while "bible scholars should conduct their deliberations in public" and then report their findings to the public (the non-scholars). This they have skillfully done through the most influential media outlets in the world.[25]

As we have seen, there is not much new in the new scholarship. These basic ideas have been around as long as our nation. But in the past, church leaders, being called both as shepherds and teachers, aspired to be "pastor-scholars." As brokers of truth, pastors served as mediators between the solid, but often stuffy, scholarship of the theological academy and the people in the pew. They received formal theological training, learned Greek and Hebrew, practiced textual criticism, examined the arguments and agenda of skeptical scholars, learned to defend the veracity of the Bible, and protected the flock of God from false doctrine. Since liberal scholars were largely contained in academic institutions, they were blocked by the pastors from reaching the "uneducated" masses.

Many of those institutions were still church-related, founded and funded by faithful church members holding to the orthodox faith "once for all entrusted to the saints."[26] Liberal professors in church-related schools, unwilling to risk careers or pensions, often lacked the intellectual integrity to inform the school supporters that their beliefs were at odds

---

25. Weststar Institute, "Mission."
26. Jude 3.

with the school's original mission. On the other hand, professors in secular colleges and universities discovered early on that a scholarly defense of the Bible would not advance their careers. The party line for the last one hundred years in higher education has decidedly been anti-evangelical, and rabidly anti-Edwards. For whatever reason, there exists today an undeniable and overt bias against orthodox Christianity among faculty members of universities. In fact, fifty-three percent admit to an unfavorable view of evangelicals, with Mormons running a distant second at thirty-three percent. University professors view Muslims more positively with just a twenty-two percent unfavorable rating. Atheists seem to be the darlings of the academic hierarchy with only an eighteen percent unfavorable rating.[27] In fact, university faculty feelings toward evangelicals are significantly more unfavorable "than any other religious group."[28] But even with this advantage, tenured academicians in religion departments of well-endowed schools who seek to advance an alternative Jesus have never been able to connect in an influential way with Americans at a popular level. Until the Jesus Seminar.

So the Weststar Institute was formed to do an end run around church leaders who were doing their biblical duty. "Many scholars," says their mission statement, "fearing open conflict or even reprisal, talked only to one another. The churches often decided what information their constituents were 'ready' to hear."[29] Instead of distributing the results of their biblical "scholarship" in the traditional way through local pastors, or even peer reviewed journals, they began to use the very untraditional means of *Time*, *Newsweek*, and *ABC News*. So when ordinary people read in a reputable magazine or hear on a network documentary that this man or woman saying these things about Jesus is a "New Testament scholar," who are they to disagree? The implied message is rather clear: this revised Jesus is the one you accept if you are smart.

What a lot of people forget, or never knew, is that Jonathan Edwards was a scholar. George Marsden remarks that "no one could have surpassed the relentlessly logical young Edwards,"[30] who graduated at the top of his undergraduate class at Yale and three years later, again at Yale,

27. Tobin and Weinberg, "Religious Beliefs and Behavior of College Faculty," 81.

28. Ibid.

29. All the quotes from the Westar Institute are from their website: www.westarinstitute .org.

30. Marsden, *Jonathan Edwards*, 82.

defended in Latin his M.A. thesis. In fact, no figure in colonial America exceeds Edwards in terms of scholarship, and nearly three hundred years later, his alma mater is graced with the Jonathan Edwards Center at Yale University,[31] an honor bestowed on none of his ministerial contemporaries. Yet in many quarters, the stereotype persists that the choices are limited to two: you can be a scholar or you can believe the Bible, but you cannot do both.

ENDLESS CHALLENGES TO THE SUPREMACY OF JESUS

At Harvard in 1731, Edwards did not name the particular challenge to the supremacy of Christ that he is addressing,[32] but he makes it clear that this particular theological dispute is not the only challenge the church will face. Any scheme that "is inconsistent with our entire dependence on God for all . . . is repugnant to the design and the tenor of the gospel, and robs it of that which God accounts its luster and glory."[33] There were many schemes in Edwards's lifetime that would challenge the supremacy of Christ, but the greatest threat of all would be deism.

Deism became a Declaration of Independence from Jesus. It was just beginning to take root in eighteenth-century soil, but Edwards had remarkable insight into the damage it would do if it flourished: Jesus Christ would be demoted from his rightful place of exalted honor. For this reason, Edwards ended his lecture on that hot July day in Boston with a final admonition: "Let us be exhorted to exalt God alone, and ascribe to him all the glory of redemption." And then, in a sweeping statement on human nature, he affirmed that "Man is naturally exceeding prone to exalt himself and depend on his own power."[34]

Almost three hundred years later we can say that Jonathan Edwards told us so. In the church in America, confidence in the supremacy of Christ is widely shaken. On one hand, some Christians meet the challenges with silence and surrender. On the other hand, some Christians

31. See www.edwards.yale.edu.

32. Most historians believe Edwards was addressing the growing popularity of Arminianism. The Puritans were originally Calvinists. Though many Arminians held to an orthodox Jesus, Edwards detected a slippery slope. In order for a Calvinist to move *to* deism, for example, he had to move *through* Arminianism to get there. In Edwards's view, Arminianism took God down a notch in order to move man up.

33. Edwards, *Works,* 17:211.

34. Ibid., 17:214.

meet the challenges with shrill anger and insecure arrogance. The way of Christ, the way Jonathan Edwards tried to go, is to meet the challenges with a humble and informed confidence.

Edwards was not surprised that people would reject the message of the Scriptures on the pretense of scholarship. After all, the apostle Paul had asked, "Where is the wise man? Where is the scholar? Where is the philosopher of this age? Has not God made foolish the wisdom of the world? For since in the wisdom of God the world through its wisdom did not know him, God was pleased through the foolishness of what was preached to save those who believe."[35] So the problem is not that the message of the Bible is unreasonable. The problem is that people who read the Bible, including—and perhaps especially—scholars, are naturally proud and inclined to overestimate their abilities. "Indeed," wrote Edwards, "it is a glorious argument of the divinity of the holy Scriptures, that they teach such doctrines, which in one age and another, through the blindness of men's minds, and strong prejudices of their hearts, are rejected, as most absurd and unreasonable by the wise and great men of the world; which yet, when they are most carefully and strictly examined, appear to be exactly agreeable to the most demonstrable, certain, and natural dictates of reason."[36] Jonathan Edwards spent a lifetime proving that there is no final conflict between biblical faith and rigorous scholarship.

35. 1 Corinthians 1:20–22.
36. Edwards, *Works,* 1:439.

4

Gospels: "They Ridicule the Story about Jesus"

*The Gospel has never been without enemies from without or within; and
as it is usually by means of human learning that they make the attack, it is
necessary that some should be ready to meet them, and able to unravel the
subtlety which they lie in wait to receive.*

—John Witherspoon, President, Princeton College from 1768 to 1794[1]

*Many wicked men hear arguments enough from time to time to convince
them, if they are not prejudiced. But that prejudice remaining, bring what
arguments you will, argue never so wisely,
and they will never be fully convinced.*

—Jonathan Edwards[2]

SAM HARRIS, ONE OF America's most widely published atheists, is clear
about the point and purpose of Jesus's life work. "Jesus's principal message," writes Harris in his bestselling book, *The End of Faith*, is "loving one's
neighbor and turning the other cheek."[3] In fact, this is Jesus "as we find
him in the New Testament, healing the sick and challenging those without
sin to cast the first stone."[4] So Sam Harris accepts the New Testament account of the life of Jesus? Not exactly. When it comes to loving neighbors,
turning cheeks, caring for the sick, and excoriating religious hypocrites,
Sam Harris likes to quote the New Testament. But if the testimony of the
New Testament does not advance his agenda, he claims it is because the

---

1. Witherspoon, *Works*, 7:23–24. Witherspoon, the only active clergy member to sign
the Declaration of Independence, was the sixth president of Princeton College (now
Princeton University).

2. Edwards, MS Sermon on 2 Peter 1:16 (1729), 18.

3. Harris, *The End of Faith*, 85.

4. Ibid., 84.

New Testament authors had an agenda of their own. "There is no evidence whatsoever," pronounces Harris, "apart from the tendentious writings of the later church that Jesus ever conceived of himself as anything other than a Jew among Jews."[5]

An interesting word, "tendentious." It sounds rather sinister. We are shocked, shocked that the Gospel authors wrote to promote a particular cause. Never mind that *The End of Faith* is tendentious in the extreme. Yet the Gospel writers never try to hide the fact. "But these are written," John's Gospel announces, "that you may believe that Jesus is the Christ, the Son of God, and that by believing you may have life in his name."[6] It seems the Gospel writers were able to convince Sam Harris that Jesus existed and that he had a "principal message" of peace and social justice. But Harris remains unconvinced that "Jesus is the Christ, the Son of God." Take from the Gospels what fits your worldview, damn the rest.

But where does Sam Harris get the idea that Jesus never claimed to be anything other than an ordinary man? The New Testament is a collection of the earliest documents relating to the life of Jesus and it presents him as quite extraordinary. So what "evidence" does Sam Harris have that Jesus only considered himself a "Jew among Jews?" If Harris has any historical documents on the life of Jesus that are earlier than the New Testament, he fails to mention them. So how close, or far, is the New Testament to what actually happened?

BENJAMIN FRANKLIN AND THE GOSPELS

"The glory of young men," wrote Solomon, "is their strength."[7] There are hints of that strength in the well-worn face that gazes at us from our hundred dollar bills. Unlike Jonathan Edwards, who was often sick and weak, Benjamin Franklin's health was robust, his body strong and vigorous. But in March of 1789, it was clear that the once powerful body of Benjamin Franklin was going the way of all flesh. Eighty-three years on the earth had taken its inevitable toll. Confined to the bed on which he would soon die, friends sent letters or came to visit one last time. Ezra Stiles, the president of Yale College (later Yale University), was particularly concerned about Benjamin Franklin's religious views and wrote to Franklin

5. Harris, *The End of Faith*, 94.

6. John 20:31.

7. Proverbs 20:29.

about his faith. In a famous letter, Franklin replied, "You desire to know something of my religion. It is the first time I have been questioned upon it."[8] Really? Perhaps Franklin's memory was failing him, but we know at least that his sister had clearly questioned his religion years earlier, and he responded by making an appeal to Jonathan Edwards to help make his case. Additionally, his parents, upon hearing of his involvement with the Freemasons, wrote a concerned letter in 1738 inquiring as to his religious beliefs.[9] Or maybe Franklin's memory served him well, but until this point he had managed to avoid making a clear public statement regarding his unorthodox opinion of Jesus Christ. Stiles knew Franklin would soon meet his Maker and was direct in his questioning. Franklin obliged.

> Here is my Creed. I believe in one God, Creator of the Universe. That he governs it by His Providence. That he ought to be worshipped. That the most acceptable Service we render Him is doing good to His other Children. That the soul of Man is immortal, and will be treated with Justice in another Life respecting its Conduct in this. These I take to be the fundamental Principles of all sound Religion and I regard them as you do in whatever Sect I meet with them.[10]

So far, so good. On the face, this creed is within the bounds of orthodox Christianity. But the letter does not stop there.

> As to Jesus of Nazareth my Opinion of whom you particularly desire, I think the System of Morals and his Religion, as he left them to us, the best the World ever saw or is likely to see; but I apprehend it has received various corrupt Changes, and I have, with most of the present Dissenters in England, some doubts as to his divinity ...[11]

So Franklin came to believe that the Gospels had been corrupted, that the actual teaching of Jesus had been changed. Changed by whom? Franklin does not say, but a fashionable explanation of the day was that Jesus's followers, including the apostles, twisted his words and claimed things for Jesus that Jesus never claimed for himself. At the end of his life and on the most fundamental point of orthodox doctrine, Franklin aligned himself with the alternative Christianities of his day. Jesus was a good man, but

---

8. Franklin, *Writings*, 1179.

9. Van Doren, *Benjamin Franklin*, 784.

10. Franklin, *Writings*, 1179.

11. Ibid.

not God. Franklin arrived at this conclusion, like everyone else who arrives there, by "cherry-picking"[12] the Gospels.

AN EXAMPLE OF AN ALLEGED DISCREPANCY

What did Jonathan Edwards think of the trustworthiness of the Gospels? In his notes on Luke 18, Jonathan Edwards anticipated the objections of New Testament critics. He acknowledges that there is a difficulty when this account is compared with other Gospels, and sets to work on reconciling all of the testimony. Take a moment to read the three accounts below to discern the problem.

> Luke 18:35–38: As Jesus approached Jericho, a blind man was sitting by the roadside begging. When he heard the crowd going by, he asked what was happening. They told him, "Jesus of Nazareth is passing by." He called out, "Jesus, Son of David, have mercy on me!"

> Matthew 20:29, 30: As Jesus and his disciples were leaving Jericho, a large crowd followed him. Two blind men were sitting by the roadside, and when they heard that Jesus was going by, they shouted, "Lord, Son of David, have mercy on us!"

> Mark 10:46, 47: Then they came to Jericho. As Jesus and his disciples, together with a large crowd, were leaving the city, a blind man, Bartimaeus (that is, the Son of Timaeus), was sitting by the roadside begging. When he heard that it was Jesus of Nazareth, he began to shout, "Jesus, Son of David, have mercy on me!"

So, was there one blind man or two? Mark, being the earliest Gospel, mentions Bartimaeus and his father by name so that his readers can verify the story. They can go to Jericho and check it out if they want to. But Mark never says Bartimaeus was alone. It may be that Bartimaeus first said "have mercy on me," and then his friend said, "have mercy on me too!", and before it was over, they were both saying, "have mercy on us." They may have started out by addressing "Jesus, Son of David" and switched to "Lord, Son of David," using the names and titles interchangeably. None of the Gospel writers pretends to give every detail of every event. Mark

---

12. I borrow this phrase from Sam Harris (who certainly borrowed it from someone else). "People have been cherry-picking the Bible for millennia to justify their every impulse, moral or otherwise." Sam Harris, *Letter,* 18. I have no quarrel with Harris on this point, and neither, I think, would Jonathan Edwards.

chooses to leave out the companion for reasons of his own, just as every historian does at some time or another. There is no contradiction here.

When the miracle took place, was Jesus entering Jericho as Luke says, or leaving Jericho, as Mark and Matthew say? Is this a hopeless contradiction that renders the Gospels useless as reliable witnesses to history? While deist critics would see this as damning evidence that the Bible is historically unreliable, Edwards sees it as a "difficulty and seeming inconsistency." Edwards did not avoid the issue, but met it head on with a possible solution. First, Jesus traveled from Galilee on his way to Jerusalem along the west bank of the Jordan River and arrived on the northern or eastern outskirts of Jericho late afternoon or early evening, tired and dusty. Here, Jesus "lodged in the suburbs" of Jericho, which would be commonly referred to as Jericho itself. If Jesus had gone on into the town's more populated center, recent experience told him the crowds would gather and he and his disciples would get no rest. After all, writes Edwards, the people "were in a great disposition to flock after him and throng him."[13] So he spent a quiet night on the outskirts of Jericho getting some much needed rest.

The next morning, he woke up and left the suburbs of Jericho (which is to say, he left Jericho) for Jerusalem, but the road passed right through downtown Jericho. In between the place he spent the night (suburbs) and the city gates (downtown), he encountered the two blind men and healed them. He then proceeded from there through Jericho toward Jerusalem. In the transition area between the Jericho suburbs and downtown Jericho, it might be said that Jesus was leaving Jericho (the suburbs) and entering Jericho (downtown) simultaneously. In the downtown area of Jericho, Jesus encountered Zaccheus and then went with him to his house, which was likely between Jericho and Jerusalem, for the rest of the day and evening.

If this sounds rather far-fetched, consider that my sister lives in Oswego, but she tells most people who do not live in the area that she lives in Chicago, and she is not wrong. I have friends who live in Dacula, a suburb of Atlanta, but they tell most people they live in Atlanta, and we do not think them liars. Suppose my friend comes to visit me, and as he leaves his neighborhood, heading toward downtown Atlanta, I call him on his cell phone and ask, "Where are you"? He may reply, "I'm just now leaving Atlanta," because he is in between the suburbs and downtown. Seconds af-

---

13. Edwards, *Works,* 15:182–84.

ter speaking with me, his wife calls from their home and asks, "Where are you?" He may reply, "I am just approaching Atlanta." In neither case would we consider him to be deceitful or inaccurate. As Edwards wrote, "this is not disagreeable to our customary way of speaking." Edwards concludes, "thus the seeming inconsistency between the evangelists is solved."[14]

It may not be solved to the satisfaction of people with an anti-supernatural prejudice who do not believe blindness can be miraculously healed, and it may not even be *the* answer. But it is *an* answer. Edwards did some scholarly work to reconcile an apparent contradiction between the Gospels. He was not the first to attempt it, and he was most certainly not the last. Of this difficulty, Craig Blomberg suggests that "probably Luke has just abbreviated Mark, as he does consistently elsewhere, leaving out the reference to the departure from Jericho."[15] After all, the Gospels never claim to "set out to supply a detailed itinerary of Jesus's ministry with every event in its proper chronological sequence."[16] It is perfectly legitimate for Luke to smooth out Mark's inelegant style by excising this clause. This is another good explanation, though I find myself more strongly drawn to Edwards's option. The bottom line is this: Matthew, Mark, and Luke agree that Jesus healed the very real Bartimaeus, son of Timaeus, in the very real city of Jericho before hundreds of eyewitnesses who could confirm this account in the same generation it was written. That John does not mention the incident at all in his Gospel does not mean he denies it happened. All it means is that he does not mention it. My point in this single example is that in the two hundred and fifty years since Edwards defended the historical reliability of the Gospels, many scholars have examined the apparent contradictions in the Gospels and found them to be more "apparent" than contradictory.

JOSEPH PRIESTLY

If Christopher Hitchens is right, Thomas Paine's *The Age of Reason* had "tremendous worldwide effect"[17] that certainly included Thomas Jefferson. But Paine was no more a Bible scholar than Jefferson. So which Bible scholars influenced Jefferson? In the spring of 1801, just after be-

---

14. Edwards, *Works*, 184.

15. Blomberg, *Historical Reliability*, 128.

16. Ibid., 127.

17. Hitchens, *God is Not Great*, 268.

ing elected as the third president of the United States, Jefferson wrote a letter in which he called Joseph Priestly the "great apostle" of "science and honesty" and it is clear from Jefferson's correspondence, that Priestly had the president's ear when it came to his view of the Gospels. Priestly, like Paine, was another British citizen Franklin had recruited to move to America. Credited with the discovery of oxygen, Priestly began his career as a Presbyterian minister, formally trained in theology, and ended it as a deistic scientist-philosopher. In a letter to Priestly, Jefferson tested some ideas he had entertained for several years. Jesus, according to Jefferson had attempted to bring his followers to "the principles of pure Deism."[18] But Jesus experienced a severe disadvantage in that he did not write down his doctrine himself. Instead, that was left to "the most unlettered of men, by memory, long after they had heard them from him." By the time they did write it down, Jefferson concluded, "much was forgotten, much misunderstood, and presented in every paradoxical shape."[19] More damage was done to the original teaching of Jesus by "those who pretended to be his special disciples" and who have misrepresented Jesus "from views of personal interest."[20] Therefore, the Jesus presented in the New Testament is an "imposter." To be sure, there are "fragments remaining" in the New Testament, pure reflections of Jesus's life and teaching, but these must be identified by educated men. As we will see in a moment, Jefferson considered himself qualified for the task.

DID THOMAS JEFFERSON BELIEVE IN JULIUS CAESAR?

If you are a skeptic of the Bible looking for a refutation of every alleged discrepancy and apparent contradiction in the Gospels, this chapter may disappoint you. My purpose in this chapter has been to demonstrate how the founding of alternative Christianities in America began with an attack on the historical reliability of the Bible in general, and the Gospels in particular. It is beyond my scope to answer each charge against the Bible raised by skeptics like Lessing, Paine, Franklin, and Jefferson. Besides, there are so many others who can do that so much better. One of the great blessings of our generation has been the vast output of scholarship answering the charges of modern skeptics like Sam Harris and Christopher

18. Jefferson, "Letter to Joseph Priestly," 9.

19. Ibid., 10.

20. Ibid.

Hitchens who, for the most part, are simply recycling the same old, tired deist arguments. But there are more scholarly answers than most people know. To be sure, the Bible has many difficulties, and they will not be resolved by the intellectually lazy. But these scholarly defenses of the reliability of the New Testament are available to anyone who desires to give a fair hearing to both sides of this centuries-old debate.[21] However, to introduce you to the superior historical reliability of the Gospels, let me tell you about two letters Thomas Jefferson wrote in the 1770's.

The first letter, to his brother-in-law, Robert Skipwith, was in response to Skipwith's request of Jefferson to recommend the best books to purchase for his library. Under the category of religion, Jefferson recommended works such as Xenophon, Seneca, Cicero, and the deist, Lord Bolingbroke. Under the category of "history," Jefferson directed him to Bayle's *Dictionary*, Plutarch's *Lives*, Caesar, Livy, Sallust, Tacitus, and the Bible.[22]

In another letter in 1787, Jefferson advises Peter Carr to "read the Bible then, as you would read Livy or Tacitus."[23] Each work of history should be judged by the same criterion and measured by the same standard. No work should get special treatment, but each should be treated equally. When we follow Jefferson's advice, are we forced to renounce the reliability of the New Testament?

I answer with another question: Did Thomas Jefferson believe that members of the Roman Senate in or around 44 BC assassinated Julius Caesar? If Jefferson is consistent with himself, he would have to believe this. His counsel is clear: "The facts which are within the ordinary course of nature you will believe on the authority of the writer."[24] Most Americans agree with this maxim, and so most would say they believe Julius Caesar was assassinated by the Senate. But try asking them why they believe this. They were not there to see it. They believe it because someone who was there and did see it either wrote it down or told someone else what they saw who subsequently recorded it in writing. But who recorded it? In a casual survey, you will probably discover what I have. Most Americans believe in Julius Caesar because in high school, they were compelled to

---

21. For example, see Bauckham, Blomberg, Bock, Craig, Eddy and Boyd, Habermas, Roberts, Komoszewski, Strobel, and Witherington. Roberts is a good non-technical introduction.

22. Jefferson, *Papers*, 1:80.

23. Jefferson, *Papers*, 12:15.

24. Ibid.

read Shakespeare's tragedy. But Shakespeare wrote *Julius Caesar* in 1590, well over sixteen hundred years after the event, so he could not have seen the murder. Who, then, was Shakespeare's source?

I once called a college literature department and asked this question of several professors. None of them knew the answer. So I kept digging to find out that Shakespeare's source was Sir Thomas North's 1579 translation of Plutarch's *Lives*. This work, which Thomas Jefferson recommends for your library, was presumably authored by Plutarch, a Greek biographer, in about AD 75, one hundred and nineteen years after Caesar's death. Since Plutarch was born in AD 46, over ninety years after Caesar's death, he is precluded as an eyewitness to the event. It also precludes Plutarch interviewing any eyewitnesses, who would have been dead by the time of his writing. So who was Plutarch's source? This is where my trail ran cold. I have yet to find an authoritative answer, but let's speculate.

Was Plutarch's source Tacitus, whom Jefferson recommended to Skipwith? Tacitus was a Roman historian who focused his work on the first century AD, which is too late for Julius Caesar. Importantly, Tacitus records in AD 109 that in Nero's reign a group of people in Rome "called Christians by the populace" were hated and tortured by Nero. "Christus, from whom the name had its origin, suffered extreme penalty during the reign of Tiberius at the hands of one of our procurators, Pontius Pilatus."[25] So here is a source outside of the Bible (and inside Jefferson's library) confirming the execution of Jesus Christ, even if it does not confirm the assassination of Julius Caesar.

Let's assume Plutarch got most of his information from the Roman historian Seutonius, who wrote *The Twelve Caesars*. The problem is that Seutonius, like Plutarch, was born about a hundred years after Caesar died so he could not have witnessed the event either. At the time of his writing, there was no living eyewitness who could either confirm or deny the story. While Seutonius was in charge of the imperial archives under the emperor Hadrian—who ruled from AD 117 to 138—and wrote a biography of Julius Caesar, it is not clear that Plutarch used him as a source.

Could it be Sallust? This Roman historian served under Caesar and knew him personally, but apparently Sallust wrote no histories of Julius Caesar.

---

25. Tacitus, *Complete Works*, 380. "Annals, 15.44."

So let's suppose Plutarch got his information on Julius Caesar from Julius Caesar, since Caesar wrote a great deal about himself. His *Commentaries* on his own military conquests boast of his prowess and advance his political agenda. But the textual evidence for Caesar's works are slim. There are ten known copies of manuscripts in existence today, and the earliest of these is dated at about AD 900, almost a thousand years after Caesar's death. Sadly, the vast majority of his works are lost to history. But even if we could establish that the copies of Caesar's works we have today accurately represent the original and that Caesar was Plutarch's main source, we still have pesky problem. It is highly improbable that Caesar wrote very much about his own death.

And what about the textual evidence for the works of Seutonius? Is it better than Caesar's? There are over two hundred surviving copies of Seutonius's works, the oldest copied manuscript being dated to sometime in the ninth century, over eight hundred years after Caesar's death.[26] A little better, but still rather weak. A lot can happen to a text in that time span. And keep in mind that none of these ancient historians had an exceptionally strong motive to be precise, since they were not risking their lives for the message they were writing or encouraging anyone else to do so.

Perhaps you are beginning to get a sense of standards that historians use for determining which ancient documents are reliable. Now compare the data on Julius Caesar's assassination with data of the New Testament. Hold on. This gets tricky.

There are over fifty-seven hundred Greek manuscripts and ten thousand Latin copies of the New Testament or portions of the New Testament in existence today. This does not include over one million quotations of the New Testament in the writings of the early church fathers. The earliest copy, a portion of John's Gospel, which you can see in the John Rylands Library in Manchester, England,[27] is dated at around AD 125, less than one hundred years after the ministry and execution of Jesus. Nothing in ancient literature compares to that short of a time span between the event and the earliest existing copy that records the event. Remember, the time span between Seutonius's death and the oldest manuscript copy we possess of his work is eight hundred years. And since Julius Caesar was killed well over one hundred years before Seutonius wrote about it, that brings

---

26. Komoszewski, Sawyer, and Wallace, *Reinventing Jesus*, 70, 71.

27. This portion of John's Gospel is called Papyrus 52. See Roberts, *Can We Trust the Gospels?* 29.

the total time span between the actual event and our earliest existing copy to over nine hundred years. Contrast that to less than one hundred years for the New Testament.

Furthermore, since the portion of John's Gospel we possess is a copy, it is probable that the original was written within the generation that witnessed the execution of Jesus. Since John's Gospel is considered to be the latest of the four, this means that even a Gospel writer such as Luke, who did not personally meet Jesus, had access to people who had personal knowledge of Jesus.[28] While Luke was writing during the time that living eyewitnesses were available, Plutarch and Seutonius were writing long after the eyewitnesses had died.

The authors of the New Testament either claim to be eyewitnesses or to record the testimony of eyewitnesses to the birth, life, death, and resurrection of Jesus Christ. Luke tells his readers that even before he began writing his Gospel, many had already "undertaken to set down an orderly account of the events that have been fulfilled among us."[29] These written sources were no doubt useful to Luke as he set down his own orderly account. One of the sources may have been the Gospel of Mark, which was probably the earliest Gospel, written around AD 60. And since these writers lived during the time that living eyewitnesses were still accessible, we can have more confidence in the accuracy of the accounts. Additionally, as we will see in chapter 7, these writers ran the risk of great suffering as a consequence of propagating this story, so the motive for precision is extreme.

The comparison of the New Testament documents with similar ancient works is instructive because a common charge of the proponents of alternative Christianities is that we cannot really know what the New Testament originally said, since we 1) do not possess the original manuscripts, 2) there is such a large time span between Jesus's death and the writing of the Gospels, and 3) there is a large time span between the writing of the original and our earliest existing copy. In the view of many New Testament experts, if this reasoning is applied consistently, "then we must deny that most facts of ancient history can be recovered, because whatever doubts we cast on the text of the New Testament must be cast a hundredfold on virtually any other ancient text. The New Testament manuscripts stand closer to the original and are more plentiful than vir-

---

28. Blomberg, *Historical Reliability*, 18.
29. Luke 1:1.

tually any other ancient literature. The New Testament is far and away the best-attested work of Greek or Latin literature in the ancient world."[30]

As someone who has great confidence in the historical reliability of the Gospels, I am not asking for special treatment to be given to the Bible. I am rather drawn to Thomas Jefferson's advice here. I do not feel threatened if someone reads the Bible as they do Livy or Tacitus. Help yourself. But keep in mind that there is, as Craig Blomberg has observed, "no body of literature in the world that has been exposed to the stringent analytical study that the four Gospels have sustained."[31] And none has better stood the test.

CONFUSED? UNCONVINCED?

Though Edwards had great confidence in the preponderance of historical evidence supporting the reliability of the Gospels, he was not overly optimistic about the power of that evidence to change made-up minds. "Men may argue the truth of the Gospel with great strength of reason, and so as cannot be answered," Edwards told his congregation in a sermon in 1729. "We may argue from the impossibility of men's forging such a story as that of Christ" in the same generation as it happened and then declaring "it through the world without being by everybody contradicted . . . and much more the impossibility of a few illiterate men's imposing such a forgery upon the whole Roman Empire so as to make them all believe it and to cast away their idols."[32] But in the end, many will not be persuaded because they are prejudiced against the message of Jesus, so "they will never be fully convinced."[33] That is because "the heart is naturally greatly prejudiced against the Gospel . . . [it] is so corrupt and [has] such enmity

---

30. Komoszewski, Sawyer, and Wallace, *Reinventing Jesus,* 70, 71. These arguments have been available to non-specialists for years. A landmark book that expresses them clearly is F. F. Bruce, *Are the New Testament Documents Reliable?* Bruce's significant work was popularized most effectively by Josh McDowell in *Evidence that Demands a Verdict.* I was prompted to follow this line of evidence by hearing Josh McDowell say years ago that there is more historical evidence for the resurrection of Jesus Christ than for the proposition that Julius Caesar ever lived.

31. Blomberg, *Historical Reliability,* ix.

32. Edwards, MS Sermon on 2 Peter 1:16, 46, 47.

33. Ibid., 18.

against everything that is holy and divine that the truths of the Gospel don't suit it."[34]

Besides, if God required all people to grasp and embrace such an elaborate defense of the Gospels as I have outlined in this chapter in order to glorify and enjoy God, that would leave most people out. God did not give the gospel "only for great men and men of learned education. The rest of mankind, which make the far greater part of the world, have souls as precious as they." After all, God "sent Christ to preach the Gospel to the poor and Christ thanked the Father that he had hid these things from the wise and prudent and had revealed them to babes."[35] Ironically, "poor fisherman" came to full assurance that Jesus was God and followed him, while "men of learning" like the "Pharisees and lawyers"[36] did not.

That is not to say that a scholarly defense of the historical reliability of the Gospels is not valuable. In fact, in the same sermon, Edwards made it plain that what he has said should not be used as an excuse for Christians to be intellectually lazy.

> Not but that the generality of men might get a great deal more knowledge than they do, and other arguments for the truth of the Gospel are not to be neglected, but to be diligently improved. And men are exceedingly to blame in indulging themselves so much in a slothful neglect of knowledge, and that they don't more acquaint themselves with the reasons and arguments that may be given for the truth of what they profess to believe.[37]

What I think Edwards is saying to his church, full of busy merchants, worried farmers, weary homemakers, tired laborers and concerned community leaders, is that the information—the scholarly argument and historical evidence—is there if you think you need it to make a decision about the supremacy of Jesus. Perhaps when people reject Jesus it is not because they followed the evidence, but because they did not follow the evidence far enough. At least examine the evidence before you summarily dismiss the veracity of the Gospels. But if you don't need all of this information, if you feel drawn to Jesus without a complicated defense of him, don't worry. Just start by reading the Gospels and behold his glory!

34. Edwards, MS Sermon on 2 Peter, 16.

35. Ibid., 28.

36. Ibid., 29.

37. Ibid., 34, 35.

The longer you follow him, the more opportunities you will have to learn about him.

THE PREJUDICE OF THOMAS JEFFERSON

So why did Thomas Jefferson not accept the testimony of the New Testament concerning Jesus? Perhaps he was not aware of the superior attestation. After all, most of this scholarship and archaeological evidence has been developed since Jefferson's day. He may never have questioned Plutarch's source or compared the textual evidence of Plutarch to that of the New Testament documents. We can only speculate what he would have done with the textual evidence available to us today. But given Jefferson's deistic bias against the possibility that God occasionally and miraculously intrudes on the laws of nature, he probably would have rejected the witness of the New Testament anyway. As he advised, "those facts in the bible which contradict the laws of nature, must be examined with more care, and under a variety of faces."[38] For Thomas Jefferson, that did not mean that the historical evidence for the reliability of the Gospels was to be carefully examined. That meant it was be summarily dismissed.

FROM LESSING'S DITCH TO THE JESUS SEMINAR

Jefferson's religious heirs are growing in abundance these days. John Dominic Crossan is an original member of the Jesus Seminar. Building on ideas advanced by Reimarus and Lessing, the Jesus Seminar, beginning as a group of about thirty scholars, who had already decided the New Testament was not historically reliable, began to meet and discuss which words of Jesus recorded in the Gospels are authentic. After each debate, they would vote by dropping colored beads in a box. As the Seminar came to a saying or parable of Jesus in the New Testament, each scholar dropped in a red bead if he was certain these were the words of the real, historical Jesus. If he or she believed Jesus probably said it, they dropped in a pink bead. A gray bead was dropped if Jesus probably did not say it but the idea is close to his own, and a black bead if he definitely did not say it. The results were published in 1993 as *The Five Gospels: The Search for the Authentic Words of Jesus.*

---

38. Jefferson, *Papers*, 12:16.

The Jesus Seminar has breathed new life into the old deistic distinction between the Jesus of history and the Christ of faith. For people like Crossan, the Easter story is not an actual historical event, but a helpful metaphor. He believes that Jesus's body was discarded in a common graveyard and probably consumed by dogs. Then Mark fabricated the story of the women's visit to the tomb. Furthermore, the disciples never saw a risen Jesus, never believed in his literal resurrection, and never intended for their accounts of Jesus to be taken literally.[39] Armed with that set of presuppositions, it is easy to imagine how the *Five Gospels* turns out.

Crossan considers himself a Christian, even if he considers the Gospels a myth. The Jesus of history was a Jewish peasant who lived and died in the first century, what remains of his bones still scattered across the Judean countryside. However, the Christ of faith still lives in our legends, and, like Aesop's fables, the stories about him offer us helpful and inspiring moral guides to live by and cheer us up at funerals even if they never happened. In the end, however, our Christian fables, while good for us Christians, are no better than the Buddhist fables are for Buddhists.[40]

Though deism died out as a movement in the early nineteenth century, the damage was done. Confidence in the Gospels had been severely shaken by deists in the eighteenth and nineteenth centuries, and it seemed to many New Testament scholars in the twentieth century that Jesus needed to be rescued and revised for a modern world. Early in the twenty-first century, ably employing the media and mass marketing, their influence is only growing. John Dominic Crossan and the Jesus Seminar believe they have saved Jesus.

"DIAMONDS IN A DUNGHILL"

While Benjamin Franklin was only willing to say publicly that he had some doubts about the Gospel accounts of Jesus, Thomas Jefferson bought the deist argument in full. Having closed his mind to the possibility of God's supernatural intervention into the natural world, Jefferson rejected anything in the Gospels he considered a miracle. The verses of the Gospels that spoke of the Jesus that Jefferson received were the diamonds. The verses of the Gospels that spoke of the Jesus that Jefferson rejected were dung.

---

39. Crossan, *Historical Jesus,* 392–93; 415–16; 404.

40. Crossan, "Opening Statement," 39.

On October 13, 1813, Jefferson wrote to John Adams that "we must reduce our volume to the simple evangelists, select, even from them, the very words only of Jesus." Jefferson believed that Jesus was misunderstood by the Gospel writers who lived in the first century and that he, living in the nineteenth century, had clearer insight into the mind of the real Jesus than they did. "I have performed this operation for my own use," he told Adams, "by cutting verse by verse out of the printed book, and by arranging the matter which is evidently his, and which is distinguishable as diamonds in a dunghill."

That's right. In January of 1804, President Thomas Jefferson, Benjamin Franklin's spiritual heir, sat down at his desk in the White House with two King James versions of the New Testament, a razor, and paste, and made for himself an alternative Bible, because the only way to revise Jesus is to revise the New Testament. Although that first Jefferson Bible is lost, he did it again in 1819 or 1820, and that version was later published by the U.S. Congress. I have a copy open on my desk even now as I type these words. Gone is the virgin birth, gone are the miracles, gone is the feeding of the five thousand, gone is the healing of Bartimaeus, and gone is the resurrection of Jesus Christ. The last verse of the Jefferson Bible is Matthew 27:60: "There laid they Jesus, and rolled a great stone to the door of the sepulcher, and departed," which is, I suppose, a comforting thought for John Dominic Crossan and the members of the Jesus Seminar.

5

God: "If Not, the Greatest Imposter"

To suppose Him not to be the Person he profess'd Himself to be is to make Him the greatest Imposter that Ever was. This should make us the more careful that we may have right Thoughts of Him.

—Jonathan Edwards[1]

A man who was merely a man and said the sort of things Jesus said would not be a great moral teacher. He would be either a lunatic—on a level with a man who says he is a poached egg—or else he would be the devil of hell.

—C. S. Lewis[2]

RICHARD DAWKINS, PERHAPS THE world's most renowned atheist, treats his readers to a theology lesson in the first chapter of his best-selling book, *The God Delusion*. Theism, he explains, is the belief in a supernatural intelligent being who created and now sustains the universe. This deity "answers prayers; forgives or punishes sins; intervenes in the world by performing miracles; frets about good and bad deeds, and knows when we do them."[3] Deism also acknowledges a supernatural, intelligent deity, but one who initially set up the laws of nature, and never intervenes in those laws, having "no specific interest in human affairs."[4] Pantheism believes in no God at all, but uses the word "god" as a "synonym for Nature," a kind of metaphoric symbol for obvious natural laws. Atheism, like pantheism, does not believe in God and sees no use for the

---

1. Edwards, "It Concerns All," 39.
2. Lewis, *Mere Christianity*, 56.
3. Dawkins, *The God Delusion*, 18.
4. Ibid.

word "god." Dawkins observes these views on a continuum: "Pantheism is sexed-up atheism. Deism is watered-down theism."[5]

Dawkins argues for a religious evolution to higher forms of world-views. The most primitive of the views, theism, evolves into deism, then into pantheism, and finally, to the apex of the intellectual elite, atheism. Richard Dawkins, Oxford University professor, is a self-appointed spokesman for the intellectual elite. And in making his argument to a very theistic America, Dawkins employs a brilliant tactic: Appeal to the Founding Fathers.

So, in the second chapter of *The God Delusion*, the British Dawkins combines his theology instruction with a lesson on American history. "Thomas Jefferson, as so often, got it right when he said, 'Ridicule is the only weapon which can be used against unintelligible propositions. Ideas must be distinct before reason can act upon them; and no man ever had a distinct idea of the Trinity. It is the mere Abracadabra of the mountebanks calling themselves the priests of Jesus.'"[6]

Let's gather up what Dawkins has pointed out to us so far. First, a move from theism to deism is a move in the direction of atheism. This tends to support the thesis of this book that atheistic writers like Richard Dawkins, Christopher Hitchens, and Sam Harris often borrow the arguments of eighteenth century deists to make their case, laboring to convert, by degree, theists to deists, and deists to atheists. Second, an effective strategy for advancing atheistic arguments in theistic America is to recruit beloved Founding Fathers. Third, Thomas Jefferson believed that "no man ever had a distinct idea of the Trinity."

Really? No man?

"HE RIDICULES THE DOCTRINE OF THE TRINITY"

In 1750, Jonathan Edwards wrote a letter to a Scottish pastor, John Erskine, in response to Erskine's inquiry regarding Edwards's view of the Westminster Confession. "As to my subscribing to the substance of the Westminster Confession," replied Edwards, "There would be no difficulty."[7] The Westminster Confession was the product of the English Parliament's call upon distinguished biblical scholars and Puritan church leaders to

---

5. Dawkins, *The God Delusion*, 18.

6. Ibid., 34. Dawkins offers no source documentation.

7. Edwards, *Works*, 16:355.

meet at Westminster Abbey in 1643 to provide guidelines for doctrine, worship and order in the Church of England. This is what the Confession states concerning the Trinity:

> In the unity of the Godhead there be three persons, of one substance, power, and eternity: God the Father, God the Son, and God the Holy Ghost: the Father is of none, neither begotten, nor proceeding; the Son is eternally begotten of the Father; the Holy Ghost eternally proceeding from the Father and the Son.[8]

Strong stuff, this confession, and every word selected with precision. Serious Christians spend a lifetime unpacking its meaning and implications, and few have given it as much attention as Jonathan Edwards.

By 1757, Edwards was alarmed at the inroads deistic doctrine had made into American life. He implored Edward Wigglesworth, a divinity professor at Harvard, to take action against the Boston pastor Jonathan Mayhew because "he ridicules the doctrine of the Trinity."[9] The implications of abandoning Trinitarian doctrine must have weighed heavily on him, for on the same day, February 11, he wrote another letter to the Reverend Thomas Foxcroft expressing his fear for America's future "if none should now appear to attempt a full vindication of the doctrine of Christ's divinity."[10] By 1757, a few months before his death, Jonathan Edwards had spent many of his days doing just that.

DEALING WITH THE DATA

The doctrine of the Trinity is an intellectually honest attempt to deal with all the data. The Bible is clear on five facts that somehow need to be reconciled with one another.

1. God is three distinct persons, Father, Son, and Holy Spirit.

2. The Father is God.

3. The Son is God.

4. The Holy Spirit is God.

5. God is one; there is one God.

---

8. *Westminster Confession of Faith*, "Of God and of the Holy Trinity," 2.3.

9. Edwards, *Works*, 16:698–700.

10. Edwards, *Works*, 16:695.

The Bible everywhere assumes these facts. In one of the most famous passages of Scripture, sometimes called the Great Commission, Jesus says to the apostles, "Therefore go and make disciples of all nations, baptizing them in the name of the Father and of the Son and of the Holy Spirit."[11] The singular form of "name" is subtle but significant. This is not a grammatical oversight. Rather, it is an intentional theological statement. If there are three gods, we would be baptized in their names. But because there is one God, we are baptized in his name.

Furthermore, each of these persons is fully God. The Father is fully God. "This, then, is how you should pray," instructed Jesus, "Our Father in heaven, hallowed be your name."[12] The Son, Jesus Christ, is fully God. "In the beginning was the Word, and the Word was with God, and the Word was God . . . The Word became flesh and made his dwelling among us."[13] And finally, the Holy Spirit is fully God. After Peter asked Ananias why he had lied to the Holy Spirit, Peter explained the offense: "You have not lied to men but to God."[14] All three persons of the Godhead are fully God.

And each person, while equal in essence, is different in function. The Father has sent the Son to reconcile sinful man to holy God. "There is one God," wrote Paul, "and one mediator between God and men, the man Jesus Christ."[15] The Son has sent the Spirit to teach and comfort those he has reconciled. "When the Counselor comes," Jesus told his disciples, "whom I will send to you, the Spirit of truth who goes out from the Father, he will testify about me."[16] Operating in perfect unity, each person of the Trinity complements the other as they function together. "God eternally exists as three persons," writes theologian Wayne Grudem, "Father, Son, and Holy Spirit, and each person is fully God, and there is one God."[17] A difficult concept to be sure, but wholly logical.

11. Matthew 28:19.
12. Matthew 6:9.
13. John 1:1, 14.
14. Acts 5:3, 4.
15. 1 Timothy 2:5.
16. John 15:26.
17. Grudem, *Systematic Theology*, 226.

WHY THE TRINITY IS NOT ILLOGICAL

Far from being unreasonable, the doctrine of the Trinity is the only reasonable way to organize the available data. And properly understood, it represents no violation of the laws of logic. It commits no formal fallacy. Some have argued that the doctrine of the Trinity is a logical contradiction. Either God is one or God is three but he cannot be both! But the law of non-contradiction states that A cannot be non-A at the same time and in the same sense. If we say that God is one person and God is three persons, that would be contradiction. But that is not what we are saying. We are saying that God is one God and he exists as three persons. Likewise, some might argue that either Jesus was God or Jesus was man but he could not be both. If we say that Jesus was God and Jesus was not God, then that would be a contradiction. But that is not what we are saying. We are saying that Jesus was God and Jesus was man. There is no contradiction here.

Granted, there is a great deal of mystery. That is not an intellectual dodge. We just cannot quite wrap our finite minds around all God is. But full comprehension has never been a prerequisite for belief in any field. For centuries, man did not fully comprehend lightning. Benjamin Franklin's generation gained unprecedented understanding of lightning, but the lightning was just as real and true a thousand years before. Deists like Jefferson should have known this better than anyone. There are many aspects of nature that scientists do not fully comprehend, but that does not make them untrue. Jonathan Edwards recognized the two-edged sword when he chides the deists for their inconsistency: "To reject everything but what we can first see to be agreeable to our reason, tends, by degrees, to bring everything relating not only to revealed religion, but even natural religion, into doubt."[18]

EDWARDS PATRIOTS ON THE DEITY OF JESUS

John Jay, equipped with a trained, legal mind, embraced similar arguments for the deity of Jesus. Jay differed from Edwards, however, in that he sought to avoid confrontation with those who held opposing religious beliefs. As an ambassador of the United States he was often placed in

---

18. Edwards, *The Works of Jonathan Edwards*, 2:496. As Edwards puts it, "So, doubtless many truths will hereafter appear plain, when we come to look on them by the bright light of heaven, that now are involved in mystery and darkness," 2:495.

delicate diplomatic situations that required a different approach. While in Paris negotiating the treaty, along with Franklin, that would end the Revolutionary War, Jay often visited in Franklin's home. One evening, while another visitor was in conversation with Franklin, the topic turned to religion and the visitor laughed at the proposition that Jesus is God. At that, "Jay glared and said nothing, arose, turned on his heel and walked away."[19] Unwilling to jeopardize diplomatic relations with the French, the best defense he felt he could make for the deity of Jesus and the doctrine of the Trinity was a silent protest.

By 1809, Elias Boudinot was concerned that because of publications from skeptics like Paine attacking orthodox Christianity, the next generation of young Americans were being "led to deny the doctrine of the Saviour's Divinity and Atonement."[20] When Boudinot wrote those words in his diary, all but one of the Congregational churches in Boston had rejected the doctrine of the Trinity and the deity of Christ.[21] His concern has a contemporary ring.

"WE HOLD THESE TRUTHS TO BE SELF-EVIDENT"

So Thomas Jefferson could not have truthfully said that no man ever had an idea of the Trinity. Jonathan Edwards certainly did. But Jefferson added an important qualifier: "no man ever had a *distinct* idea of the Trinity." To Jefferson, the doctrine of the Trinity was unintelligible and unreasonable; it was not distinct. But was Jefferson right? If by the word distinct, Jefferson meant, "easy to understand," then he is right. The doctrine of the Trinity, like quantum physics, is not easy to understand. But if by distinct, Jefferson meant logical, then Thomas Jefferson was wrong. The doctrine of the Trinity violates no formal rule of logic. Jonathan Edwards took great pains to demonstrate how this was true.

Edwards freely acknowledged that on the surface, a proposition that is actually true might seem to be false; it may appear to be a contradiction of common sense. To prove his point, he once asked a thirteen-year-old boy in his church if he believed a two-inch cube was eight times larger than a one-inch cube. The boy responded as most of us would at that age: Of course, not.

19. Monaghan, *John Jay*, 218.
20. Boudinot, *Journey to Boston*, 52.
21. Ibid., 50, fn. 111.

So Edwards took a block of wood that was two inches by two inches, and cut it into eight equal cubes, one inch by one inch. The boy even after handling and counting the cubes for himself could not bring himself to believe his eyes: "He seemed to [be] astonished as though there were some witchcraft in the case and hardly to believe it after all, for he did not yet at all see the reason of it." [22] The mystery of the cubes, Edwards concluded, was a greater mystery to a thirteen-year-old boy than the Trinity is to grown and learned men, "and there seemed to him more evidently to be a contradiction in it than ever there did in any mystery of religion to a Socinian or deist." Edwards continued his musing: "And why should we not suppose that there may be some things that are true, that may be as much above our understandings and as difficult to them, as this truth was to this boy. Doubtless, there is a vastly greater distance between our understanding and God's, than between this boy's and that of the greatest philosopher or mathematician." [23]

It was Thomas Jefferson who forever enshrined that hyphenated word of the Enlightenment in the American vocabulary: self-evident. [24] To be self-evident means that a proposition made sense on the face of it. It could be quickly grasped by human reason. "We hold these truths," Jefferson wrote in the Declaration of Independence, "to be self-evident, that all men are created equal, that they are endowed by their Creator with certain unalienable rights." It was obvious to Jefferson and the founders that the grounds for armed revolt were both logically reasonable and morally right. It was not obvious that "all men" should include Jefferson's own slaves. Some things are true that are not immediately self-evident.

HOW THE TRINITY IS LIKE A CELL PHONE

Imagine you can travel back in time to the summer of 1776 and you catch Benjamin Franklin and Thomas Jefferson in a room together as they are editing the Declaration of Independence. They want to consult with John Adams on a particular phrase and you say that you wish you had your cell

22. Edwards, *Works*, 16:192–93.

23. Ibid.

24. The original rough draft of the Declaration reads: "We hold these truths to be sacred and undeniable," but was later changed to read, "We hold these truths to be self-evident." While some historians attribute the change to Franklin, others note that there is no "conclusive evidence, and there seems to be even stronger evidence that the change was made by Jefferson or at least it is in his handwriting." See fn. 2 in Jefferson, *Papers*, 1:427.

phone so you could just call him. "What's that?" asks Jefferson. You try to explain: "A cell phone is like a hybrid between a phone and a two-way radio." "Unintelligible," says Jefferson. "Unreasonable," says Franklin. Of course it would have been to them, because in explaining something that is unknown, we almost always depend on relating it to something that is known. A cell phone is like a telephone in your home, hard wired to the phone company's main trunk. But it is mobile, so it is like the walkie-talkies we played with as children. Once we become familiar with the technology of each, it is a shorter reach to comprehend how the technologies might be integrated into a cell phone. What would be unintelligible and subject to ridicule in 1776, is now an understandable, every-day tool of modern life. Cell phones are not illogical now that they are understood, but neither would they have been illogical in 1776 when they would not have been understood.

Such is the doctrine of the Trinity for us. "God requires us to understand no more than is intelligibly revealed," wrote Edwards. "That which is not distinctly revealed, we are not required distinctly to understand. It may be necessary for us to know a thing in part, and yet not necessary to know it perfectly."[25] In the end, our failure to understand it does not mean it is not true. To hold such a position is to hold oneself and one's own intellect in stunningly high esteem.

"NO OTHER SAVIOR"

Of the many implications of the doctrine of the Trinity, I focus on one. Jesus of Nazareth was God in the flesh. That is the uniform testimony of the most reliable historical records. In a notebook called the *Miscellanies*, Edwards stockpiled an enormous amount of biblical data and deductive reasoning that he likely intended to use on later writing projects he did not live long enough to complete. I will offer just a sample of Edwards's thinking on this topic. The evidence that Edwards amasses can be divided into four categories.

First, *Jesus said things only God can say.* Edwards gives numerous instances in which Jesus applied to himself the Old Testament references to God. For example, God, through Malachi, foretells the sending of a messenger "who will prepare the way for me."[26] Jesus, speaking of John

25. Edwards, *The Works of Jonathan Edwards*, 2:497.
26. Malachi 3:1.

the Baptist, publicly declared "this is the one about whom it is written, 'I will send my messenger ahead of you, who will prepare your way before you.'"[27] Clearly, John the Baptist was preparing the way for Jesus, so Jesus, in applying this passage to himself, is claiming to be God. "But who," asks Edwards, "is this person that is called the Lord, the God of Israel, whose forerunner, John the Baptist, is to prepare his way? And nothing is more manifest than that it is Jesus Christ."[28] What the Old Testament scriptures "foretell is a forerunner to prepare the way for the only true and supreme God."[29] Jesus is claiming to be God.

Second, *Jesus did things only God can do.* The multiple miracles that Jesus performed demonstrate his authority over nature, disease, and death. He is the sovereign over all creation. "Raising of the dead is spoken of as an instance of the exceeding greatness of the mighty power of God," observes Edwards, "But this very power is often ascribed to Christ."[30] In fact, Jesus claimed to have this power himself when he announced "just as the Father raises the dead and gives them life, even so the Son gives life to whom he is pleased to give it."[31] No wonder then that the religious leaders of his day tried to kill him. He was, after all, "calling God his own Father, making himself equal with God."[32] Not long after that, Jesus issued a command to a dead man to "come out" of his tomb and the dead man obeyed.[33] As we will see in the next chapter, the final and crowning miracle is Jesus's own resurrection. His miraculous works validate his claim to be God.

Third, *Jesus received worship and adulation of which only God is worthy.* When the rich young ruler called Jesus "Good Master," Christ, notes Edwards, did not "reject it and reprove him."[34] Rather, he simply responded that "no one is good—except God alone."[35] When Thomas saw and touched the risen Jesus, he exclaimed, "My Lord and my God!"[36] and Jesus did not rebuke him for idolatry, but instead received his praise. When

27. Matthew 11:10.
28. Edwards, *Works*, 23:419.
29. Ibid., 23:420.
30. Ibid., 23:425–26.
31. John 5:21.
32. John 5:18.
33. John 11:43, 44.
34. Edwards, *Works*, 23:412.
35. Mark 10:18.
36. John 20:28.

Jesus spent two days teaching in the hometown of the Samaritan woman, the result was that her neighbors came to believe and publicly confess that Jesus "really is the Savior of the world"[37] and Jesus did nothing to persuade them to think otherwise. However, God had declared through Isaiah centuries earlier "I am the Lord, apart from me there is no savior."[38] Edwards restates the truth that "there is no other Savior besides the one, only Jehovah."[39] We can only conclude that Jesus is willfully receiving the honor that is due to God alone. "But now nothing," reasoned Edwards, "is more evident by the express and abundant doctrine of Scripture than that Jesus Christ is most eminently and peculiarly the Savior of God's people and the Savior of mankind, the Savior of the world."[40]

Fourth, *Jesus's followers referred to him as only God should be.* Edwards systematically, doggedly, stacks up one biblical reference after another that prove beyond all reasonable doubt that Jesus's earliest followers believed him to be God. Scripture consistently and repeatedly ascribes to Jesus the adjectives and titles that belong only to God. Edwards points out that Jesus is called in the Scripture,

> he that [is] true, the Amen, the faithful and true witness, the mighty God, the everlasting Father, the Prince of Peace, the blessed and the only potentate, the King of kings and Lord of lords, the Lord of life that has life in himself, that all men might honor the Son as they honor the Father, the wisdom of God, the power of God, the Alpha and Omega, the Beginning and the End, God, Jehovah, Elohim, the King of Glory.[41]

A WATERED DOWN JESUS

There is no evidence that either Benjamin Franklin or Thomas Jefferson attempted any careful examination of the biblical evidence for the deity of Jesus. They had eschewed the authority of Scripture years earlier. Granted, Edwards's argument in *Miscellany* 1349 has not proved to a skeptic's satisfaction that Jesus is God. But what it does prove is that the historical evidence overwhelmingly supports the assertion that Jesus *claimed* to be God.

37. John 4:42.
38. Isaiah 43:11.
39. Edwards, *Works*, 23:618.
40. Ibid., 23:619.
41. Ibid., 23:412.

Franklin and Jefferson were no doubt familiar with the claim that Jesus of Nazareth was God in the flesh. They just didn't believe it. They had a high regard for Jesus and found him to be a good source of ethical teaching, but other than that, Jesus was not unique. Like Socrates, he had a wide influence on many people, and there is much to be admired, but there is nothing there to inspire worship. Jesus was a great man, but he was, in the end, just a man.

As a young man, Benjamin Franklin developed a list of virtues which he resolved to attain. As he later wrote in his autobiography:

> These names of virtues, with their precepts, were: 1. TEMPERANCE. Eat not to dullness; drink not to elevation. 2. SILENCE. Speak not but what may benefit others or yourself; avoid trifling conversation. 3. ORDER. Let all your things have their places; let each part of your business have its time. 4. RESOLUTION. Resolve to perform what you ought; perform without fail what you resolve. 5. FRUGALITY. Make no expense but to do good to others or yourself; i.e., waste nothing. 6. INDUSTRY. Lose no time; be always employ'd in something useful; cut off all unnecessary actions. 7. SINCERITY. Use no hurtful deceit; think innocently and justly, and, if you speak, speak accordingly. 8. JUSTICE. Wrong none by doing injuries, or omitting the benefits that are your duty. 9. MODERATION. Avoid extremes; forbear resenting injuries so much as you think they deserve. 10. CLEANLINESS. Tolerate no uncleanliness in body, clothes, or habitation. 11. TRANQUILITY. Be not disturbed at trifles, or at accidents common or unavoidable. 12. CHASTITY. Rarely use venery but for health or offspring, never to dullness, weakness, or the injury of your own or another's peace or reputation.[42]

But the list was to be amended. A friend later informed him that Franklin had a reputation for being a proud man, and that the arrogance manifested itself often in his conversations with others. He was often "overbearing" insisting on winning every argument. After hearing his friend produce a few examples, Franklin was convinced and consequently added a final virtue to his list:

> 13. HUMILITY. Imitate Jesus and Socrates.

Never mind for now that Jesus, if he was not God, resembled anything but humility in claiming to be God. The point to take away is that Jesus was, in

---

42. Franklin, *Writings*, 1384–85.

the mind of Benjamin Franklin, in the same league with Socrates, merely a great human teacher. When deism gave us what Richard Dawkins called "a watered-down theism," it also gave us a watered-down Jesus.

THE SHOCKING ALTERNATIVE

But a watered-down Jesus is not a viable option for the intellectually honest. If Jesus claimed to be God and wasn't, he was either a deceiver or self-deceived, unworthy of adoration. If Jesus claimed to be God and was, then the implications are breathtaking. C. S. Lewis, the Cambridge scholar and author, famously made this point with his trilemma in *Mere Christianity* in 1943. In a chapter entitled "The Shocking Alternative," Lewis made his case:

> I am trying here to prevent anyone from saying the really foolish thing that people often say about him: "I'm ready to accept Jesus as a great moral teacher but I don't accept his claim to be God." That is the one thing we must not say. A man who was merely a man and said the sort of things Jesus said would not be a great moral teacher. He would either be a lunatic—on a level with a man who says he is a poached egg—or else he would be the devil of hell. You must make your choice: Either this man was, and is, the Son of God; or else a madman or something worse. You can shut him up for a fool, you can spit at Him and kill Him as a demon; or you can fall at His feet and call him Lord and God. But let us not come with any patronizing nonsense about his being a great human teacher. He has not left that open to us. He did not intend to.[43]

That seems rather clear to most people, but not to Christopher Hitchens. Labeling C. S. Lewis's defense of orthodox Christianity as "absurd," he reminds his readers again that some founders like Thomas Jefferson took the very position that Lewis says you cannot take: that Jesus was a great moral teacher without being God. He then proceeds to unleash his vitriol on Lewis.

> Least of all, do I accept his reasoning, which is so pathetic as to defy description and which takes his two false alternatives as exclusive antithesis, and then uses them to fashion a crude non sequitur ("Now it seems to me obvious that He was neither a lunatic nor a

---

43. Lewis, *Mere Christianity*, 56.

fiend; and consequently, however strange or terrifying or unlikely
it may seem, I have to accept the view that He was and is God.")[44]

There is a fourth alternative, Hitchens might say: Jesus never said this sort
of thing. Of course, the problem with this option is that the earliest documents are in agreement that Jesus did say this sort of thing. Who has a
clearer view of what Jesus said? Those New Testament authors in the first
century or Christopher Hitchens in the twenty-first century?

One wonders how Lewis, who died in 1963, might respond to Hitchens's
rant. By 1943, Lewis had become convinced of the superior attestation of
the New Testament documents. He was, after all, a professor of literature at
Cambridge University, and familiar with the discipline of textual criticism.
As we saw in chapter 4, if the New Testament is not historically reliable,
then no history from the ancient world is. That issue was already settled for
Lewis when he framed the trilemma, and it is the assumption from which
he works. Yet, if he were alive today, there is little doubt that Lewis would
take Hitchens's objection seriously. Possibly, he could satisfy Hitchens by
adding a small phrase to the proposition: "A man who was merely a man
and said the sort of things *that the best and earliest historical documents
confirm* Jesus said would not be a great moral teacher."

But two centuries earlier Jonathan Edwards was already spotlight-
ing the logical impossibility, given the historical evidence, of Jesus being
merely a great moral teacher. "There are," he warned his church family
in 1749, "very various opinions about him, so in those days, so in these
days." Throughout history, some have labeled Jesus "a crafty subtle deceiver, a wizard, a very good man, but no more than a mere man."[45] And
now Edwards's own "shocking alternative": "To suppose him not to be
the person he professed himself to be is to make him the greatest impostor that ever was. This should make us the more careful that we may
have right thoughts of Him."[46] In his sermon notes, Edwards reminds
himself to remind the congregation at the close of the message with a
curt summary: "If not, the greatest impostor."[47]

---

44. Hitchens, *God Is Not Great*, 7.
45. Edwards, "It Concerns All," 37.
46. Ibid., 33.
47. Ibid., 39.

THE SUPREMACY OF JESUS CHRIST

The absolute uniqueness and supremacy of Jesus Christ is the *sine qua non*—the *without which not*—of historic Christianity. In fact, if it does not confess Jesus Christ as Lord and God, it cannot rightly be called Christianity. The Apostle Paul, writing in about AD 61, incorporates an early Christian poem in his letter to the church at Colossae.

> And he is the head of the body, the church; he is the beginning and the firstborn from among the dead, so that in everything he might have the supremacy. For God was pleased to have all his fullness dwell in him, and through him to reconcile to himself all things, whether things on earth or things in heaven, by making peace through his blood, shed on the cross.[48]

The historic creeds and confessions of the church throughout all generations have affirmed this truth. Again we turn to the Westminster Confession of Faith to which Edwards subscribed:

> It pleased God, in his eternal purpose, to choose and ordain the Lord Jesus, his only-begotten Son, to be the Mediator between God and men, the prophet, priest, and king; the head and Savior of the Church, the heir of all things, and judge of the world; unto whom he did, from all eternity, give a people to be his seed, and to be by him in time redeemed, called, justified, sanctified, and glorified.[49]

For Edwards, the supremacy of Jesus Christ, due to his deity, was a non-negotiable element of the Christian faith. "If we take only a part of Christianity," affirmed Edwards, "and leave out a part that is essential to it, what we take is not Christianity; because something that is of the essence of it is wanting. So if we profess only a part, and leave out a part that is essential, that which we profess is not Christianity."[50]

THE DIFFERENCE BETWEEN LAMBS AND LIONS

In 1736, Edwards wrote *The Excellency of Christ*, a discourse demonstrating how diverse and seemingly contradictory traits find perfect resolution in Jesus. For example, think about how high Christ is. "Christ, as he

---

48. Colossians 1:18–20.

49. *Westminster Confession of Faith*, 28–29.

50. Edwards, *Works*, 2:413.

is God," writes Edwards, "is infinitely great and high above all."[51] Here Edwards affirms again, the deity, and thus, the supremacy of Jesus Christ. It's too good to paraphrase, so I'll let you read it in Edwards's words:

> He is higher than the kings of the earth; for he is King of kings, and Lord of lords. He is higher than the heavens, and higher than the highest angels in heaven. So great is he, that all men, all kings and princes, are as worms of the dust before him; all nations are as the drop of a bucket, and the light dust of the balance; yea, and angels themselves are as nothing before him. He is so high, that he is infinitely above any need of us; above our reach, that we cannot be profitable to him; and above our conceptions, that we cannot comprehend him."[52]

But at the same time, think about how low Jesus Christ is. He comes down to the level of the weakest of people and he meets them at their point of need. He does not require them to lift themselves up, or make themselves attractive, or powerful, or rich. Jesus comes down to the lowest, the poorest, the weakest, the most despised, and he loves them. "Christ condescends," says Edwards, "to take notice of beggars . . . and people of the most despised nations . . . and little children . . . His condescension is great enough to become their friend; to become their companion, to unite their souls to him in spiritual marriage."[53]

Edwards goes on like this for several pages. Christ is high but low, just but gracious, majestic but meek, deserving of good treatment but patient in mistreatment, obedient but dominant, sovereign to decree but resigned to the decrees, self-sufficient but God-reliant. And so, Edwards observes, "there is an admirable conjunction of diverse excellencies in Jesus Christ."[54]

This discourse is built on Revelation 5:5, 6 where Jesus is called both the Lion and the Lamb in the same breath. What could be more different than a lion and a lamb? And yet in Christ they come together in "admirable conjunction." As a lamb he condescends, loves, obeys, suffers, resigns himself to the will of God, relying on him for strength to do his will. As a lion he rules, judges, takes dominion, and depends on nothing and no one in creation. He does what he wants, says what he wants, goes where

51. Ibid., 19:565.
52. Edwards, *Works,* 19:565.
53. Ibid., 19:566.
54. Ibid., 19:565.

he wants, gives what he wants, takes what he wants, and no one can thwart him or stand in his way. With no comparable rivals, he is supreme.

American culture, largely because of the influence of founders like Franklin and Jefferson, has been generally friendly to Jesus the Lamb. Lambs can be penned up, fenced in, and pushed around. Lambs can be fit into a life where and when it is most convenient, and if you don't want the lamb around, you can just avoid him. Lambs are soft, safe, warm, and dependent. They make no demands, only requests, and if you do not meet their requests, they are powerless to make you feel consequences. Lambs can give good examples to live by, but they give no commands to obey. No one is offended much by Jesus the Lamb.

It is Jesus the Lion that the world hates. This lion is untamable. He cannot be conveniently ignored, managed, or manipulated. Lions depend on no man and they are unimpressed with human accomplishments. Lions are hard and strong and dangerous. They do not need to be led to green pastures or still waters. With the flick of a paw and the slash of a claw, the lion can rip the life from the human heart. Lions do not present meek requests. They roar out authoritative warnings, and the wise will give heed. Lions conquer, because lions are supreme.

The good news is this: for those of us who trust the Lamb, the Lion will be supreme for us. His strength is our safety. His dominion is our defense. His power is our protection. And so Edwards bids us to surrender: "Let the consideration of this wonderful meeting of diverse excellencies in Christ induce you to accept of him, and close with him as your Savior."[55] He continues, "Christ is the Lion of the tribe of Judah; he is strong, though we are weak; he hath prevailed to do that for us which no creature else could do."[56]

Of course, the reason he can do for us what we cannot do for ourselves is this: Jesus is God. Jesus Christ has done for us what no one else could do. Abraham cannot do this. Moses cannot do this. David cannot do this. Mohammed cannot do this. Buddha cannot do this. Angels cannot do this. Neither can scholars nor statesmen, preachers or prophets, philosophers or scientists. We cannot do it for ourselves. Only Christ can do this for us. This is the supremacy of Jesus Christ.

---

55. Edwards, *Works*, 19:583.
56. Ibid.

"PAY DIVINE REGARDS TO *SOMETHING*"

In 1728, Benjamin Franklin drew up his own personalized "Articles of Belief and Acts of Religion."[57] In it, he sets out his personal statement of faith and liturgy. He offers model prayers that might be recited to "some unseen power" that surely created the universe.

Through human reason, Franklin concluded that this power is "a *good Being,* and as I should be happy to have so wise, good and powerful a Being my Friend."[58] Furthermore, just as this Being created animals, creatures beneath us who are inferior to us, he also created other Gods, creatures over us who are superior to us, who rule in other solar systems we have not discovered.

Yet not once in his "Articles of Belief and Acts of Religion" does Franklin mention Jesus. Search in vain for even a passing reference to the one who is arguably the most influential person who ever lived, and demonstrably the most important religious figure in history. It is as if the arrival of Jesus on the human scene is unnecessary to Franklin's faith. And that is the point. In Franklin's concept of God, Jesus is quite unnecessary.

Franklin discerns that he has a duty to "pay divine regards to SOMETHING"—that something being what we commonly call God—and to give him thanks. In fact, said Franklin, because "Ingratitude is one of the most odious of Vices, let me not be unmindful gratefully to acknowledge the Favours I receive from Heaven."[59] He continues his personal liturgy by giving thanks for food and clothes, corn and wine, air and light, fire and water, and so on. In other words, he gives thanks for the kinds of things that are acknowledged in every kind of religion to every kind of idol that has ever been imagined by humans. Yet Franklin gives no thanks for what the Bible calls the greatest gift of all. "For God so loved the world that he gave his one and only Son, that whoever believes in him shall not perish but have eternal life."[60] And again, "Thanks be to God for his indescribable gift!"[61]

On this, Jonathan Edwards would agree with Benjamin Franklin: "Ingratitude is the most odious of vices."

57. Franklin, *Papers,* 1:101–11.
58. Franklin, *Papers,* 103.
59. Ibid., 109.
60. John 3:16.
61. 2 Corinthians 9:15.

6

Grave: "The Grand Evidence"

These are facts related by them, not in a secret history, or in a corner; not for their private or personal advantage in this life, but at the risk of their reputation, peace, comfort, and even of their lives.

—Elias Boudinout,
President of the Continental Congress, 1782–1783[1]

Christianity is built on certain great and wonderful, visible facts, such as Christ's resurrection from the dead, and the great and innumerable miracles wrought by him and his apostles and other followers in Judea and in many parts of the world. These facts were always referred to as the foundation of the whole, and Christianity always pretended to be built on them.

—Jonathan Edwards[2]

More dependably, when a statement is prejudicial to a witness, his dear ones, or his cause, it is likely to be truthful.

—Louis Gottschalk,
former Professor of History, University of Chicago[3]

That is one of the reasons I believe Christianity. It is a religion you could not have guessed. If it offered us just the kind of universe we had always expected, I should feel we were making it up.

—C. S. Lewis[4]

1. Boudinot, *The Age of Revelation*, 54.

2. Edwards, *Works*, 23:332.

3. Gottschalk, *Understanding History*, 161. Cited in Eddy and Boyd, *The Jesus Legend*, 408 n. 2.

4. Lewis, *Mere Christianity*, 48.

Marcus Borg, professor of Religion and Culture at Oregon State University and member of the Jesus Seminar, believes in the resurrection of Jesus. Sort of. In this age of revising Jesus, there are two main types of resurrections to choose from: bodily resurrection or spiritual resurrection. Borg opts for a spiritual resurrection of an improved Jesus. "I do believe in the resurrection of Jesus," says Borg, "I am just skeptical that it involved anything happening to his corpse."[5] For Borg, and others like him, the New Testament account of the resurrection of Jesus is not really fiction, the way we understand the word today. Rather, the New Testament represents an "ancient storytelling technique where you use a story to express a truth of something that has happened."[6] What happened? After the resurrection, those original followers of Jesus had "experiences of Jesus as a living reality," Borg tells us, "visionary experiences." Borg would like for us to believe, on the shaky foundation of the subjective, emotional, collective liver-quiver of a band of demoralized fisherman, tax-collectors, and prostitutes, the world was turned upside down. To convey their inner experience to the world, they made up a myth about a resurrection to use as a metaphor for new beginnings.

Not so fast, says N. T. Wright, former Lecturer of New Testament at Oxford University and presently the Bishop of Durham. Hundreds of men had claimed to be the Messiah before Jesus did. When they died, so did their movement. A self-proclaimed Messiah was exposed as a fraud when he stopped breathing. No one expected a crucified Messiah. So what was so different about Jesus? Why did his followers continue to believe Jesus was the Messiah after his death? It was not because of some subjective visionary experience. Only the literal, physical, bodily resurrection can make sense of it. "Historically speaking," says Wright, "it's actually impossible to explain the rise of Christianity without it."[7] In the end, either the bones of Jesus are still on the earth, in some form or another, or they are not.

THE BONES OF JESUS IN THE SUBURBS OF JERUSALEM

In 2007, the Discovery Channel aired a documentary, *The Lost Tomb of Jesus*, which claimed that archaeologists had found the family tomb of Jesus in a suburb of Jerusalem called Talpiot. The bone boxes (ossuar-

---

5. Borg and Wright, "The Resurrection of Jesus."
6. Ibid.
7. Ibid.

ies) found in the tomb are empty, but several of them bore the engraved names of Joseph, Mary, Jesus, the son of Joseph, Mariamne (the filmmakers suggested this was another name for Mary Magdalene), and Judah, son of Jesus. Christians and skeptics alike see the implications clearly. But they were even clearer to the Apostle Paul almost two thousand years ago. If that ossuary contained the bones of Jesus, then Christ has not been raised. "And if Christ has not been raised," wrote Paul, "our preaching is useless and so is your faith."[8] The Christian faith is built squarely on this non-negotiable doctrine.

The problems with the documentary's hypothesis are numerous. The ossuaries, discovered in 1980, were catalogued, stored, and not examined again for over twenty years. No one knows what happens to the bones. Also, the names on the boxes were extremely common in the first century. Twenty-five percent of the women were named Mary, and one out of every seventy-five males in Jerusalem at that time was a "Jesus, son of Joseph."[9] Furthermore, Jesus's family was from Nazareth, so what is his family tomb doing in Jerusalem? For these and other reasons, scholarly consensus does not support the claim that this is the actual tomb of the biblical Jesus.

But the possibility is intriguing, to say the least. If the bones of Jesus are still on our planet, Christianity falls like a house of cards. Unless, like Marcus Borg, you opt for the spiritual resurrection of an improved Jesus. So when James Charlesworth, professor at Princeton Theological Seminary, was asked if this really is the tomb where Jesus's bones were finally deposited (after Jesus and Mary Magdalene had a son), this Methodist minister did not seem too concerned that it would bother many Christians. "I don't think it will undermine belief in the resurrection, only that Jesus rose as a spiritual body, not in the flesh."[10] And then, in the deistic tra-

---

8. 1 Corinthians 15:14.

9. Strobel, *Case for the Real Jesus*, 148–49.

10. McGirk, "Jesus 'Tomb' Controversty Re-Opened." Notice that Charlesworth is redefining the word "resurrection." Hijacking the terms of orthodox Christianity and giving them new meaning is a common practice among those who seek to present a revisionist Jesus. I am reminded here of Jonathan Edwards's comments about the importance of defining terms: "If a man is going on a journey and inquires on a great number of paths which is the right and is told 'tis that which leads south, it can determine him nothing at all if the word south as used in that place has 32 different and inconsistent significations, one by the word means what another calls north, another what he means by northwest, and so it is understood of all the thirty-two points of the compass (MS "Controversies" Notebook, 798).

dition of Benjamin Franklin and Thomas Jefferson, Charlesworth adds: "Christianity is a strong religion, based on faith and experience, and I don't think that any discovery by archaeologists will change that."[11] In other words, facts don't have much to do with faith, and reason should not get mixed up with religion. Evidently, alternative Christianities presenting a new and improved Jesus don't need the bodily resurrection, while historic Christianity owes its very existence to it.

THE DEIST CONNECTION

What has Charlesworth done? He has separated the Christ of faith from the Jesus of history. In chapter 3, we saw that Lessing's Ditch set religious experience on one side of the ditch and real, actual history on the other. It doesn't matter if the two don't match up. In fact, they never will. The miracles of the New Testament, including the resurrection, never happened, but that is okay. What matters is that these legends, myths, and fables about Jesus are useful vehicles for conveying important spiritual truth that God wants us to know. For Jefferson, those important spiritual truths were diamonds that he displayed in his very own cut-and-paste Bible. Jesus's claims to deity and the miracles that allegedly validated those claims were the dunghill. Keep the dunghill if you want. Common laborers who fall from the loft may find it to be soft and warm and safe. But educated, gentleman-plantation-owners have no need for such things.

The deist attack on the resurrection provoked an avalanche of treatises defending the historical evidence that Jesus was bodily raised from the dead. Fourteen hundred years earlier, the church historian Eusebius had laid the foundation for that defense, but according to William Lane Craig, he appears to have been "the last great champion of the historical argument for the resurrection of Jesus until the dawning of the Renaissance."[12] In response to deism, many orthodox apologists in England resurrected Eusebius's defense and added more substance. Jonathan Edwards, being a voracious reader and committed to staying abreast of current theological disputes, no doubt drew much of his own material from these ancient and contemporary sources. While his arguments are not entirely original,

11. Ibid.

12. Craig, *Historical Argument*, 49. Eusebius's refutation of the conspiracy theory echoes to this day in the writing of modern apologists, many of whom may be unaware that these arguments were made about AD 300.

Edwards attempted to bring that scholarly defense down to the level of the people in his congregation in order to encourage and equip them. That is the duty of every faithful pastor.

EDWARDS PATRIOTS ON THE RESURRECTION

It is unclear how much Professor James Charlesworth is aware of his debt to Jonathan Edwards. There would be no Princeton Theological Seminary if not for the College of New Jersey. The College of New Jersey, where Edwards was installed as its third president shortly before his death, was established in response to the departure of Harvard and Edwards's alma mater, Yale, from the orthodox Jesus. Later to be called Princeton College, and then Princeton University, the focus of the school was to train men for the ministry, teaching them, among other things, to declare and defend the bodily resurrection of Jesus Christ. One of Edwards's successors at Princeton, John Witherspoon, the only clergy member to sign the Declaration of Independence, also signed the Westminster Confession. "Jesus was crucified," states the Confession, "and died, was buried, and remained under the power of death, yet saw no corruption. On the third day he arose from the dead, with the same body in which he suffered."[13]

By 1812, Princeton College had deviated from its original mission, as orthodox theology was growing dimmer and the number of clergy students was becoming slimmer. In response, several orthodox trustees of Princeton, including Elias Boudinot, established a seminary in Princeton that was formally separate from the college where sound doctrine could be more carefully guarded by the Presbyterian church.[14] Boudinot, who had grown up in Philadelphia as a neighbor and friend of Benjamin Franklin, was a remarkable statesman and patriot, serving as a colonel in the Revolutionary War, a New Jersey delegate to the Continental Congress, and, it can be argued, as the first president of the United States.[15] He wrote a long treatise, *The Age of Revelation*, in response to Thomas Paine's deistic *Age of Reason*[16] in which he pointedly defends the reliability of the

13. *Westminster Confession of Faith*, 8:4.

14. Marsden, *Soul of the American University*, 74.

15. The Treaty of Paris, in which Great Britain recognized the independence of the United States, was concluded while Boudinot was serving as president of the Continental Congress, making Boudinot the *de facto* president of the United States.

16. Boudinot writes in his introduction: "I am averse to increasing the number of books, unless it be on important occasions, or for useful purposes; but an anxious desire

New Testament, the deity of Jesus, and the bodily resurrection. In fact, in Boudinot's estimation, the extraordinary measures taken by the authorities to secure the tomb were God-ordained. "And this they did," explains Boudinot, "as if directed by the providence of God to establish and confirm the evidence of the great facts, beyond contradiction, which of all things these leaders of the Jews most dreaded."[17] There is no question how Elias Boudinot would react to Professor Charlesworth's intriguing theory that most Christians would be undisturbed if it is proven that Jesus was not bodily raised from the dead.

IS THE RESURRECTION LIKE A PEANUT SHELL?

We have a restaurant in our town where we can eat while we wait for our order. There on the table is a galvanized bucket filled with peanuts. We crack the shells, devour the contents, and throw the remains on the floor, all with the restaurant's permission. Likewise, deists believed that their unaided reason would infallibly lead them to the valuable core of truth in the Bible. But around that core were wrapped the traditions, myths, and legends that biblical authors added for a variety of reasons. In particular, the Gospel writers fabricated the Easter story. It is as if the truth were the peanut and the stories of miraculous events were the shell that carried the central truths safely from one generation to another. Once you get to the peanut, you can toss the shell.

It gets even better. The peanut is that core of religious truth found in all the major religions, the ethical systems built around the Golden Rule, "Do unto others as you would have them do unto you." You can wrap the nut in any kind of shell you want: a Muslim shell, a Hindu shell, a Jewish shell, a Confucian shell, a Christian shell. It doesn't matter, really. Take your pick. If you choose the Muslim shell, you get Muslim myths, like Muhammad flying on his horse to Jerusalem.[18] Of course, to classify this as a myth would be an affront to most Muslims. (A Muslim tour guide once showed me where

---

that our country should be preserved from the dreadful evil of becoming enemies to the religion of the Gospel, which I have no doubt, but would be introductive of the dissolution of government and the bonds of civil society; my compliance with the wishes of a few select friends, to make this work public, has been more easily obtained." Boudinot, *Age of Revelation*, Introduction.

17. Ibid., 170.

18. See Qu'ran, Surah 17:1. Muslim tradition embellishes this passage with the "Night Journey."

he earnestly believed the horse's hoof set down on the rock over which the Dome of the Rock mosque stands in Jerusalem, convincing me it is not a myth to him.) But if you pick the Christian shell, you get the Christian myths, like the resurrection of the Son of God. That is how deists, and their spiritual heirs, can still claim to be Christians with a straight face while simultaneously denying the bodily resurrection of Jesus.

WHAT'S AT STAKE?

By now you may discern some progression in this book. In chapter 4, we saw that if the Gospels are reliable, then Jesus really did make the audacious claim to be God. But making the claim is one thing and proving it is another. Anyone can make that claim. Why should we believe him? Why did anyone who heard and saw Jesus during his ministry on earth come to the conclusion that Jesus was indeed the one he claimed to be? What evidence did Jesus offer to validate his claim to be God? The answer is in the miracles he performed, especially his own bodily resurrection. As a miracle in itself, he predicted to his disciples he would be raised, even though they could not comprehend what he meant at the time.[19]

In the face of the deistic charge that believing Jesus's claim to be God is unreasonable, Edwards asks, "What can be more reasonable than to believe a man, when he comes and tells us that he is sent from God" who then did the sort of things he did? He claimed he would heal the "diseases of our souls," so in his earthly ministry he healed "the diseases of our body." He claimed that he would deliver us "from spiritual and eternal death, and also from temporal death; that he will raise us from the dead, and give us eternal life" so that we might live forever with him. "And to prove this," Edwards points out, "he gives us sensible evidence that he has power over men's lives," not only by raising others from the dead, but by rising "from the dead himself."[20] Perhaps it is the deist who is being unreasonable by raising the bar of historical evidence so unrealistically high, that he summarily dismisses the claims of Jesus without examining the evidence. His prejudice against miracles prevents him from being objective. We could ask with Edwards, "What more could we desire of a man that pretends to come from God, and to have power to do these things for

---

19. John 2:19.
20. Edwards, *Works*, 18:119–20.

us, than to give us such evidences of his power as these?"[21] In other words, believing in the claim of Jesus to be God is a reasonable response to the evidence supporting his bodily resurrection.

Edwards knew what was at stake. "If Christ were not risen," he concluded, "it would be an evidence that he was an impostor, for the grand evidence of his mission and appointment as our Savior was his resurrection which Christ foretold as such."[22] Believers and doubters alike can agree: If Jesus was bodily raised from the dead, his claims are patently true. If Jesus was not bodily raised from the dead, his claims are certainly false.

"IT CONCERNS ALL TO DETERMINE WHO JESUS WAS"

On a Sunday morning in January, 1749, Jonathan Edwards delivered a sermon on Matthew 16:15, where Jesus asks Peter, "Who do you say that I am?" It's hard to imagine January in Massachusetts without a chill in the air, so it is easy to visualize the Northampton church full of worshipers, listening to the sermon, still bundled in their coats. Though the sermon, "It Concerns All to Determine Who Jesus Was,"[23] does not mention deism by name, it seems that Edwards is concerned that some of the people in Northampton were being influenced to think along deistic lines concerning the identity of Jesus. Perhaps some of his hearers that day were harboring doubts about whether Jesus was accurately portrayed in the New Testament. That Sunday, Edwards aimed to "evince and clear the matter."[24]

While some deists rejected Jesus as a fraud or magician, others, like Franklin and Jefferson, held a revised Jesus in high esteem. They spoke admiringly of his moral teaching and ethical example. But in the end, Jesus was merely a man, not God. "There are very various opinions about him," declared Edwards, "so in those days, so in these days. Some a crafty subtle deceiver, a wizard, a very good man but no more than mere man. Some a great prophet, but inferior to Muhammad. Some a glorious creature made

---

21. Edwards, *Works*, 120.

22. Ibid., 24:1059.

23. Edwards, "It Concerns All," 1. As of this date, the online version is only partially edited. Since Edwards did not prepare this for publication, this manuscript is merely his sermon notes, unpublished and often in shorthand or outline form. I have taken the liberty to edit an occasional phrase or word to make it more readable. For example, Edwards, in typical eighteenth century fashion, spelled Muhammad as "Mahomet."

24. Ibid.

in time." The never-ending list of these alternative Jesuses shows "how liable men are to mistake."[25]

In typical Edwards fashion, he moves doggedly from point to point, pressing in on his conclusion and appealing to his listeners for a verdict. Edwards is out to prove that there is a core set of facts proposed in the New Testament that were believed to be true by both the friends and enemies of Jesus during the first generation of the church. For example, the crucifixion of Jesus and the declaration by his followers that he was raised from the dead are indisputable facts. In the literature of first-century Roman and Jewish historians, there is no denial that a man named Jesus was crucified by Rome or that his followers claimed they had seen him alive three days later. The persecution of the early church by Roman emperors is well documented and even the Roman emperors "suppose the facts to be true."[26] All the extra-biblical evidence, explains Edwards, corroborates the account of events presented in the Gospels.

The report of these early followers would not have been so "quickly and publicly received" by so many in those years during the administration of Pontius Pilate if these facts were not true. There were thousands in and around Judea who "could have confuted" their accounts, but even those who crucified Jesus never denied crucifying him. All of these things were done openly, not in private, for the world to see. In those early days after Jesus's own resurrection when many came from other nations to Jerusalem, Lazarus, whom Jesus had raised from the dead, "was yet alive near to Jerusalem."[27] If Lazarus had denied the story that was circulating about him, Christianity could have been stopped dead in its tracks.

As the gospel spread and the world was being "turned upside down," most of those eyewitnesses were still living and could confirm the message. For Edwards, "the greatest evidence that it was done" was that "it now remains."[28] That is, the existence of the Christian church today, bearing witness to the Gospel, is evidence in favor of the central claims of historic Christianity. Those eyewitnesses to the crucifixion and resurrection are crucial to Edwards's defense of the orthodox Jesus. Why? Because those eyewitnesses, more than "any in the world, would not have had any heart"

---

25. Edwards, "It Concerns All," 38.

26. Ibid., 8.

27. Ibid., 6.

28. Ibid., 7.

to proclaim these facts "if they had known that they were false." By doing so they "exposed themselves"[29] to unnecessary suffering, loss, and violent death. What possible motive could they have to say they saw Jesus bodily raised from the dead, when in fact, they knew they had not?

If the deist says that the original disciples never made such claims and that later church leaders fabricated the Easter story to gain more power and profit, they still have a problem. The written texts that record the story remain. Even before Luke wrote his Gospel, many had "undertaken to draw up an account of the things that have been fulfilled among us, just as they were handed down to us by those who from the first were eye-witnesses and servants of the word."[30] Those documents were written and distributed when eyewitnesses were still alive who could have—and would have—refuted them if they were not true. The altering of those many documents, the rewriting of history, could not have been done without a "conspiracy of multitudes" that "could not have been managed," and even if managed, "could not have been concealed."[31] It would have required all types of various and competing sects to agree with one another to deceive the world and then keep it a secret. Yet, scholarly consensus today is overwhelming that the Gospels were written in the first century[32] while there were still living witnesses to the events both inside and outside of the church.

At this point, Edwards offers his cold congregation an illustration. Suppose someone had decided to fabricate a story in 1749 that a "very great and extraordinary public" event had occurred in London just a few years earlier "in the lifetime of the present living generation." He makes his proclamation "in the city of London, before the Parliament and in the universities" and takes the message to all parts of the United Kingdom before millions. In his account, he tells how the Royal family was involved and the nation was affected. And suppose he recruits many messengers who pretend to be eyewitnesses and sends them out into the world. They are able to make converts in other nations by the millions. What is the

---

29. Edwards, "It Concerns All," 8.

30. Luke 1:1, 2.

31. Edwards, "It Concerns All."

32. The Gospel of John was most likely the last to be written, probably between AD 75 and AD 100.

likelihood of that happening when there are thousands of people alive who are "able to confute them?"[33]

These confuters could and would say they were in London when these alleged events supposedly occurred and they saw and heard no such thing. Even greater, is it possible that those messengers pretending to be eyewitnesses would voluntarily "die the most cruel death" to maintain their testimony? That is what deists are asking us to believe, when they invite us to reject the bodily resurrection of Jesus. That event affected the house of Caesar, not the Royal Family. It took place in Jerusalem, not London, but it is equally preposterous to think that "any should go about to invent now at this day a new history" that had "never been heard of before."[34]

Midway through the sermon, Edwards reaches a conclusion. "Therefore," he announced, "undoubtedly there was such a person."[35] Not only that, "it is certain he was a most remarkable and wonderful person." He is remarkable for many things, especially for what happened after his crucifixion. Jesus was "declared to be risen; the stone sealed, watch set, declared to be seen ascending into Heaven."[36] There is no record that either Roman or Jewish authorities denied the stone was sealed, the watch was set, or that Jesus's followers declared they had seen him alive after the crucifixion. Not everyone saw the stone sealed, but if the stone was not sealed, someone who was there would have said, "It's not true. I was there. No one sealed the stone." Not everyone saw the guard posted at Jesus's tomb, but if no guard had been posted, someone who was there that night would have said, "It's not true. I was there. No guard was posted at the tomb." And not everyone saw Jesus risen from the dead, but if Jesus had not been raised, there would have been many among those first disciples who would have said, "It's not true. I was there with the disciples in Jerusalem for those forty days after the crucifixion. It never happened." There is no historical evidence of any such testimony; no hint of defection. Even the enemies of Jesus admitted the fact: those early followers unanimously declared to all who would listen that they had seen Jesus bodily raised from the dead. Doubters today may not believe that Jesus was raised from the dead, but

33. Edwards, "It Concerns All," 14.
34. Ibid., 15.
35. Ibid., 23.
36. Ibid., 27.

they cannot convincingly deny that those early followers of Jesus adamantly believed in his bodily resurrection.

Skeptics have complained that if Jesus really was bodily raised he would have appeared to others besides those who were already committed to the cause. For some, this is strong evidence that the resurrection was merely spiritual and not physical. But Thomas was not there when Jesus first appeared to his disciples and would not believe until he could see and touch Jesus himself. Don't miss the point here. The Gospel writer takes pains to let us know that Thomas did not believe that any kind of resurrection had taken place, spiritual or bodily, until he had personally seen and touched the material body of Jesus himself. Once given that opportunity, he could only address Jesus as "My Lord and my God!"[37]

Thomas is not alone. Paul was an enemy of Jesus and of all who claimed to see him risen. He was certainly not pre-committed to Jesus or his cause. But when the risen Jesus appeared to Paul, he became a believer. And James, the brother of Jesus, was a doubter of Jesus during Jesus's earthly ministry,[38] but after the risen Jesus appeared to him,[39] James became a key leader in the early church. What turned these doubters into believers if not the bodily resurrection of Jesus? True, Jesus did not appear to all, but all to whom he appeared believed.

The manuscript of Edwards's sermon is actually in the form of a rough draft that every pastor recognizes. When you write a sermon or two every week, you don't have time to dot all the i's. It is unpolished and unfinished, and we can only wonder what would have happened if he had refined the grammar, sharpened his argument, clarified his points, and offered it for publication. No doubt he would have deleted a few things and restated others. Yet it has the raw ingredients of a valuable apologetic. His main idea is that the most reasonable explanation for the rise of Christianity, and its inestimable impact on history, is the bodily resurrection of Jesus Christ. And this brings us back to N. T. Wright and a host of modern scholars who agree with Edwards.

37. John 20:28.
38. Mark 6:3, 4; John 7:5.
39. 1 Corinthians 15:7.

N. T. WRIGHT ON THE RESURRECTION

Wright's massive book, *The Resurrection of the Son of God* (2003), dedicates the first six hundred and eighty pages to making the scholarly case that for the first two hundred years after the death of Jesus, Christians everywhere and at every time, consistently and uniformly, believed in his bodily resurrection. Skeptics may not believe that Jesus was literally raised from the dead, but the evidence is overwhelming that these Christians believed that, and to deny that they did is irresponsible scholarship.

Furthermore, they said they believed in the bodily resurrection of Jesus for two reasons. First, on the third day after his execution, the tomb in which Jesus's corpse had been laid was empty. Second, Jesus appeared to many people in different locations and at different times in such a way as to convince them that they were not hallucinating or experiencing a vision. If this was a spiritual resurrection only, his corpse would still be in the tomb and his appearances would not have convinced them that what they were seeing was a physical body. "This belief about Jesus," notes Wright, "provides a historically complete, thorough and satisfying reason for the rise and development of the belief that he was Israel's Messiah and the world's true lord."[40]

Wright is not a lonely scholar, but one who works in the company of a growing number of New Testament experts who are adding flesh and blood to the bare bones of Edwards's argument. The following is a survey of reasons being offered by contemporary scholars to accept the bodily resurrection of Jesus.

THE CASE FOR THE RESURRECTION

1. *Something happened.* We may disagree on what it was, but we all must agree that something unprecedented happened in Jerusalem in the middle of the first century that "turned the world upside down." No single man or movement has influenced more people in the history of the world. The world measures the years by counting how many of them have passed since Jesus was born. Today, of the six and a half billion people on this planet, over two billion of them call themselves Christians. No religion on earth has more adherents. Whatever it was that happened, it motivated hundreds of people to persuade others in nation after nation, culture after culture, to make great sacrifices in following the way of Jesus.

40. Wright, *Resurrection*, 681–82.

2. *The testimony of the eyewitnesses who claimed to see what happened was secured in writing within their lifetime.* Through a combination of oral tradition and note-taking,[41] the testimony of these eyewitnesses was preserved and passed from person to person, town to town, region to region. It is difficult to grasp, in our age of print and video, the accuracy of oral tradition. However, in the first century, when so many people could not read or write, memorization was a way of life. They lived in an oral culture.

When I was a boy I memorized the beginning of the Gettysburg Address. Without consulting any written source (I promise), I'll type it right now: "Four score and seven years ago, our fathers brought forth on this continent a new nation, conceived in liberty, and dedicated to the proposition that all men are created equal." After forty years, I can quote it perfectly. If you ask me again this time next year, I'm confident I can do it again. For some reason (which still eludes me), it was important that I remember that opening line to one of the greatest, and shortest, presidential speeches in history.

Now suppose I was there at Gettysburg, November 19, 1863, and I heard those words. Along with what I hear, I will never forget much of what I see that day. I will remember it is a Thursday. I will remember if the day was warm or cold. I will remember how the program started with a prayer by a Reverend. I may or may not remember his name, but I know he was a Reverend. I will remember the Marine band played, and a choir sang a dirge. And I will never forget Edward Everett's forgettable oratory. He was a professional speaker they asked to give a speech before Abraham Lincoln spoke a few words of dedication. I will not remember every word of Everett's two-hour speech, but I will be able to give the gist of it. I will also remember that it was very long. I may not remember all of these things in the exact order they happened, but I will remember that they did happen. Or I may remember the exact order, but when I recount that day, I may change the order so I can end on the part I want to emphasize to my listeners.

And since we are supposing, suppose that as Lincoln leaves the crowd, he walks up to me and asks me to ride with him back to Washington. On the way, I tell him I want to memorize the inspiring speech he just gave. Can he help me at least learn the first few lines? Can he repeat it until I have it? When he comes to that place where he says, "The world will

---

41. Bauckham, *Jesus and the Eyewitnesses*, 287–89.

little note, nor long remember what we say here" I smile and think to myself, "I'll prove you wrong." I tell this story to my children and later, my grandchildren. Over the years, I jot down a few notes to remind me of what I know. I am kept from getting the story wrong; restrained from elaboration and exaggeration, because thousands of others were there as well who are still alive and will correct my distorted account. And in my old age, my family and friends will ask me, "Tell us the story again. We want to write down all the details, so that when you are gone, we will tell it to our children as well." I know what I saw and heard that day, and now, they will too.

That is not unlike the process that gave us the Gospels and the eyewitness accounts of the bodily resurrection of Jesus. Frankly, that is the way *most* of ancient history has come to us. In about AD 55, Paul recites a list of eyewitnesses to the death, burial, and resurrection of Jesus to the church in Corinth. Most scholars believe this is a section of memorized oral tradition, in creed form,[42] that had already been passed down for nearly twenty years. "For what I received," wrote Paul, "I passed on to you as of first importance." At this time, most of the eyewitnesses were still accessible to those who wanted to confirm the story. Paul takes care to note that most of them "are still living."[43] While Paul gives a brief summary of the Easter story, a fuller account would be completed in the Gospels between about AD 60 (Mark) and AD 90 (John), just as those original eyewitnesses to the resurrection were dying out.[44]

In the end, no matter how frail our memories, there are some things we just will not forget. My parents will never forget the day John F. Kennedy was assassinated. They remember exactly where they were and

42. Anyone who has memorized the Apostles' Creed, knows how accurate this form of transmission (oral tradition) can be. "I believe in God the Father, Almighty, Creator of Heaven and Earth," will not easily slip from my memory and I can teach it to children who have not yet learned to read. Keep in mind that the risen Jesus ministered to the disciples for forty days after his resurrection and before his ascension. We know that on occasion, during these post-resurrection appearances, he taught them from the Scripture (Luke 24:27). Perhaps this was a period of review in which the apostles either committed large portions of Jesus's teaching to memory or took notes on what he taught, or both. Matthew, being a tax-collector, had to be literate. On top of all this, Bible-believing Christians have no trouble believing that God gave these early witnesses a supernatural recall ability and providentially preserved the recording of their testimony. If there is a God who raised Jesus from the dead, this would be a small feat.

43. 1 Corinthians 15:6.

44. 1 Corinthians 15:3.

what they were doing when they heard the news. I will never forget the day that terrorists flew passenger jets into the Twin Towers in New York. I remember exactly where I was, what I was doing, and who was with me. And the disciples would have never forgotten the first Easter. They knew what they saw: an empty tomb and a risen Lord. So they spent the rest of their lives telling the world what they knew.

3. *The testimony of the eyewitnesses contains "embarrassing" elements about the eyewitnesses.* As Edwards has noted, if the tomb was not empty and Jesus did not appear to hundreds of eyewitnesses after the resurrection, then a diverse group of people entered into a conspiracy to convince the world these things had happened. The motive for conspiracy is always to protect or enhance one's status. When anyone lies, it is because they believe it to be in their self-interest. When someone persuades another to join in the lie, it is because both are convinced they will benefit from the deception. For example, when a man has an affair, he will lie to his wife about where he has been, whom he was with, and how he spent his money. He does this to protect and enhance his status. When he convinces his partner in adultery to lie to her own husband, it is because both of them believe this to be in their self-interest. The lie is designed to put them in the best possible light and make their story most believable.

If these eyewitnesses lied about the first Easter, it is because they were seeking to protect and enhance their status in the community Jesus had organized. But if this is the case, there are some troubling features in the story that are hard to explain. Paul Rhodes Eddy and Gregory A. Boyd remind us "the presence of self-damaging details in a document usually suggests to historians that the author was willing to risk damaging his own cause for the sake of remaining faithful to history."[45] The more "self-damaging" details that are included in the document, the greater our confidence that the information is accurate. If they were inventing the story, they would avoid putting themselves in a negative light in order to guard their status. Yet, as Eddy and Boyd note, "the disciples who were to form the foundation of the new community consistently seemed dull, obstinate, and eventually cowardly."[46] In the end, it was a member of the

---

45. Eddy and Boyd, *The Jesus Legend*, 408.

46. Ibid., 411. The examples offered from Mark's Gospel are 8:32–33; 10:35–37; 14:37–40, 50; 14:43–46; 14:66–72.

inner circle, Judas, who betrayed Jesus, and his most vocal disciple, Peter, denied that he even knew him.

Along these lines, our confidence in the veracity of the Gospels is also bolstered by some surprising omissions. When the Gospels were being written, there were serious theological and practical debates raging in individual local churches. There were controversies over the role of women, what men and women should wear, speaking in tongues, eating meat sacrificed to idols, church government, and the place of Gentile believers in relation to Jewish believers. If the Gospels were the inventions of co-conspirators, this is the perfect opportunity to write in some "red-letter" words they could attribute to Jesus that would settle the debates. If the Gospels were being fabricated by those who held power in the growing movement, "these are precisely the sorts of issues we would have expected the Jesus of the Gospels to address."[47] These embarrassing inclusions and surprising omissions in the Gospel accounts seem counterproductive if the writers are conspiring with others in order to convince the world to esteem them and believe their lie.

There are numerous other examples of "embarrassing" details in the Gospel accounts, but I'll focus on one that involves women. All the Gospels agree that Jesus was crucified by the Romans. That by itself is a hindrance. "It is hard to imagine," write Eddy and Boyd, "a more effective way to convince people in a first-century Jewish context that someone is *not* the Messiah than by telling them that the would-be savior was executed by Israel's military oppressors!"[48] But to make matters worse, the Gospels want us to know that all the male disciples, except one, had fearfully abandoned Jesus as he was dying, while a band of women followers courageously remained near the cross.

On Easter morning, while the men remained in hiding, the women went alone to the tomb. They were the first to discover the tomb to be empty and when they reported this finding to the men, the men did not believe them and considered their words to be "nonsense."[49] This response is understandable for several reasons. For example, no one, even among

---

47. Eddy and Boyd, *The Jesus Legend*, 412. Furthermore, notes Craig Blomberg (*Historical Reliability*, 105), no Gospel describes the actual resurrection itself. If the disciples fabricated the resurrection story and wanted others to believe it, would they not fabricate an eyewitness to be there when Jesus stepped out of the tomb?

48. Eddy and Boyd, *The Jesus Legend*, 411.

49. Luke 24:11. See also Matthew 27:55–56; Mark 16:4–8.

his closest followers, was expecting a bodily resurrection. They may have seen Jesus raise Lazarus from the dead, but who among them had the power to raise Jesus?

Furthermore, most men in the first century did not consider the testimony of a woman to be reliable. Josephus, the first century Jewish historian advised, "let not the testimony of women be admitted, on account of the levity and boldness of their sex."[50] Even if we grant that Mark invented most of his Gospel in the early 60s, "it will not do to have him, or anyone else at that stage, making up a would-be apologetic legend about an empty tomb and having women be the ones to find it."[51] Not only did the women find an empty tomb, but the Gospels also present Mary Magdalene as the first eyewitness to the risen Jesus.[52]

Think about that for a moment. If you are writing fiction in the first century that you want people to accept as fact, then you have your choice of anyone to be the first witness to the resurrection. Why would you choose a woman? Yet there it is in all of the Gospels. The first witnesses to the empty tomb and the risen Jesus are women.

This may seem like a small thing to twenty-first century Americans, but recall that women were not trusted to vote in this nation from its founding. The Nineteenth Amendment, providing a constitutional guarantee of a woman's right to vote, was not ratified until 1920. Imagine then, the impact of the Gospel accounts on eighteenth century deist authors, all of whom were men. When Thomas Jefferson wrote "all men are created equal" in the Declaration of Independence, he did not mean his black male slaves[53] or women of *any* color. Benjamin Franklin liked the ladies, but it is not clear how much he respected them.[54]

---

50. Josephus, *Complete Works,* 97. "Antiquities of the Jews, Book 4, chapter 8, Paragraph 15."

51. Wright, *Resurrection,* 607.

52. Matthew 28:1, 9; Mark 16:9; John 20:14.

53. In fact, John Wesley, a loyal British citizen, chided his rebellious American brethren for their hypocrisy in this regard, asking them: "Who then is a slave? Look into America, and you may easily see. See the Negro, fainting under the load, bleeding under the lash! He is a slave. And is there no difference between him and his master Yes. The one is screaming, "Murder! Slavery!" the other silently bleeds and dies." Wesley, *A Calm Address.*

54. In 1938, Carl Van Doren (*Benjamin Franklin,* 657) said that Franklin "treated every woman as if she was a person too." Not only that, he "loved, valued, and studied women" (657). Perhaps he studied them a bit too much. In 1725, Franklin lost one of his best friends when he tried to seduce his girlfriend (Isaacson, *Franklin,* 44). He entered into a common-

Even for eighteenth century skeptics, the Gospel portrayal of women as the first witnesses to the empty tomb and the risen Jesus might have been one more stumbling block to belief. But it is precisely for this reason that the Gospel accounts of the resurrection are more believable. If the Gospel writers are fabricating a story that they want other people to believe, they can write it any way they want. A leading explanation for why the Gospel writers presented women as the first eyewitnesses to the empty tomb and risen Lord is that this is exactly what happened.

4. *Sources outside the Christian community corroborate the early Christian testimony.* As we saw in chapter 4, Thomas Jefferson likely had in his own library the history written by Tacitus, which confirmed the crucifixion of Jesus. Beyond that, Tacitus, writing about AD 112, also fixes the time of Jesus's execution as being "during the reign of Tiberius, at the hands of one of our procurators, Pontius Pilate."[55] Tacitus, who had access to official archives of the Roman Senate, also confirms that the message of the early followers of Jesus, though "checked for the moment, again broke out not only in Judaea, . . . but even in Rome."[56] The bodily resurrection of Jesus is the best explanation for why the movement broke out in spite of Jesus's awful and demoralizing death.

Pliny the Younger, in his official correspondence as a Roman administrator in about 110 AD, describes the worship of early Christians and mentions how they sing to Jesus "as if to a god."[57] This extra-biblical corroboration that the early church believed in the deity of Jesus is further

---

law marriage with Deborah Read in 1730, but he was often away from her. Their union was "mutually useful" (Ibid., 75), but fifteen of the last seventeen years of their marriage, Deborah remained alone in Philadelphia while Franklin lived an ocean away, in London and Paris, where he gained a "reputation for lecherousness that he did little to dispel" (Ibid., 165). Historians are still uncertain as to the identity of the mother of Benjamin Franklin's only son, William Franklin (Ibid., 76). William followed his father's example, producing an illegitimate grandson for Benjamin, William Temple Franklin. Temple continued the family tradition, when he fathered, with a married woman, an illegitimate son, Theodore, who died in childhood of smallpox. "Theodore Franklin," writes Isaacson, "the illegitimate son of the illegitimate son of Franklin's own illegitimate son, was, albeit briefly, the last male-line descendant of Benjamin Franklin, who would in the end leave no family line bearing his name." In the end, it might be asked, though never answered, how much Deborah Franklin felt loved, valued and studied by Benjamin Franklin.

55. Tacitus, *Complete Works*, 380. "Annals, 15.44."

56. Tacitus, *Complete Works*, 380.

57. Pliny, *Letter to Emperor Trajan*, Book 10, Letter 96. Quoted in Eddy and Boyd, *The Jesus Legend*, 175.

evidence for his resurrection. What else would lead them to believe this crucified Jewish peasant was God?

Seutonius is another Roman historian whose work Jefferson recommended. Around AD 120, Seutonius, who also had access to Roman archives and official libraries, notes that Claudius "expelled the Jews from Rome, since they were always making disturbances because of the instigator Chrestus."[58] If the world was in the process of being turned upside down by the Christian message, it is not surprising that Seutonius would at least make a passing reference to it.

These sources are examples that support Edwards's assertion that even enemies of Jesus confirm the central facts of the Gospels. Although these ancient historians did not believe all of what Christians said about Jesus, they do confirm that the earliest Christians actually said these things. Though they are skeptical, not one of these ancient sources produces an eyewitness to refute the testimony found in the Gospels.

5. *Those who testified to what happened suffered for their testimony.* The idea that the earliest Christians were proclaiming a spiritual resurrection faces formidable evidence to the contrary. The multiple post-resurrection appearances over forty days are designed to convince people that this is a walking, talking, eating, drinking, breathing body. Furthermore, the spiritual resurrection simply cannot explain the empty tomb. The corpse of Jesus was gone.

A natural reading of the text leads us to conclude that the resurrection proclaimed by the disciples was physical and they appealed to an empty tomb to make their case more persuasive. If the disciples stole the body[59] and then invented the Easter story, they knew that what they were proclaiming was false. If someone else stole the body,[60] and the disciples proclaimed the bodily resurrection based merely on the empty tomb, we might see how they deceived themselves with wishful thinking. They did not, however, merely announce an empty tomb. They also proclaimed that they had seen Jesus alive. Christianity is not just built on the empty tomb, but on the empty tomb *plus* the resurrection appearances. So if someone else stole the body, and the disciples claimed to see him alive, they knew

---

58. Seutonius, *Lives of the Caesars*. Quoted in Eddy and Boyd, *The Jesus Legend*, 176.
59. Matthew 27:64.
60. John 20:2.

that what they were proclaiming was false. Either way, the disciples were lying, and they knew it.

As I mentioned earlier, behind nearly every lie is the desire to preserve or enhance our own status. We must perceive that somehow fraud is in our best interest, helping us gain some pleasure or escape some pain. In other words, we always have a motive for lying. But what did the disciples gain by perpetuating this fraud? Jonathan Edwards reminded his congregation that if the disciples were only pretending to be eyewitnesses, they, and many who believed them, gained a "most cruel death."[61] This does not make sense. Even if the movement had begun as a conspiracy, the sustained persecutions from religious, social, and political leaders would have shortly shattered the conspiracy like glass. The deists were asking the world to believe that the disciples lied, even though their only gain was loss.

First, consider the loss of possessions. Was there a profit motive to concoct this elaborate hoax? Did the early Christians lie for money? Everything we know about them works against this theory. To a would-be follower, Jesus once said, "Foxes have holes and birds of the air have nests, but the Son of Man has nowhere to lay his head."[62] Paul assures the Corinthians that "what I want is not your possessions"[63] and reminded the Thessalonians that he had "worked night and day,"[64] probably making tents, in order not to be a financial burden to them. In fact, those early eyewitnesses to the resurrection often suffered severe financial reversals and experienced "hunger."[65] It is hard to imagine how the first disciples could gain much of a following if they were living in luxury while at the same time extolling a Jesus that owned only the clothes on his back.[66]

Second, consider the loss of freedom. In the earliest days of the Christian church, Peter and John, eyewitnesses to both the empty tomb and the risen Jesus, proclaimed the good news in Jerusalem. Their message was

61. Edwards, "It Concerns All," 14.

62. Luke 9:58.

63. 2 Corinthians 12:14.

64. 1 Thessalonians 2:9.

65. 2 Corinthians 6:5.

66. Someone may object by pointing to those who preach a "prosperity Gospel" which results in the preacher's luxurious lifestyle. Keep in mind that modern "prosperity theologians" insist that Jesus was not poor, but, contrary to what we read in the Gospels, was very wealthy. "Health and wealth" advocates do more damage than they know to the spread of the Gospel by giving skeptics a motive for the disciples to lie about the resurrection, when no such motive existed in actual history.

deeply threatening to the religious and political leaders who had, just weeks earlier, been responsible for the execution of Jesus. They were arrested, brought before the authorities and asked, "By what power or what name did you do this?" Peter did not miss this opportunity to declare the good news even to these enemies of Jesus as he boldly and clearly answered: "It is by the name of Jesus Christ of Nazareth, whom you crucified, but whom God raised from the dead."[67] They were warned to stop their preaching and then released. Not long after this, all the apostles were arrested, and again called to account. The reply? "The God of our fathers raised Jesus from the dead—whom you killed by hanging him on a tree . . . we are witnesses of these things."[68] Notice the centrality of the bodily resurrection. These men who hid in fear from these same authorities weeks earlier are now confronting them with eyewitness testimony of a risen Jesus.

Before Jesus appeared to him, Paul put many Christians in prison in an effort to destroy the nascent church. He went "from house to house" and "dragged off men and women."[69] Until this point, the persecution is mainly coming from Jewish leadership, but eventually Roman authorities join in as these eyewitnesses continue to proclaim the resurrection of Jesus. King Herod arrested a number of church members, including James, the brother of John, and had him beheaded.[70] Until this point the eyewitnesses had demonstrated a willingness to die for their testimony, but this is the first mention of an eyewitness who actually did.[71] James's execution was a political success for Herod, so he arrested Peter with the same intentions, though Herod was unsuccessful in this attempt. Eventually, the apostle Paul would spend a great portion of his ministry in prison, more than any of the other leaders in the church.[72] The persecution he experienced was directly due to the success he had in persuading people that Jesus's corpse had been laid in a tomb, and that Jesus had later been bodily raised from the dead.[73] His defense was not only a clever legal

---

67. Acts 4:10.

68. Acts 5:29.

69. Acts 8:3.

70. Acts 12:2.

71. While Stephen is recorded as the church's first martyr and certainly believed in the resurrection of Jesus, it is not clear whether or not he was an eyewitness to the empty tomb and the risen Jesus.

72. 2 Corinthians 11:23.

73. Acts 13:29, 30.

maneuver, but a theological truth: "I am on trial because of my hope in the resurrection of the dead."[74]

Third, consider the loss of life. James, the brother of John, was the first eyewitness to die for his testimony, but he would not be the last. The only historical sources we have tell us that Peter was eventually crucified by Rome, upside down by his own request. James, the brother of Jesus, was clubbed to death in Jerusalem. Thomas was reportedly run through with a spear. Judas, the son of James (sometimes called Thaddeus) was shot to death with arrows, possibly while hanging on a cross. Matthew was slain with a halberd (an ax and pick with a spearhead). Matthias was stoned and beheaded. Andrew was crucified without nails, protracting the torture. Simon the Zealot, Philip, and Bartholomew were crucified. Paul was beheaded in Rome during Nero's tyrannical reign. Of the original disciples, only John escaped a violent end, and died of natural causes at nearly one hundred years of age. Their willingness to maintain their testimony, even when it resulted in their violent deaths, only enhances the credibility of their testimony.[75]

THE TESTIMONY OF JAMES THE BROTHER OF JESUS

The bone boxes found in Talpiot in 1980 contained several common names from the first century. In this public discussion, many people, Christians and non-Christians alike, have been surprised to find out that Jesus had brothers. They should not have been. The Bible has never hidden the fact. "Isn't this the carpenter?" asked the good people of Jesus's hometown. "Isn't this Mary's son and the brother of James, Joseph, Judas and Simon? Aren't his sisters here with us?"[76] The Gospels are intended,

---

74. Acts 23:6.

75. Ancient sources reporting the suffering and martyrdom of the disciples include Josephus, Eusebius, Clement, Origen, Gaius, Dionysius. For example, writing just before AD 300 and drawing from earlier written sources available to him, Eusebius writes: "Thus Nero publicly announcing himself as the chief enemy of God was led on in his fury to slaughter the apostles. Paul is therefore said to have been beheaded at Rome and Peter to have been crucified under him. And this account is confirmed by the fact that the names of Peter and Paul still remain in the cemeteries of that city even to this day." (*Ecclesiastical History*, 2:25:5). While some of the details of the deaths in the different accounts are difficult to reconcile, the tradition of the early church and non-Christian sources are unified in the proclamation that all of the original apostles suffered and all but John died for their testimony.

76. Mark 6:3.

among other things, to document specific living eyewitnesses in the first century, to the words and works of Jesus. And what did these four brothers think of their oldest brother? John tells us: "For even his own brothers did not believe in him."[77] And yet, James and Judas would later become central leaders in the Christian church. There is broad scholarly opinion that Judas authored the little New Testament book of Jude[78] and exhorted his readers to "contend for the faith that was once for all entrusted to the saints."[79] Likewise, Jesus's brother, James, is the most likely author of the book of James. Luke and Paul both note that James presided at the Council of Jerusalem.[80]

So what happened? How is it they went from being non-believing, half-brothers, to being fully devoted followers and worshippers of Jesus Christ, leaders in the church and authors of sacred text? What happened in between that made the difference? It was not how Jesus lived, taught, or died. In fact, his undignified death on a Roman cross likely confirmed their initial suspicion that Jesus was emotionally disturbed. What made the difference is the bodily resurrection of Jesus. "Then he appeared to James," Paul asserts, "then to all the apostles."[81] And from the moment they saw their brother raised from the dead, they publicly worshipped him as God. Were they just pretending? Had Jesus's own brothers joined the conspiracy?

The first century Jewish historian, Josephus, tells us what James gained for his testimony. Ananus, the Caesar-appointed High Priest in Jerusalem, "assembled the Sanhedrin of judges, and brought before them the brother of Jesus, who was called Christ, whose name was James, and some others, [or, some of his companions] and when he had formed an accusation against them as breakers of the law, he delivered them to be stoned."[82]

---

77. John 7:5.

78. The author of Jude identifies himself as a "brother of James" (Jude 1). While the very common name for Judas is exactly the same in the original language (Greek), there is a long-held tradition of translating Judas as Jude in the English text when seeking to avoid confusion with Judas Iscariot.

79. Jude 1:3.

80. Acts 15; Galatians 1:19.

81. 1 Corinthians 15:7.

82. Josephus, *Complete Works*, 423. "Antiquities, 20:9:1."

Since Josephus was not a Christian, this supports Edwards's assertion that even those who were not the friends of Jesus corroborate the facts of the New Testament. This is an extra-biblical source that confirms there really was a man named Jesus who really did have a brother named James and this Jesus was believed by many to be the Christ. The belief in Jesus as the Messiah was so firm, that many, including Jesus's own brother, were willing to die for it. Importantly, the "James Passage" of Josephus demonstrates that far from being some later invention, Jesus was considered to be God even while his brothers were still alive.[83]

WHO DIES FOR A LIE?

The point is that all of these eyewitnesses could have avoided the loss of their possessions, freedom, health, and lives if they had just stopped telling the world they had seen an empty tomb and a risen Jesus. The most plausible explanation for why they did not stop saying this is that their testimony was true. If they had not seen these things, they knew they were lying.[84] Someone may protest, "But religious people die all the time for what they believe. Just look at the hijackers on 9/11!" That is certainly true, but that is not what I am saying. As many before me have noted, while many people may die for what they believe is true, no one dies for what they know is false. If the disciples had not seen an empty tomb and a bodily risen Jesus—if they had

---

83. Eddy and Boyd, *The Jesus Legend*, 199. See also their defense of the authenticity of both references to Jesus by Josephus against the charge that these are later Christian interpolations in 185–98.

84. What Edwards advanced in 1749 was developed more fully by Elias Boudinot in 1801: "Besides, the disciples, in taking away the body, must have only deceived others; they could not have deceived themselves; and of all men, they must have acted the most absurdly, to lay down their lives in support of facts they knew to be false . . . Here again, it requires the belief of a miraculous fact, to disbelieve the miracle of the resurrection of our Lord and Savior—there can be no possible cause assigned, why men, simple in their manners, honest and upright in their lives, and totally cut off from every temporal advantage, should voluntarily bring on themselves the hatred and detestation of their government and fellow-citizens, by asserting and steadily professing through their whole lives a fact which they knew of their own knowledge to be false, and finally to seal the truth of it with their blood. Add to this, that they should within a few days of the transaction, be able to convince thousands of their countrymen of all ranks and characters, under every advantage of examination and detection, of the truth of what they asserted, so as to lead them, also, to forsake every personal advantage and expose themselves to contumely and reproach for the sake of him who was the great object of this miraculous event, and that with his express declaration before their eyes, 'that they should suffer persecution for his sake'" (*Age of Revelation*, 173–74).

merely invented the stories—they knew their claim was false. What possible motive did they have to maintain that testimony?

"DEATH WILL RESOLVE THINGS"

In typical fashion, Edwards closes his sermon "It Concerns All to Determine Who Jesus Was" with an urgent appeal to his listeners. He exhorts them "never to give themselves any ease til they come to a full determination in the points whether he was an imposter," or whether he was of the devil, "or whether a mere man." Edwards makes it clear: "Either he was a divine person or he was not."[85] There is much hanging in the balance. "If Christ is what he professed himself to be" and you have "determined that he is not" what he professed, "how doleful is your state if he is God." Whatever you choose today, "death will resolve things for you," but then, if you are wrong, "it is too late."[86]

Benjamin Franklin never seems to have come to what Edwards called a "full determination." In that famous letter to Ezra Stiles, just days before his death, he expresses only doubt. On the question of whether Jesus was God, Franklin said, "I think it needless to busy myself with it now, when I expect soon an opportunity of knowing the truth with less trouble."[87] Nearly twenty thousand mourners in Philadelphia watched as his funeral procession worked its way to the cemetery at Christ Church. Leading the processional were the clergymen of the city, "all of them, of every faith."[88] Five weeks after writing to Ezra Stiles, for better or worse, death resolved things for Benjamin Franklin.

---

85. Edwards, "It Concerns All," 47.

86. Ibid., 50.

87. Franklin, *Writings*, 1179.

88. Isaacson, *Benjamin Franklin*, 470.

7

Grace: "A Free Gift"

*For there is no other way, there is nowhere else that you can go. You must
come hither or perish. You had better, therefore leave off all attempts
at getting salvation in any other way, leave off building upon your own
righteousness and yield yourself to Christ Jesus. . . . He is willing to receive
you; he calls you, he nears you, he opens his arms to receive you.[1]*

—Jonathan Edwards

God helps them that help themselves.[2]

—Benjamin Franklin

It's the easiest thing in the world for a man to deceive himself.[3]

—Benjamin Franklin

POLLSTER GEORGE BARNA HAS made a good living taking the spiritual
pulse of Americans for over twenty years. In that time, a cascade of
Barna surveys has charted the trends in our religious beliefs. Of particular
interest to Barna has been the state of biblical literacy among Americans.
How well do we know our Bibles? In 2000, Barna asked America if the
Bible teaches that "God helps those who help themselves." Three out of
four Americans agreed that it does.[4] Although the statement had existed

---

1. Edwards, *Works*, 10:531.
2. Franklin, *Papers*, 2:140.
3. Franklin, *Writings*, 1238.
4. Barna Group, "Americans' Bible Knowledge," 66. See also: Lutzer, *Ten Lies*, 173–75.
To show that Franklin's thought was not original, Lutzer also cites Aesop ("The gods help
them that help themselves"), Euripides ("Try first thyself, and after, call on God."), George
Herbert ("Help thyself and God will help thee").

in various forms for centuries, it cannot be found in the Bible. Rather, the present version of that proverb comes to us from Benjamin Franklin who, in the parlance of the eighteenth century, pronounced that "God helps them that help themselves."

THE ROOTS OF THE AMERICAN SELF-HELP MOVEMENT

Franklin used this line on several occasions in his life, the first being in Poor Richard's Almanac. The almanac, a collection of pithy proverbs in which Franklin, by way of the pseudonym, Richard Saunders, offers such gems as "He's a fool that makes his doctor his heir"; "Great talkers, little doers";[5] "Fish and visitors stink in 3 days"; "Diligence is the mother of good luck"; "None preaches better than the ant, and she says nothing";[6] "A countryman between 2 lawyers, is like a fish between two cats";[7] and, "Haste makes waste."[8]

In these clever nuggets of common sense, Franklin reflects and strengthens the foundation of virtues that would give rise to America's dominance in later years. The spirit of America is marked by action, a Puritan work ethic devoid of Puritan dogma. While citizens in other nations depended on powerful central governments for protection and provision, Americans like Franklin wanted to grow up, throw off these parental constraints, along with their high taxes, and take personal responsibility. The aristocracy, made up of doctors, lawyers, ministers, and landed gentry, could be defied in America. Franklin, who succeeded without a college education, was living proof that regardless of family name, Americans who worked hard and exercised self-discipline would find no end to what they could achieve. If these virtues are in place, if individual citizens are governing themselves in their private lives, there is less need to be governed by public officials.

And so in 1758, the year that Jonathan Edwards died in Princeton, Franklin made Poor Richard to say that as onerous as Great Britain's taxes were on Americans, Americans were taxed even more by their own idleness. It is well and good to pray for relief, but "God helps them that help

---

5. Franklin, *Papers,* 1:312–13.

6. Ibid., 2:137–40.

7. Ibid., 2:166.

8. Ibid., 4:405.

themselves."[9] Franklin advised his fellow citizens that they would be in better financial condition if they were not so lazy: "Sloth, like rust, consumes faster than labor wears, while the used key is always bright," "Lost time is never found again"; "Early to bed, and early to rise, makes a man healthy, wealthy and wise"; "There are no gains without pains"; "God gives all things to industry"; "Plow deep, while sluggards sleep, and you shall have corn to sell and keep."[10] In other words, stop blaming the government for all of your problems, take responsibility for yourself, and get to work!

But working hard is not enough. Making money will not liberate if you spend it faster than you make it. "A penny saved is a penny earned,"[11] after all. Americans must be frugal, taking care to live within their means. "Beware of little expenses; a small leak will sink a great ship"; "Buy what thou hast no need of and ere long, thou shalt sell thy necessities"; "A child and a fool imagine twenty shillings and twenty years can never be spent"; "When you run in debt, you give to another power over your liberty"; "The second vice is lying, the first is running in debt"; and never forget that "Creditors have better memories than debtors."[12]

In retrospect, the times of greatest economic prosperity and political freedom in the United States have been those seasons when Americans have followed Franklin's advice on fiscal discipline. On the other hand, ignoring Franklin's advice has, on several occasions in our history, brought us to the brink of catastrophe. For some years now, Americans have maintained a negative savings rate, lived beyond their means, pursued extravagance, piled up massive debt, expected luxury, and nursed a sense of entitlement in ways that would have drawn a strong scolding from Benjamin Franklin.

Poor Richard's Almanac is not the only place that Franklin called on men to help themselves. On May 23, 1775, one month after the battles

9. Franklin, *Papers*, 7:341. This proverb appeared in Poor Richard twenty-two years earlier, in June 1736. See Franklin, *Papers*, 2:140. "Poor Richard, 1736."

10. Ibid. 7:340–55.

11. I cannot discover the source of this commonly accepted version of the quote that is often attributed to Franklin. The closest I find is "A penny saved is a penny got," which Franklin uses twice. The first is under the alias of Celia Single, July 24, 1732 (Franklin, *Papers*, 1:242), and the second is in a letter to Edward Bridgen, October 2, 1779 (Franklin, *Papers*, 30:430). In the letter to Bridgen, Franklin suggests that new coins be minted with wise proverbs, such as "Honesty is the best policy." In Franklin's mind, this will tend to "make an impression on the mind" and "regulate the conduct" especially of young people.

12. Franklin, *Papers*, 7:340–50.

of Lexington and Concord, in a letter to Humphry Marshall, Franklin warns that the colonies must be "prepared to repel force by force" and he is confident they can be successful as long as they stay united. The colonies cannot passively wait for God to intervene. Rather, Franklin reminds Marshall, "God helps them that help themselves."[13] Self-help in this situation was armed revolution against the crown.

"THE SPIRIT OF OUR PEOPLE"

The last record I have found of Franklin's use of this famous phrase is in a letter to John Adams in 1780. Franklin writes from Passy, France, while serving as an ambassador for the United States. Four years into the Revolutionary War, one of Franklin's duties was to solicit financial and political support from other nations in Europe. But the nations of Europe had been hesitant to ally themselves with the upstart United States, waiting on the sidelines to see if the American cause was viable. Franklin is encouraged that his countrymen have come "to depend on themselves" and that "the Spirit of our people was never higher than at present." Then Franklin reminds Adams that "The Proverb says, 'God helps them that help themselves,' and the world too in this sense is very godly."[14]

This use of the proverb gives us some insight into Franklin's understanding of it. The nations of the world were waiting to see if America could help herself, if she was committed to the cause. Of course, she could not do it alone. She would need a little help from nations like France. In doing her best, America would do most of the work. Yet with a little assistance from other nations who do the rest, she would be victorious. In the end, victory over Great Britain is the product of an alliance between the self-reliant nations of America and France. This spirit of self-dependence, self-trust, self-help, and self-improvement is the spirit of America.

In this way, Franklin tells Adams, France is like God. God waits on the man to see if he is willing to work hard, helping himself. If the man performs acceptably, God will throw in some aid, just enough to tip the scales in favor of the man. That is, just as France will help the United States because the United States deserves it, God helps the man who helps himself because the man deserves it. Salvation is the product of an alliance between man and God. We do our best and God does the rest.

---

13. Franklin, *Papers*, 22:51. "Letter to Humphry Marshall, Tuesday, May 23, 1775."
14. Ibid., 33:354.

IS SELF-HELP BIBLICAL?

There is a sense in which Franklin's call to action and personal responsibility is aligned with the Bible. Scripture consistently denounces laziness and presumption. "Lazy hands make a man poor," said Solomon, "but diligent hands bring wealth."[15] Paul gave the church a universal principle: "If a man will not work, he shall not eat."[16] The church is not obligated to help someone who is not willing to help himself. Also, James condemns the mere profession of faith while not acting on that faith when he says that "faith by itself, if it is not accompanied by action, is dead."[17] He who says he trusts in God but takes no action is deceiving himself.

But scripture also denounces self-reliance. "It is better to take refuge in the Lord than to trust in man."[18] "I do not trust in my bow," prays David, "my sword does not bring me victory, but you give us victory over our enemies."[19] Again, the psalmist warns "Do not put your trust in princes, in mortal men, who cannot save."[20] You must "Trust in the Lord with all your heart and lean not on your own understanding."[21] When it comes to the salvation of sinners, it does not "depend on man's desire or effort, but on God's mercy."[22] It was not when we could help ourselves, but when we were helpless, "powerless, Christ died for the ungodly."[23] Paul writes to the Colossians that before they became Christians, they were "dead" in their sins, but God made them "alive with Christ."[24] In what way can a dead man help himself? In no way! And that seems to be the point. When it comes to doing good works that somehow merit the favor of God, earning a place in heaven, the Bible teaches we are completely helpless and totally unable.

---

15. Proverbs 10:4.

16. 2 Thessalonians 3:10.

17. James 2:17.

18. Psalm 118:8.

19. Psalm 44:6.7.

20. Psalm 146:3.

21. Proverbs 3:5.

22. Romans 9:16.

23. Romans 5:6. In commenting on this verse, C. E. B. Cranfield notes: "Christ's work was not according to 'God helps them that helps themselves' of *Poor Richard's Almanac*. He did not wait for us to start helping ourselves, but died for us when we were altogether helpless" (*Critical*, 263–64).

24. Colossians 2:13.

In other words, God helps those who *cannot* help themselves. By biblical standards, Franklin was far too optimistic about his own abilities.

George Whitefield, the renowned evangelist of the Great Awakening, and colleague of Jonathan Edwards, had developed a warm friendship with Franklin. Whitefield once told Franklin that if his offer to Whitefield to lodge at his house was for Christ's sake, it would be rewarded in heaven. "Don't let me be mistaken," replied Franklin, "it was not for Christ's sake, but for your sake."[25] Franklin, who believed Whitefield to be "a perfectly honest man," wrote in his autobiography that Whitefield used "indeed sometimes to pray for my Conversion, but never had the Satisfaction of believing that his Prayers were heard."[26] Whitefield repeatedly presented the orthodox Jesus to Franklin and inquired as to Franklin's faith, and Franklin assured Whitefield that he had "no doubt" that he would experience eternal happiness in heaven. Franklin's confidence did not rest on the finished work of Jesus Christ, but rather on the temporal happiness he had enjoyed the first sixty years of his life on earth. For Franklin, the material blessings he had received were proof that God loved him, and "if he loves me, can I doubt that he will go on to take care of me, not only here but hereafter?"[27] The problem is that many people, good and evil, lovers of God and haters of God, have experienced the earthly health and wealth that Franklin interpreted as evidence that he was destined for heaven. Whatever this is, it is not biblical Christianity.

DID FRANKLIN BELIEVE IN SELF-SALVATION?

What does self-help look like when applied to eternal salvation? To be saved from the judgment of God, the man must help himself by doing good works. The woman who would escape eternal punishment must conduct herself in a way that conforms to God's laws. No one is perfect, but if he or she obeys often enough and well enough, then God will be inclined to help the well-intentioned soul make up the deficit. It is as if our bad works, failing to meet God's moral standards, creates a debt to God. In order to pay the debt, we work it off by good works. Perhaps we can never pay the entire debt, but if we impress God with our effort and sincerity, he might pay the rest for us. For example, suppose I owe the bank $100,000.

25. Franklin, *Writings*, 1408.

26. Ibid.

27. Franklin, *Works*, 7:261.

After working diligently, I can only come up with $80,000. The bank may be so impressed with my effort to help myself that it chooses to be merciful and help me by forgiving the remaining $20,000. I do my best, the bank does the rest.

This approach to God, sometimes called moralism, has several practical implications. First, moralism can produce model citizens. If our eternal salvation depends on being moral, then doing good works that benefit our countrymen will take priority. Franklin, with the other founders, knew that the form of government they were building in America would survive only as long as the people of America were both educated and moral. The less moral the people, the more the people would need to be governed. The more government required, the more taxes would be raised. If people did not use their power to govern themselves in their private lives, then their power would be taken from them and given to the government, which in turn would force their compliance. Only moral people can be trusted to govern themselves, and since Franklin viewed the moral system taught by Jesus as superior to all others, he valued the political usefulness of Christian ethics, the moral system taught by Jesus.

A second implication of moralism is religious relativism. All the religions of the world, it is commonly held, teach the same basic moral principles. Though they often differed in their rituals, Franklin believed that all religions shared an ethical core of doing good works for your fellow man. Don't steal his property, lie to his face, sleep with his wife, or take his life. These rules are found in every religion and, frankly, in Poor Richard's Almanac. Therefore, Christianity is not unique or distinct.

A third implication of moralism is a ground for human pride. If a right relationship with God is earned by keeping these rules, then the people who do the best at keeping the rules will feel superior to the people who break them. More importantly, they may feel justified in sharing some of God's glory. If salvation is a joint effort where, for example, I do eighty percent of the work and God does twenty percent of the work, then I am entitled to eighty percent of the glory. Therefore, I have some grounds for boasting in the presence of God, rather than being overwhelmed with gratitude for his kindness. In the end, moralism, to borrow and revise Franklin's famous proverb, is the belief that God saves those who save themselves.

Franklin's sister, Jane, a strong supporter of Jonathan Edwards, was greatly concerned that Franklin had in fact embraced moralism. In July 1744, Franklin wrote to settle his sister's concern. As to salvation by good works, Franklin noted that "there are few, if any, in the world so weak as to imagine that the little good we can do here, can *merit* so vast a reward hereafter."[28] It is not clear what Franklin intends to say here. By saying what he does, he may be able to dodge the charge of human pride. In self-salvation, since no one is perfect, there is still need for at least a measure of grace, and therefore, some humility. Franklin knows enough to not put *all* of his trust in his good works. Perhaps he means that the reward in the hereafter will be greater than what is deserved, but he will deserve some of it nonetheless. Possibly, Franklin is saying that the best we can do, the "little good," is about twenty percent and God covers the remaining eighty percent. But the result is the same: I do my best, God does the rest.

Franklin's friend, Thomas Paine, did not share Franklin's ambiguity when he confessed that, "the only true religion is Deism . . . the belief in one God . . . the practice of what are called moral virtues;—and that it was upon this only . . . that I rested all my hopes of happiness hereafter. So say I now—and so help me God."[29]

While Franklin may have vacillated in his views of salvation during his life, he finally seems to have settled on a deistic version of self-help salvation. Take another look at that letter Franklin wrote, shortly before his death, to Yale president Ezra Stiles.

> Here is my Creed. I believe in one God, Creator of the Universe. That he governs it by His Providence. That he ought to be worshipped. That the most acceptable Service we render Him is doing good to His other Children. That the soul of Man is immortal, and will be treated with Justice in another Life respecting its Conduct in this. These I take to be the fundamental Principles of all sound Religion and I regard them as you do in whatever Sect I meet with them. As to Jesus of Nazareth my Opinion of whom you particularly desire, I think the System of Morals and his Religion, as he left them to us, the best the World ever saw or is likely to see; but I apprehend it has received various corrupt Changes, and I have, with most of the present Dissenters in England, some doubts as to his divinity . . .[30]

Enclosed with the letter to Stiles in 1790 was a copy of a letter Franklin had written nearly forty years earlier to a "zealous religionist." Franklin

28. Franklin, *Papers*, 2:385. Emphasis is in the original.

29. Paine, *Age of Reason*, 150.

30. Franklin, *Writings*, 1179.

believed he had healed this man, Joseph Huey, of paralysis by way of electrical shocks. In 1753, Huey feared that Franklin would become proud, relying on good works such as healing the sick, to get him into heaven. Franklin assured Huey that in his "notion of good works" he is far from expecting that he "shall merit heaven by them." Franklin is clear: "I can do nothing to deserve such a reward." To expect heaven for his good works would be like expecting a plantation in exchange for giving a thirsty man a drink of water. The happiness of heaven will come "rather from God's goodness than our merit."[31]

But where does Jesus fit into all of this? Franklin reminds Huey that "your great Master thought much less" of outward appearances, like "holiday-keeping, sermon-reading or hearing, performing church ceremonies, or making long prayers … than many of his modern disciples. He preferred the doers of the Word to the mere hearers." Some people who do good works will be accepted in the final judgment "though they never heard of his Name." In fact, Franklin asserts that Jesus believed "there were some in his time so good that they need not hear even him for improvement."[32]

The problem with the deist system is that it cannot explain how anyone might be "treated with justice in another life respecting its conduct in this" and still end up in heaven. Crimes must still be punished. Suppose you are stopped by the police for driving 60 miles an hour in a 45 mile an hour speed zone. Can you escape a ticket by promising to drive 30 miles an hour all the way home? Does that balance the score? Or suppose a murderer seeks to escape justice by pointing out that for 364 days of the year he murdered no one? On what basis will this holy and perfect God forgive sin? How can God be just and yet overlook man's catastrophic failure to keep his laws? The Christian's answer is that God is able to be both merciful and just by executing justice on a willing and worthy substitute. Because justice was done on the cross, mercy can be extended to sinners.

So it is what Franklin did *not* say that is most telling. Interestingly, Franklin does not say, "Our great master," but "Your great Master." Franklin's creed uses Jesus as a moral guide but does not bow before him as Savior. That's why he told Stiles he considered "the System of Morals and his Religion, as he left them to us, the best the World ever saw or is likely to see." Franklin knew his good works did not fully merit heaven,

---

31 Franklin, *Papers*, 4:505–6.

32. Ibid.

but he also seems to believe his bad works did not merit hell. In Franklin's view, surely a good and loving God would show mercy, cut him some slack, because Franklin had sincerely tried to do "real good works, works of kindness, charity, mercy, and public spirit."[33] In the end, Franklin's creed advocates a salvation that is Christ-less and cross-less. After all, if you can save yourself, you really don't need a Savior. You just need a little help.

EDWARDS PATRIOTS ON GRACE AND GOOD WORKS

The Bible is clear that all who go to heaven do so on the basis of good works. The Bible is also clear that the good works that merit our place in heaven are not our own. Rather, anyone who goes to heaven will enjoy that grace because of the good works of Jesus Christ. The Judge of the universe cannot be unjust. Sin cannot be overlooked, but must be punished. On the cross, the guilt of sinners was transferred, or imputed, to Jesus who experienced the wrath of God against sin in perfect justice. "God made him who had no sin to be sin for us, so that in him we might become the righteousness of God."[34] As a willing substitute, Jesus offered himself "unblemished to God"[35] as a sacrifice in the place of lawbreakers. Not only that, the righteousness of Jesus, his perfect life of keeping God's law at every point, is imputed to sinners who come to him. This is why Paul can say that he is "found in him, not having a righteousness of my own that comes from the law, but that which is through faith in Christ."[36] While Jesus got the blame for Paul's law-breaking, Paul got credit for Jesus's law-keeping.

Though Franklin was right to deny that his good works merit heaven, I have yet to find him affirming his trust in the good works of Jesus. What makes Franklin's failure to publicly profess his trust in the merits of Jesus even more glaring are the clear confessions of other patriots in Franklin's day. Samuel Adams made it a point to leave his confession of faith in his will. He recommended "my soul to that Almighty Being who gave it, and my body I commit to the dust, relying on the merits of Jesus Christ for pardon for all my sins."[37] But Adams's confession was not just private.

---

33. Franklin, *Papers*, 4:505–6.
34. 2 Corinthians 5:21.
35. Hebrews 9:14.
36. Philippians 3:9.
37. Samuel Adams, *Writings*, "Last Will and Testament," 3:379.

When John Hancock died in office as Governor of Massachusetts in 1794, his Lt. Governor, Samuel Adams, was immediately handed the duties of governor. In his letter to the state legislature, Adams referred to his placement as "a sovereign act of God."[38] Less than a month later, Adams issued a "proclamation for a day of public fasting, humiliation and prayer." With stunning boldness, Adams did not hesitate, as so many of his fellow patriots had, to publicly speak the name of Jesus. He counseled his fellow citizens to seek the "gracious and free pardon" of God "thro' Jesus Christ."[39] Furthermore, he implores the people of Massachusetts to ask God "above all, to cause the religion of Jesus Christ, in its true spirit, to spread far and wide, till the whole earth shall be filled with his glory."[40]

Elias Boudinot, in addition to serving as President of the Continental Congress, served as the president of the General Assembly of the Presbyterian Church in the United States of America. As a tireless defender of orthodoxy, he faithfully guarded the Westminster Confession's clear pronouncement that those who are accepted by God are received "not for anything wrought in them, or done by them, but only for the perfect obedience and full satisfaction of Christ, by God imputed to them, and received by faith alone."[41] Likewise, John Witherspoon, signer of the Declaration, followed the example of his predecessor, Jonathan Edwards, and was faithful to teach his Princeton students, including Aaron Burr and James Madison, that their only hope of eternal salvation was the "acceptance of the pardon and peace through Christ Jesus, which they neither have contributed to the procuring, nor can contribute to the continuance of, by their own merit."[42]

John Jay, the first chief justice of the Supreme Court, and co-negotiator with Franklin and John Adams of the Treaty of Paris, was an "evangelical Episcopalian"[43] who did not hide his loyalties. The *Thirty-Nine Articles of Religion* as a statement of faith of the Episcopal Church, leaves no doubt about the relationship of grace and good works. "We are accounted righteous before God," states Article Eleven, "only for the merit

38. Samuel Adams, *Writings*, "Last Will and Testament," 4:354. "To the Legislature of Massachusetts, January 17, 1794."

39. Ibid., 4:361.

40. Ibid., 4:362.

41. *Westminster Confession of Faith*, "Larger Catechism, Q.70," 37.

42. Witherspoon, *Works*, 1:36.

43. Holmes, *Faiths of the Founding Fathers*, 154.

of our Lord and Savior Jesus Christ by faith, and not for our own works or deservings. Wherefore, that we are justified by faith only, is a most wholesome doctrine, and very full of comfort."[44]

Benjamin Franklin would have been familiar with the biblical relationship between good works and God's grace, but intentionally avoids affirmation of it.

BY GRACE ALONE

Against the popular cliché "God helps them that help themselves," Jonathan Edwards represented another view: We are saved by grace alone through faith alone in Christ alone to the glory of God alone. As an heir of the Protestant Reformation, Edwards saw this cluster of slogans as the rallying point of orthodox Christianity.

By grace alone, the Reformers meant that our salvation is not a cooperative effort between God and us. Rather it is all of God and none of us. God does not help those who help themselves because all of us are helpless. God starts, sustains, and completes our salvation. Even my very best effort has no merit in the sight of God. "All have turned away," Paul reminded the Romans, "they have together become worthless; there is no-one who does good, not even one."[45]

Edwards did not share Franklin's optimism about human good works. Even the good things we do are often tainted with self-interest and impure motives. "If we love not God because he is what he is, but only because he is profitable to us, in truth we love him not at all."[46] To say that a man is good because he frequently does good things, is like saying that a ship is good because it sails most of the way across the Atlantic before it breaks apart and sinks.[47] We would not say it was a good ship. Likewise, a man who obeys most of the laws of God (if that were possible) cannot be said to be good. As Jesus pointed out, "no one is good—except God alone."[48] In the end, as Archbishop William Temple is reported to have

---

44. *Thirty-Nine Articles of Religion*, Article 11.
45. Romans 3:12.
46. Edwards, *Works*, 3:156.
47. Ibid., 3:152.
48. Luke 18:19.

said, "We contribute nothing to our salvation except the sin which made it necessary."[49]

That's why our need for God's grace is so complete. We don't need God's help added to ours. Our only hope is God's help only. We have a duty to respond to his grace, but even our ability to respond is a gift from God. "We are saved wholly and entirely by Christ's righteousness," proclaimed Edwards.[50] It is not that Christ's righteousness covers the twenty percent or even eighty percent we did not attain for ourselves. This is no joint venture between Jesus and me where I put in my righteousness and he puts in his, and together we get me to heaven. Rather, I am morally bankrupt and Christ's righteousness covers one hundred percent of the debt.

Edwards defined grace as "the free love and goodness of God."[51] There is no condition for his love or prerequisite for his goodness. God does not wait to see if I perform correctly, strive sincerely, or in some other way help myself. Rather, God loves and does good to me in spite of the fact I have done absolutely nothing to deserve his kind attention. I am saved by grace alone.

THROUGH FAITH ALONE

Throughout history, many individuals, being overwhelmed by the biblical evidence, concede that we have no merit of our own and only the merit of Christ on our behalf can save us. But how do we receive the merit of Christ? Do we work for it so that we merit the merit of Christ? Or do we combine faith with work so that we receive the merit of Christ as a result of faith plus works? Or do we receive it by faith alone, simply trusting God to freely give us the merit of Christ upon our belief in him? Edwards could not be clearer that we receive God's grace, including the merits of Christ, by faith alone.

In this, he is faithful to the teaching of the apostles. "For it is by grace," Paul wrote the Ephesians, "you have been saved, through faith—and this not from yourselves, it is the gift of God—not by works, so that no-one can boast."[52] Even our faith is a gift of God! "A man is justified by faith

---

49. Source unknown.
50. Edwards, *Works*, 14:337.
51. Edwards, "Jesus Christ Full of Grace and Truth," 18.
52. Ephesians 2:8, 9.

apart from observing the law"[53] and "a man is not justified by observing the law, but by faith in Jesus Christ."[54] When the jailer asked Paul and Silas what he must do to be saved, the response was clear as crystal: "Believe in the Lord Jesus, and you will be saved." They did not say "Believe and do good works," or, "Believe and go to church," or, "Believe and give to the poor." The only instrument by which we receive the grace of God is faith.[55] When we believe that Jesus died for us, God justifies us, declaring us to be righteous in his sight, giving us credit for the good works of Jesus. We are saved because of works, affirms Edwards, "but not our own. It is on account of the works which Christ has done for us."[56] When we put our faith in Christ, then God, according to his "sovereign grace" regards us, who have no righteousness, as if we do.[57] This is pure grace, declared Edwards, "a free gift,"[58] and the package in which God wrapped this gift to us is Jesus who is "full of grace and truth."[59]

Patrick Henry came to understand this most ultimate truth. His wife, after witnessing his death, wrote to her step-daughter:

> "Oh my dear Betsy, what a scene I have been witness to—I wish that all the Heroes of the Deistical Party could have seen my Ever-Honored Husband pay his last debt to Nature ... My loss, my dear Betsy, can never be repaired in this life. But oh that I may be enabled to imitate the virtues of your Dr. and honored Father; and that my end may be like his—He met death with firmness and in full confidence that through the merits of a bleeding Saviour his sins would be pardoned."[60]

FAITH THAT IS ALONE: THE PROBLEM OF HYPOCRISY

While Edwards believed we are justified by faith alone, he also believed that we are not justified by faith that is alone. Genuine faith is always accompanied by good works. Good works are not the *condition* of justifica-

---

53. Romans 3:28.
54. Galatians 2:16.
55. The verb form of the Greek noun for *faith* is often translated as *believe* in English.
56. Edwards, *The Works of Jonathan Edwards*, 2:53.
57. Edwards, *The Works of Jonathan Edwards*, 1:622.
58. Edwards, "Jesus Christ Full of Grace and Truth," 26.
59. John 1:14.
60. Mayer, *Son of Thunder*, 472.

tion, but rather the *consequence*. Good works are the fruit, the evidence, of God's grace in a person's life. When it comes to discerning who has genuinely received God's grace, Jesus warned his disciples, "by their fruit you will recognize them."[61] The fruit will be both doctrinal (what we believe) and ethical (how we behave), relating to both our creed and conduct. Genuine believers will teach the truth about God. They will also produce the "fruit of the spirit,"[62] being marked by such virtues as love, joy, peace, patience, kindness, goodness, gentleness, and self-control. They will take care of widows and orphans and feed the hungry because "faith without deeds is dead."[63] As Edwards put it, "none are true saints, but those" who are disposed "to pity and relieve their fellow creatures, that are poor, indigent and afflicted."[64] And again, some may claim to be true Christians, who are at the same time "sordid, selfish, cross and contentious spirit . . . morose, hard, close, high-spirited, spiteful," but "grace has a great tendency to restrain and mortify such sins."[65] So in fact, good works play a large role in salvation, not as a *condition*, but as a *consequence*. We do not do good works in order to *be* saved. Rather, we do good works because we *are* saved. An absence of good works is evidence of the absence of saving grace. Professing to be a Christian while not acting like one is hypocrisy, and hypocrisy was a big problem for both Benjamin Franklin and Jonathan Edwards.

"THE WICKEDNESS OF ITS MEMBERS"

When orthodox Christianity is perceived to hold an inordinate amount of political and social power in a culture, when it seems to influence the making and enforcing of laws, when it appears to open doors for business and financial success, there is almost always a reaction against it by those who feel left out. In England, church and state had developed a long reputation for each using the other, often for ignoble purposes. Thomas Paine's charge of the shameless use of the Christian doctrines to accumulate money and power is not altogether unfounded. In Edwards's New England, it was difficult to advance in any endeavor without the blessing of the Puritan hierarchy. Being a baptized church member in good standing was a neces-

---

61. Matthew 7:16.
62. Galatians 5:22.
63. James 2:26.
64. Edwards, *Works*, 2:355.
65. Ibid., 2:356–57.

sary social status for anyone who desired financial security and political influence. Clergy members were often wearers of "whigs," the mark of aristocracy. Magistrates and ministers, the "big-wigs," worked hand in hand.

That does not necessarily mean that the Puritan understanding of Jesus was wrong. It is my assertion that it was exactly right. But sound doctrine does not guarantee pure hearts. Then as now, corruption in the church existed at every level and hypocrisy was easy to find. In this, Paine and his philosophical kin are exactly right. And neither Benjamin Franklin nor Jonathan Edwards were bashful about blowing the whistle on the problem of hypocrisy in the church.

Writing as an apprentice printer under the pseudonym "Mrs. Dogwood," Franklin confides that "it has been for some time a question with me whether a commonwealth suffers more by hypocritical pretenders to religion or by the openly profane. But some late thoughts of this nature have inclined me to think that the hypocrite is the more dangerous person of the two, especially if he sustains a post in government . . . a little religion, and a little honesty, goes a great way in courts."[66]

Edwards was not so subtle. In 1749, he published an airtight case for returning church membership standards to a more biblical norm. For years, clergy in New England, bowing to popular pressure, had lowered the standards by degrees in an effort to permit more people to gain the church membership necessary for social status in New England. Unsurprisingly, the result was a lot of churches filled with hypocrites. Edwards's most severe opponents were church leaders who complained that higher standards would empty the churches, resulting in numerical decline. No, said Edwards, "the contrary tends to keep it small, as 'tis the wickedness of its members, that above all things in the world prejudices mankind against it; and is the chief stumbling block, that hinders the propagation of Christianity, and so the growth of the Christian church." What does the church need to be credible? "But holiness," wrote Edwards, "would cause the light of the church to shine so as to induce others to resort to it."[67] Merely professing orthodox Christianity was not enough. "Reason shows," wrote the ever-reasonable Edwards, "that men's deeds are better and more faithful interpreters of their minds, than their words."[68]

66. Franklin, *Writings*, 27.

67. Edwards, *Works*, 12:310.

68. Edwards, *Works*, 2:409–10.

For his efforts in purging the church of hypocrisy, Edwards was fired from his pastorate over the famous "Communion Controversy."[69] The difference between Franklin and Edwards, however, is that Edwards fought church hypocrisy to preserve orthodox Christianity, while Franklin used church hypocrisy to win legitimacy for an alternative Christianity. Disillusioned by hypocrisy among those who held to orthodox Christian doctrine and enamored by deist authors, Franklin found himself convinced that the best recourse was deistic religion.

Hypocrisy remains the favorite charge of skeptics today. In 2006, Sam Harris, a semi-famous atheist, continued the tradition of shining the light on the church's hypocrisy as a means of discrediting orthodox Christianity. After taking Bible-believers to task for moral shortcomings past and present, Harris reasons, "If we are going to take the God of the Bible seriously, we should admit that he never gives us the freedom to follow the commandments we like and neglect the rest."[70] On this, at least, Jonathan Edwards, Benjamin Franklin, and Sam Harris would fully agree.

IN CHRIST ALONE: THE SCANDAL OF EXCLUSIVISM

Consider the price paid by Jesus to redeem sinners: the humiliation of God taking on human flesh, the hatred from those he came to save, the rejection of the Father when the guilt of sinners was imputed to him, the cruel and excruciating death that satisfied God's demand for justice. It is natural to ask, Was there not some other way? Could God not direct us to another path of salvation and spare his own son? The biblical data confirms there is no other way. Jesus told his disciples, "I am the way and the truth and the life. No one comes to the Father except through me."[71] Peter was just as direct when he testified before the Sanhedrin, very religious people, that "Salvation is found in no one else, for there is no other name

---

69. In his argument for higher standards for church membership, Edwards drew the battle line at the Lord's Supper. His grandfather and predecessor, the beloved and revered Solomon Stoddard, had permitted many to receive communion who did not have assurance of their own salvation. Stoddard considered the Lord's Supper a "converting ordinance" that could be used to bring participants to saving faith. Edwards argued a more biblical position that only those who have examined themselves and are assured they are right with God should partake of communion. To do less is to make a mockery of the Lord's Supper. When Edwards reversed Stoddard's policy, the pursuant conflict eventually led to Edwards's dismissal after serving the church for over two decades.

70. Harris, *Letter*, 22.

71. John 14:6.

under heaven given to men by which we must be saved."[72] Apparently, being very religious is not enough. Those who are without Jesus are also "without hope and without God in the world."[73] The Thessalonians sincerely believed their religious tenets and tried to obey them, but it was not until the Gospel of Jesus came to them that they "turned to God from idols to serve the living and true God." Which means that until they put their faith in Jesus, they did not know God. Between God and men, there is only "one mediator" and that is "the man Christ Jesus."[74] Without hesitation, John declared that "He who has the Son has life; he who does not have the Son of God does not have life."[75] If there were some other way, if it were possible to live our lives well enough to save ourselves, clean enough to be accepted on the basis of our self-righteousness, then "Christ died for nothing."[76] The answer seems rather clear. There is no other way.

This clarity led the Westminster framers to insert an important question in the Larger Catechism: "Can they who have never heard the Gospel, and so know not Jesus Christ, nor believe in him, be saved by their living according to the light of nature?" The Scripture-soaked answer comes back: "They who, having never heard the Gospel, know not Jesus Christ, and believe not in him, cannot be saved, be they never so diligent to frame their lives according to the light of nature, or the laws of that religion which they profess; neither is there salvation in any other, but in Christ alone, who is the Savior only of his body the church."[77]

Because Jonathan Edwards loved the Bible, he believed that trusting Jesus is the only way to be reconciled to God. Because Jonathan Edwards loved people, he spent his life telling as many as he could about Jesus. Even if it were possible for people to sincerely seek after God, sincerity will be no excuse in the judgment. There is no compelling evidence, either from reason or from the Bible, that God will give eternal life to adherents of other religions "in their endeavors to find out the will of the deity, and to please him, according to their light, that they may escape his future displeasure and wrath."[78] In fact, "none but those that do live under the

72. Acts 4:12.
73. Ephesians 2:12.
74. 1 Timothy 2:5.
75. 1 John 5:12.
76. Galatians 2:21.
77. *Westminster Confession of Faith*, Larger Catechism, Q.60.
78. Edwards, *Works*, 1:319.

calls of the Gospel shall be saved . . . That is God's way and his only way of bringing men to salvation."[79] In the view of Scripture, the Reformed tradition, and Jonathan Edwards, the self-help, works-based religions of the world do not represent alternative ways of gaining access to heaven. For Edwards, it was clear: Trust in Jesus is the only way.

> For there is no other way, there is nowhere else that you can go. You must come hither or perish. You had better, therefore leave off all attempts at getting salvation in any other way, leave off building upon your own righteousness and yield yourself to Christ Jesus. He is the only Savior, and he is a very glorious one; he is all-sufficient, able to save to the uttermost, able to do everything for you that you need should be done. He is willing to receive you; he calls you, he [draws near to] you; he opens his arms to receive you.[80]

SELF-HELP EQUALS GOOD ENOUGH

The philosophy of self-help, with its attendant pride, is famously imbedded in the DNA of American life. Coupled with self-control, it can drive an economy to prosperity. Divorced from self-discipline, it can push a nation to ruin. Unhinged from a proper understanding of God's grace, it will lead people to eternal destruction. Apart from God we are utterly helpless and unable to help ourselves. For that reason, we have nothing for which to boast. If we are healthy, wealthy, or wise on this earth or if we experience happiness in heaven, it is only by God's grace.

Over two centuries later, Franklin's version of self-salvation thoroughly penetrates the American culture. In years past, because they retained a measure of humility before the Almighty, few Americans would claim they were so good that they deserved heaven. But it is also true that very few Americans believed they were so bad they deserved hell. Today, our culture has come farther than even Franklin might allow. Most Americans do in fact believe they have obligated God by their self-righteousness and thus deserve heaven. A Gallup Poll revealed that seventy-seven percent of Americans believed their chances of going to heaven were "good" or "excellent."[81] A Newsweek/Beliefnet.com poll announced that seventy-nine percent of Americans agreed that their religious faith was not the

79. Edwards, MS Sermon on Matthew 22:14 (1732).

80. Edwards, *Works*, 10:531.

81. Ostling, "Heaven and Hell."

only way and that a "good person" of another faith could go to heaven or attain salvation. In other words, about eight out of ten Americans are sure they will go to heaven, while seven out of ten Americans believe we get to heaven by being good persons. Even more startling is that sixty-eight percent of those in the poll describing themselves as evangelical Protestants agreed that a good person will go to heaven, no matter what they believe about Jesus. If these polls are accurate, nearly seven out of ten evangelicals in America now believe that faith alone in Christ alone is no longer required for salvation.[82] It also means that, whether they realize it or not, they really believe that Jesus came and died for nothing.[83]

This corroborates another Gallup poll revealing that seventy-five percent of Americans "say that there is a religion 'other than their own that offers a true path to God,' and of that number a substantial majority believe that this other path to God is equally as good as their own."[84] About eighty percent believe "there will come a day when God judges people and decides whether they will go to heaven or hell." Remarkably, the poll also finds that forty-four percent believe that a "good person will go to heaven"[85] *even if the person is an atheist!*

Similarly, Barna Research reports that fifty-four percent of Americans believe that "if a person is generally good, or does enough good things for others during their life, they will earn a place in Heaven," while thirty-eight percent disagree with that statement.[86] Among that thirty-eight percent, there are likely many who believe with Franklin, that even if they cannot earn a place in heaven by their good works, God will show them grace and give them a place anyway because they have sincerely done their very best. They are hoping for a little help from God in return for helping themselves, a portion of grace apart from Jesus, a measure of mercy apart from the cross, and eternal life apart from the resurrection power of the Son of God. Having breathed the air of a self-help culture for so long, what else could they conclude?

82. Newsweek/Beliefnet Poll, "Who Goes to Heaven?"
83. Galatians 2:21.
84. Gallup, "Americans Remain Very Religious."
85. Ibid.
86. Barna Group, "Beliefs: Heaven and Hell."

8

Islam as a Deist Argument

Honesty, Sincerity and openness, I esteem essential marks of a good mind.
I am therefore of opinion, that men ought, (after they have examined with
unbiased judgments, every System of Religion, and chosen one System on
their own Authority, for themselves) to avow their Opinions
and defend them with boldness.

—John Adams[1]

L IEUTENANT PRESSLEY O'BANNON, UNITED States Marine Corps, was a long way from his home in Virginia. At twenty-nine, he could have never imagined two years earlier that he would be fighting a war in this desert against Muslims who used the Qur'an to justify the capture and killing of Americans. Along with seven other American Marines, O'Bannon served in an American-led alliance that included three hundred Muslim troops. They were fighting together, Christians and Muslims, to unseat a Muslim tyrant who had been an exasperating thorn in America's side for years. Already, O'Bannon had distinguished himself as a courageous leader of men, calm under fire.

On the afternoon of April 27, O'Bannon led an attack force into a strategic town on the coast. The U.S. Navy had three ships positioned north of the harbor to maintain unrelenting fire on the enemy's shoreside defense and divert attention away from the Marines attacking from the south. After two hours of ferocious exchange, two marines were dead, three were wounded, and the American flag had been hoisted over the field of battle.

This secret mission, ordered by the President of the United States, guaranteed that O'Bannon and his detachment, America's first Marines, will forever hold the distinction of fighting in the United States' first land

---

1. John Adams, *Diary,* 1:12.

battle on foreign soil and being the first troops to raise an American flag on the field of battle outside of North America. The flag had fifteen stars and fifteen stripes. The place was Derne, on the North African "shores of Tripoli." The year was 1805. The president of the United States was Thomas Jefferson.[2]

What precipitated this violent response was a hostile aggression. For four centuries, Muslim nations along the Barbary Coast acted on the Qur'an's sanction of a holy war. They understood the Muslim scripture as instructing them to attack non-Muslim cities along the Mediterranean coast and seize the spoils of war, including the citizens whom they enslaved. The Qur'an seemed clear to them: "When you meet the unbelievers in the battlefield strike off their heads, and when you have laid them low, bind your captives firmly. Then grant them their freedom or take a ransom from them." If the Muslim warriors lost their lives in the process of enriching themselves and extending Islam's borders, they were comforted to know that "As for those slain in the cause of God, He will not allow their works to perish . . . He will admit them to the paradise he has made known to them."[3]

In addition, they believed God authorized them to stop any non-Muslim ship sailing through the Mediterranean Sea, whether military or commercial, and take what they wanted. "Of all fears," writes Richard Zacks, "of people living in the 1780's and 1790's, a fear perhaps exceeding death itself was the terror of being made a slave on the Barbary coast."[4] In fact, a rumor was widely spread in 1785 that Benjamin Franklin had been captured by Barbary pirates on his way to France.[5] Christian slaves who "converted" to Islam might gain better living conditions and perhaps their freedom, but faithful Christians could expect especially harsh treatment.

To avoid the terror of attack and enslavement by Muslim pirates, many countries, including the United States, simply paid tribute monies to the Barbary States for safe passage. By 1795, the United States was paying over a million dollars a year. Having amassed crippling debt from the Revolutionary War, U.S. foreign policy makers decided appeasement was more economical than fighting another war. But that policy began

2. Zacks, *Pirate Coast*, 229–33.

3. Qur'an 47:4–6. All quotations from the Qur'an are taken from N. J. Dawood, translator, *The Koran*.

4. Zacks, *Pirate Coast*, 4.

5. McCullough, *John Adams*, 352.

to change in October of 1803, when the *USS Philadelphia*, one of only six ships in the entire American navy, ran aground and was captured off the coast of Tripoli. Over three hundred American officers and men were captured, enslaved, and held for ransom. The pasha, or governor, of Tripoli, Yussef Karamanli, gaining the distinction of becoming the first foreign power to declare war on the United States, informed the American president he could have the men back for a ransom of $1,690,000. That amount exceeded the entire budget for the young nation's military.[6] In the end, it was diplomacy combined with the military victory at Derne that persuaded the pasha to settle for $60,000. However, Thomas Jefferson was not the first American president to negotiate with terrorists. The policy of appeasement was initiated several years before he took office.

THE TREATY OF TRIPOLI

On June 7, 1797, a treaty was sent to the floor of the Senate where it was read aloud and unanimously approved. From there, it went to the desk of President John Adams, where it was signed and later announced to the nation. Of particular interest is Article 11 of the treaty:

> As the Government of the United States of America is not, in any sense, founded on the Christian religion; as it has in itself no charac-ter of enmity against the laws, religion, or tranquility, of Mussulmen; and, as the said States never entered into any war, or act of hostility against any Mahometan nation, it is declared by the parties, that no pretext arising from religious opinions, shall ever produce an inter-ruption of the harmony existing between the two countries.[7]

Though the terminology has changed, most will recognize that the refer-ence is to Muslims and Muslim nations. The Treaty of Tripoli established an agreement in which the United States would send massive amounts of tribute money to the Barbary States while the Barbary States would cease terrorizing American ships. In 1801, the governor of Tripoli broke that treaty, and Thomas Jefferson exercised a military option.

The most intriguing feature of the treaty today is that it proves that such prominent founders as Washington, Adams, and Jefferson, and argu-ably the entire U.S. Senate in 1797, agreed that the "government of the United States of America is not, in any sense, founded on the Christian

6. Zacks, *Pirate Coast*, 30.
7. "The Barbary Treaties."

religion."[8] The treaty, originally drafted in George Washington's second term, had been negotiated by diplomat Joel Barlow, a friend of Thomas Jefferson and Thomas Paine, and by most accounts, a deist. However, it is hard to imagine that all of our nation's leaders in 1797 were denying the rich Christian heritage of the United States, the incontestable influence of biblical principles on the worldviews of the founders, or the fact that in 1797, the vast majority of Americans were professing Christians (even if not faithful church attendees). At the time, there was no Muslim constituency in America to speak of.

As an example of the founders' acknowledgment of a biblically informed government, we saw in chapter 7 that a month after Samuel Adams succeeded John Hancock as governor of Massachusetts, he issued a proclamation setting aside a day of prayer and fasting. In that proclamation he asked the citizens of his state to beseech God to "protect our navigation from the rapacious hands of invaders and robbers on the seas, and graciously to open a door of deliverance to our fellow-citizens in cruel captivity in a land of Barbarians."[9] And then he unashamedly (in a state document!) directs them to ask God "above all, to cause the religion of Jesus Christ, in its true spirit, to spread far and wide, till the whole earth shall be filled with his glory."[10]

I'll briefly mention two more historical facts that argue against the notion that the Treaty of Tripoli is a denial of the influential role of Christianity in the founding of the United States. First, in his Farewell Address of 1796, George Washington, spotting a secular trend veering away from Christianity, warned that the nation could not expect that "national morality can prevail in exclusion of religious principle."[11] The American experiment in self-government works only if the citizens are moral, and Washington could not see how they could be moral apart from the teachings of Jesus. It is not unlikely that Washington's ideas here were inspired by Benjamin Franklin's speech at the conclusion of the Constitutional Convention in 1786. Franklin agreed to the Constitution, "with all its faults" but he was certain that it would only be "well administered for a course of years, and can only end in despotism, as other forms

8. "The Barbary Treaties."

9. Samuel Adams, *Writings*, 4:362.

10. Ibid.

11. Novak and Novak, *Washington's God*, 242.

have done before it, when the people shall become so corrupted as to need despotic government."[12] Perhaps Franklin's words left an impression on George Washington.

A second event is the presidential campaign of 1800 in which Jefferson, the sitting vice-president, challenged John Adams, the sitting president. Adams and his supporters exploited Jefferson's deism to their own political advantage. Many Americans today, weary of the mudslinging in modern political campaigns, especially mudslinging with religious overtones, may yearn for a more civil past, but the election of 1800 was bitter and brutal. Newspapers endorsing Adams commonly regaled Jefferson's religious opinions with headlines such as "*GOD—AND A RELIGIOUS PRESIDENT or impiously declare for JEFFERSON—AND NO GOD.*"[13] The nation was almost evenly divided, but geography played a role, with the southern states supporting the Virginian while New England rallied behind Adams of Massachusetts, who was seeking a second term as president. But there were five candidates that year, and Jefferson's closest rival was the grandson of Jonathan Edwards, Aaron Burr, who received exactly as many electoral votes as Jefferson. In the end, Jefferson barely won the election, not because of his views on Jesus, but in spite of them. Because of the tie, the election had to be decided by the House of Representatives, which also awarded the vice-presidency to Aaron Burr. These two events, Washington's Farewell Address in 1796 and the presidential campaign of 1800, bracket the Treaty of Tripoli and give some context to the opinions of the founders.

By this time, the Constitution, including the First Amendment, had been ratified after a long struggle and vigorous debate. Patrick Henry, the Voice of the American Revolution,[14] is best known for his rousing challenge to the Second Virginia Convention in 1775, declaring, "I know not what course others may take, but as for me, give me liberty or give me death." Probably most Americans have not read the balance of the address, which is pregnant with biblical imagery. There is, however, more to Patrick Henry. He began building his legal reputation as an attorney by defending Virginia plantation owners against the Anglican clergy in 1763 in what became known as the Parson's Cause. As the established church,

12. Franklin, *Works*, 5:156.

13. *Gazette of the United States*, September 16, 1800. Quoted in Ferling, *Adams vs. Jefferson*, 154.

14. As we have seen, Samuel Adams is considered the Father, Washington the Sword and Jefferson the Pen of the American Revolution.

the Anglican Church was funded by tax revenue, and in Virginia, the clergy's salary was tied to the price of tobacco. This worked well for the parsons when the price of tobacco was up, but not so well when tobacco was down. When the parsons sued the vestry for back pay, King George and the English parliament took the parsons's side. In the trial, Henry challenged the clergy's hypocrisy and London's right to tax Virginia, especially to fund a state church.

However, Henry did not defend the planters against the parsons because he was hostile toward Christianity. His warm, evangelical faith is well documented. His argument was with the king and parliament that used the Church of England to accomplish their political agenda. Virginia ministers from other denominations might be permitted to preach, but they had to meet the approval of the established church and, unlike Anglican ministers, received no government funding.

So the "established church" in Virginia was the Church of England. The national government, based in London, taxed its subjects to pay the parsons in the colonies. American patriots had seen the results of such a system: a breeding of corruption among the Anglican clergy and a use of the church as a political tool to manipulate the people to the monarch's ends. Members of other Christian denominations that proclaimed the gospel, such as the Baptists, were hindered from worshipping God according to their conscience. This concern for religious freedom would later compel Henry to work tirelessly for a Bill of Rights to be attached to the Constitution which would insure that congress would have no power to establish a national church. The First Amendment exists largely because of the labor of Patrick Henry.[15]

---

15. Federalists like James Madison (who had studied under John Witherspoon at Princeton) were also mightily concerned with religious freedom, and, in fact, Steven Waldman writes that "no one did more to secure religious freedom" in the new nation than Madison. But Madison believed religious liberty was best secured without a Bill of Rights because the Constitution gave no explicit power to the federal government to establish a church, compel anyone to worship, or hinder anyone from worshipping according to conscience. However, Jefferson agreed with Patrick Henry (who had opposed Madison and the Constitution because of the power it gave to the Federal government) that the Bill of Rights was necessary to make sure the federal government never overstepped its bounds. In the end, Madison conceded and the First Amendment was crafted as a result of compromise on all sides. One of the more balanced explanations of how the First Amendment came to be is found in Steven Waldman's *Founding Faith: Providence, Politics, and the Birth of Religious Freedom in America*, 94–158.

The Founding Fathers learned from history and forged the First Amendment to preclude the possibility that the United States would ever establish a national church as England had done. That was the original intent of the "no establishment" clause of the First Amendment that is often ignored today. Richard John Neuhaus ably notes "the 'no establishment' clause, it needs ever to be repeated, is in the service of the 'free exercise' clause. The primary reason for the 'no establishment clause' is not to keep the church from taking over the state but to prevent the state from taking over the church."[16] In contemporary America, the debate is still very much alive, though the historical origin has been lost on most of her citizens.[17]

JONATHAN EDWARDS ON THE SEPARATION OF CHURCH AND STATE

Since Edwards died almost four decades before the First Amendment was ratified, we can only speculate on what his opinion might have been. What we do know is the Great Awakening he promoted proved to be a subversive movement, shaking up the state-supported religious status quo. In the last half of his ministry, Edwards was beginning to question the Puritan idea that God had some special theocratic covenant with America, as he had made with Israel. His teachings were for many "too dangerously revolutionary."[18]

While Edwards was making waves with his pen, his colleague in the Awakening, George Whitefield, was stirring things up with his preaching. Whitefield was banned from speaking in many churches and was relegated to preaching in the open air, attracting a diverse group of sects and denominations. This further threatened the religious establishment and amused Benjamin Franklin, who worked to raise money to build a meeting hall in Philadelphia "expressly for the Use of any Preacher of any religious Persuasion who might desire to say something to the People of Philadelphia; the Design in building not being to accommodate any

16. Neuhaus, *Naked Public Square*, 116.

17. Even though the First Amendment forbids a national church, it does not forbid a state church; that is, a church supported and promoted by individual state governments. At the time of the ratification of the Constitution, several states still supported the churches with tax money. Some of these state churches continued this practice until 1833. The idea of individual states favoring and funding particular Christian denominations did not seem unusual, and certainly not unconstitutional, in the infant years of our nation.

18. Noll, *America's God*, 47.

particular Sect, but the Inhabitants in general; so that even if the Mufti of Constantinople were to send a Missionary to preach Mahometanism to us, he would find a Pulpit at his Service."[19]

There was a certain measure of hypocrisy in the way the Puritans had dissented in Old England, suffered persecution, and then migrated to New England to establish a government that would persecute religious dissenters. Edwards was beginning to feel the sting of that persecution himself as he promoted the Awakening, making a few enemies at Harvard and Yale along the way. As it turned out, Princeton College, where Edwards would serve as the third president, began as a haven for pro-Awakening ministers-in-training, but its founders built it in New Jersey, not in Puritan New England.

Another leader who felt the sting of religious persecution was Isaac Backus. He had been born into the Congregationalist church, admired Whitefield and Edwards, and after his conversion, migrated to the Baptist church. He received baptism by immersion by 1751 and later became a renowned champion for religious freedom in the United States. Becoming a Baptist certainly did not result in his abandoning orthodoxy, and throughout his ministry he quoted from, as he put it, "our excellent Edwards."[20]

So while it would be a stretch to say that Jonathan Edwards would have promoted something like the First Amendment in 1758, by then he had sown the seeds in America that would result in exactly that. His challenge to the government-sponsored religious establishment and his willingness to cross denominational lines (such as his ministry in the Presbyterian church and alongside the Anglican Whitefield) in order to promote the gospel might have eventually led him to see the wisdom in believing God's church could thrive without being propped up by the government.

IS THE UNITED STATES A CHRISTIAN NATION?

Already in America, both before and after the Revolutionary War, the use of force to advance the gospel and enforce church discipline had given orthodox Christians several scandals for which to be embarrassed. Repeatedly, the Baptists in America bore the brunt of mistreatment from governments dominated by Congregationalists (in the North) and

19. Franklin, *Writings*, 1406–7.
20. McBeth, *Baptist Heritage*, 260.

Anglicans (in the South).[21] Consequently, Baptists like Isaac Backus were at the forefront of the effort to separate church and state. It was to Baptists in Danbury, Connecticut, that Thomas Jefferson would write a letter in 1801 containing that now famous opinion that the First Amendment built "a wall of separation between Church and State."[22] Understandably, the Baptists did not like paying taxes that paid for Congregational ministers and they wanted Jefferson to intervene. President Jefferson was unable to offer much help because, while the First Amendment prohibited a national church, it did not prohibit individual state governments, like that of Connecticut, from using tax revenue to pay Congregational ministers. Jefferson could not intervene while he was President, and the Bill of Rights would not be applied to the states until the Fourteenth Amendment was ratified in 1868. However, by 1797, when the Treaty of Tripoli was signed, even though the battle for religious freedom had not been settled on the state level, it had been reasonably settled on the federal level. And it was on the federal level that the United States dealt with foreign nations.

In this sense, as the Treaty of Tripoli states, the federal government of the United States is not founded on the Christian religion. The Declaration of Independence, whose principal authors, Thomas Jefferson, Benjamin Franklin, and John Adams, makes reference to God four times in terms acceptable to both the deists and orthodox Christians among the Founding Fathers. In fact, these terms might even be acceptable to most Muslims. There are no direct references to Jesus in the Declaration and

21. Consider a possible explanation. The Puritans (Congregationalists) had come out of the Church of England (Anglicans) and the Anglicans had come out of the Roman Catholic Church. Unlike Catholics, Anglicans, or Puritans, Baptists had no history of joining church and state. Perhaps a fundamental reason is theological. That is, Baptists saw more discontinuity between the Old and New Testaments, and thus between Israel (a theocracy) and the New Testament Church. That discontinuity is seen especially in their understanding of the Christian practice from which they derive their name: baptism. While in the Old Testament, circumcision was performed on infants as a sign of God's covenant with Israel, it was replaced by water baptism in the New Testament. Catholics, Congregationalists, and Anglicans, recognizing more continuity between the Old and New Testaments, baptize infants. However, Baptists, seeing no clear examples of infant baptism and no clear commands in the New Testament to baptize infants, reserved baptism only for professing believers. For Baptists, the kingdom Jesus established was radically different from the theocratic kingdom of Old Testament Israel. Consequently, Baptists have historically been suspicious of state involvement in promoting or regulating religion, while Christian traditions that saw greater continuity, and therefore baptized infants, were more inclined to church-state alliances.

22. Jefferson, "Letter to the Danbury Baptists."

the Constitution makes no reference to God at all. Yet the purpose of most of the founders in framing the Constitution was not to remove all references to God or the influence of Christianity from government. Sessions of Congress continued to be opened with prayer by Christian ministers, Christian military chaplains continued to be paid by the government, presidents continued to make proclamations setting aside national days of prayer and thanksgiving (except Jefferson), and several state legislatures continued to use tax revenue to support state churches (not mosques or synagogues). Not all the founders agreed with these practices, but the aim of the founders in crafting the First Amendment was to at least insure that the new federal government did not get in the business of running churches, and, as a result, use its power to exclude or persecute those whose religious ideas did not conform to state mandated religious standards. In Old England, that had proven to be detrimental for both church and state.

This is even more pertinent when we consider one of the main reasons the federal government was created in the first place. Of the six purposes of a federal government listed in the preamble of the Constitution, one is to "provide for the common defense." As we have seen, a leading proponent for the Constitution, John Jay, was a faithful follower of Jesus Christ and stalwart defender of Christian orthodoxy. As one of the three authors of the Federalist Papers, he consistently argued for a strong federal government. This government, of course, would be empowered to raise a military force that could defend the young nation. It seems clear then, that the founding patriots, whether orthodox Christians or unorthodox deists, reached a consensus that the federal government, with its authority to build a mighty military, would in no sense use the power of the sword to advance the Christian message or coerce anyone to submit to it. Breaking with the tragic history of Europe, the United States intended to separate the sword of the state from the mission of the church. That message was especially important to get across when crafting foreign policy dealing with Muslim nations like Tripoli who had a long history of attacking—and being attacked by—"Christian" nations.

This is a historic shift that needs to be emphasized. Orthodox Christians among the founders were forced to rethink their theology by the reality of forming a federal government out of a religiously diverse America. They were compelled to go back to the Bible, especially the teachings of Jesus, and consider the question of employing force—the sword of the state—to advance the spiritual objectives of the church Jesus founded. Gradually, some more reluctantly than others, they came to the conclusion that Jesus wanted them to do no such thing. Eventually, Edwards Patriots and their spiritual heirs would come to see that the apostles affirmed the sword of the state as God's ordained instrument to *protect* churches that proclaim the orthodox Jesus, but not to *promote* them. And, by application of the Golden Rule,[23] that protection should extend to all other religions, even Islam.

JEFFERSON'S QUR'AN

On January 4, 2007, Representative-elect Keith Ellison from Minnesota, the first Muslim elected to Congress, took his oath of office with his hand on the Qur'an. In response to the criticism he received for this astonishing break from tradition, Ellison pointed out the all-American roots of this particular copy of the Qur'an. It belonged to Thomas Jefferson. In using the Qur'an, said a spokesman, Keith Ellison "is paying respect not only to the Founding Fathers' belief in religious freedom, but the Constitution itself."[24] While many Americans have heard of Jefferson's Bible, few are aware of Jefferson's Qur'an.

Jefferson's Qur'an, now in the Library of Congress, is an English version translated by George Sale in 1734, published in London about 1764. What motivated Jefferson to purchase the Qur'an when he became president in 1800? Most likely, since he was going to war with Muslim people in a Muslim land, he wanted to know all he could about his opponent. Far from believing the Qur'an or seeking some spiritual solace, Jefferson's interest was political, military, and philosophical. That very practical American interest in the contents of the Qur'an would be resurrected two centuries later, on September 11, 2001.

ISLAM AS AN ATHEIST ARGUMENT

The world was forever changed that day. Before 9/11, I could drive up to the curb of my local airport, park my car, put a few coins in the meter, and leave it at that convenient location for hours. No more. Now security officers command me to keep moving and disallow unattended cars within two hundred feet of the building. That is one of a million things that were

---

23. Matthew 7:12.
24. Argetsinger and Roberts, "But It's Thomas Jefferson's Koran!" CO3.

altered after hijackers flew passenger planes into the Twin Towers of New York City.

Another thing that changed was the boldness of self-professed atheists. The events of that historic day in September instilled a new confidence in skeptics that promoting a belief in nothing is the most loving thing they can do for the human community. Religion is the problem. Religion kills. Religion must go. Let Christopher Hitchens, whose thesis is "religion poisons everything," tell you in his own words:

> The nineteen suicide murderers of New York and Washington and Pennsylvania were beyond any doubt the most sincere believers on those planes. Perhaps we can hear a little less about how "people of faith" possess moral advantages that others can only envy. And what is to be learned from the jubilation and ecstatic propaganda with which this great feat of fidelity has been greeted in the Islamic world? At the time, the United States had an attorney general named John Ashcroft, who had stated that America had "no king but Jesus" (a claim that was exactly two words too long).[25]

Hitchens is not alone. Sam Harris, whose ambitious mission is to "demolish the intellectual and moral pretensions of Christianity in its most committed forms,"[26] does not miss a chance to equate "the resurrection of Jesus" with "Muhammad's conversation with the archangel Gabriel"[27] in terms of historical reliability. For Harris, it is rather clear that faith, whether Christian or Muslim, "inspires violence."[28] In his appeal to Christians, he affirms that he and other atheists "stand beside you, dumbstruck by the Muslim hordes who chant death to whole nations of the living. But we stand dumbstruck by *you* as well."[29]

Richard Dawkins employs a similar strategy, opining that just as Muhammad founded Islam and then depended on military conquest to spread the faith, so Jesus founded Christianity and it was "spread by the sword."[30] Yet these contemporary critics of the orthodox Jesus are not original in their attempt to undermine Christianity by linking it to Islam. In fact, they are about three centuries late to the debate.

25. Hitchens, *God is Not Great,* 32.
26. Harris, *Letter,* ix.
27. Ibid., 67
28. Ibid., 80.
29. Ibid., 91. Italics are his.
30. Dawkins, *The God Delusion,* 37.

ISLAM AS A DEIST ARGUMENT

Long before Hitchens, Harris, or Dawkins made this argument, the deists were using Islam to discredit Christianity and the real Jesus. As I mentioned earlier, if Thomas Paine had a fan club, Christopher Hitchens would be the president. When he wrote *The Age of Reason* in 1794, Paine was quick to point out that he did not believe the creed professed by "the Turkish church, by the Protestant church, nor by any church I know of. My own mind is my church."[31] Paine, like most English-speakers in the eighteenth century, referred to Muslims as Turks because at the time Islam was inseparable from the Turkish Ottoman Empire, one of the purer blends of mosque and state the world has known. "All national institutions of churches," wrote Paine, "whether Jewish, Christian or Turkish, appear to me to be no other than human inventions set up to terrify and enslave mankind and monopolize power and profit."[32]

The Christians have their Jesus, "the Turks their Mahomet." The Christians say their "Word of God came by divine inspiration" while "the Turks say that their word of God (the Koran) was brought by an angel from heaven."[33] To Paine, the account of the virgin birth of Jesus was on par with the account of Muhammad's receiving the Qur'an from an angel, both of them "hearsay upon hearsay" and not worthy of belief. Then, dubiously linking Islam and Christianity as morally and theologically equivalent, Paine makes a calculated tactical move. He launches into his presentation of an alternative Jesus, according to the creed of his self-made church. This Jesus of the deists was a "virtuous and an amiable man" who preached a moral system that "has not been exceeded by any."[34] But Jesus was not God and the stories of his resurrection are "a wretched contrivance."[35] Just as we cannot trust the Qur'an, we cannot trust the Bible. Paine concludes that Adam, "if ever there was such a man, was created a Deist."[36]

Notice then that Hitchens, Harris, Dawkins, and the eighteenth century deists share a common debating strategy, sometimes called "guilt-by-association." The logic goes like this:

31. Paine, *Age of Reason*, 6.
32. Ibid.
33. Ibid., 7.
34. Ibid., 26.
35. Paine, *Age of Reason*.
36. Ibid., 84.

Premise 1: Christianity and Islam are basically the same.

Premise 2: Islam deceives and destroys people.

Therefore: Christianity deceives and destroys people.

While the logic may be valid, if one of the premises is false, then the conclusion is unwarranted, and the guilt-by-association argument becomes a fallacy. Jonathan Edwards made this observation two centuries before Christopher Hitchens's parents had children. The challenge for Edwards as well as contemporary defenders of the orthodox Jesus is to help the American public discern the blatant differences and subtle distinctions that decisively separate Christianity and Islam. If we can demonstrate that Premise 1 is false, then the argument falls apart. In the following pages, I will use the categories we have already examined (Gospels, God, Grave, and Grace) to compare Christianity with Islam. In the next chapter, I will add a fifth category, Growth, to compare the early expansion of each of these religions.

GOSPELS: DO THEY AGREE WITH THE QUR'AN?

Jonathan Edwards, I can safely say, never met a Muslim. While Edwards never traveled outside of America, the likelihood of Muslims traveling through Northampton, Massachusetts, in the first half of the 1700's is negligible. His best opportunity to encounter Muslims might have been his days in New York, where we know he had a Jewish neighbor.[37] There is a remote possibility that he could have met Turkish sailors at New York's harbor, but we simply have no record that he ever met a professing Muslim. Yet, Edwards had access to Sale's reliable English translation of the Qur'an. In the *Miscellanies*, Edwards transcribed many excerpts of the works of other authors who had studied Islam and the life of Muhammad. Was Edwards's understanding of Islam in the eighteenth century accurate?

One of the first similarities that Edwards would notice in his study is that Christians and Muslims are "people of the book." That is, their faiths are informed by what they believe to be the written revelation of God. But the differences between the two books are manifold. While the Bible has over forty authors who lived over a period of about fifteen hundred years, the Qur'an is a collection of revelations that Muhammad claims to

37. Edwards, *Works*, 2:165.

have received from God through the angel Gabriel over a period of about twenty-three years. He orally shared these revelations with his followers who transferred them orally until they were written down in Arabic a generation or so after Muhammad's death. Islam holds that only the Arabic original of the Qur'an is truly God's Word and translations are considered only interpretations. In contrast, Christianity endeavors to translate the Bible from the original languages of Hebrew, Aramaic, and Greek into every known language by scholars and linguistic experts, viewing each proper translation with equal authority. While the Bible has endured rigorous scholarly examination and textual criticism for over three hundred years, similar study of the Qur'an has only occurred recently.

The Qur'an and the Gospels of the New Testament agree on many points. For example, both teach there is one God, that Jesus was a real historical figure, born of the virgin Mary, and a miracle-working prophet who spoke for God. In fact, the Qur'an recognizes Jesus as the Messiah. But the Qur'an flatly contradicts the Gospels of the New Testament at crucial points. Therefore, anyone seeking to equate Christianity and Islam is obligated to subject the Qur'an to the same scholarly scrutiny that has been given the New Testament. Unfortunately, when such historical-critical analysis is applied to the Qur'an, scholars sometimes run the risk of a death sentence, or *fatwa*, from Muslim leaders.[38]

GOD: WHO IS MUHAMMAD'S JESUS?

Like deism, Islam presents an alternative Jesus. Islam holds Jesus in high regard as a great prophet, the predicted Messiah who will someday return to earth, though lower in authority to Muhammad. The Qur'an teaches that Jesus was born of a virgin, performed miracles, and spoke for God. But Muhammad's Jesus, like Jefferson's Jesus, is a different Jesus from the one presented by the apostles. Like "diamonds in a dunghill," Muhammad picked out features of Jesus that advanced the religion he was founding,

38. An example is Salman Rushdie who attempted to apply historical-critical analysis of the Qur'an in his novel, *Satanic Verses*. The so-called Satanic Verses refer to three verses in an early version of the Qur'an that allowed intercessory prayer to pagan idols. Muhammad later claimed to get new revelation that cancelled these verses and claimed Satan had tricked him earlier by placing the verses in the Qur'an without his knowledge. Iran's religious leader, Ayatolla Khomeini, issued a *fatwa* on February 14, 1989, calling for Muslims to assassinate Rushdie. Christopher Hitchens, a friend of Rushdie's, seems to find great motivation in this incident to write his book *God Is Not Great* (28–31).

while rejecting the rest. It is Muhammad's Jesus, not the orthodox Jesus, that is highly esteemed in the Muslim world.

Islam did not arise in a religious vacuum. Rather, Muhammad had been exposed to the Bible and influenced by a deviant form of Christianity. Consequently, many Christians will recognize much of the language and many of the characters in the Qur'an. Islam, with Judaism and Christianity, traces its roots back through Abraham, and much of the Qur'an reflects the influence of Old Testament Scripture. Unfortunately, the version of Christianity to which Muhammad was introduced presented a heretical understanding of the doctrine of the Trinity. Like Franklin who doubted and Jefferson who denied the deity of Christ, Muhammad has since persuaded millions to distrust the New Testament's full account of Jesus.

In about 610, when Muhammad claims to have experienced his first encounter with the angel Gabriel, an aberrant understanding of the Trinity was floating around the Arabian Peninsula. Instead of God being presented as one God in three persons, he was being presented as three gods. This "tritheism" affirmed the deity of Jesus at the expense of the unity of God. Muhammad, like Jews, orthodox Christians, and deists, was a strict monotheist, so it is understandable that the Qur'an contains several excoriating statements about what Muhammad understood to be Christianity. "Unbelievers," states the Qur'an, "are those who say: 'God is one of three.' There is but one God. If they do not desist from so saying, those of them that disbelieve shall be sternly punished."[39] And again, "So believe in God and his apostles and do not say 'Three.' Forbear and it shall be better for you. God forbid that he should have a son!"[40] Similarly, "God forbid that He himself should beget a son!"[41] And in another place, the preexistence and incarnation of Jesus are once again denied, since Jesus is "no more than an apostle."[42] Church historian Timothy George says, "Christians believe just as strongly as Muslims in the oneness of God. We can only agree with the Qur'an in its rejection of a concocted tritheism."[43] Sadly, there is no evidence that Muhammad was ever presented with the

---

39. Qur'an 5:73.
40. Ibid., 4:171.
41. Ibid., 19:35.
42. Qur'an 5:75.
43. George, *Father of Jesus*, 59.

orthodox doctrine of the Trinity and his rejection of the deity of Christ is his response to a heresy that advocates belief in three gods.

GRAVE: WAS JESUS RAISED FROM THE DEAD?

The heart of the gospel is that Jesus died on the cross in the place of sinners, was buried, and raised on the third day to reconcile man to God. The Qur'an presents a revised Jesus. First, it denies outright that Jesus died on the cross. While Muslims agree that Jesus was sentenced to death by crucifixion, at just the last minute, he was replaced with another convicted criminal who looked like him. Jesus escaped not only an excruciating death, but death altogether. Here is how the Qur'an describes what happened:

> And for their saying, "verily we have slain the Messiah, Jesus the son of Mary, an Apostle of God." Yet they slew him not and they crucified him not, but they had only his likeness. And they who differed about him were in doubt concerning him: No sure knowledge had they about him, but followed only an opinion, and they did not really slay him, but God took him up to Himself.[44]

In bypassing a death for Jesus, the Qur'an rules out his resurrection. Like Jefferson and Paine, Muhammad denies the central historical event in human history and presents an alternative Jesus.

GRACE: ARE WE SAVED BY GRACE ALONE?

If we are not saved by believing in Jesus, God in the flesh, who died on the cross for sinners and was raised from the dead, how shall we be saved? The gospel according to Muhammad is a combination of obedience to the teachings of the Qur'an and the mercy of God. If Muslims try their best to follow the Qur'an, God does the rest. Most assuredly, writes Timothy George, "salvation in Islam is not 'by faith alone.'"[45] Far from being unconditional, God reserves his love only for those who perform proficiently. God loves those who "deal justly"[46] with others, and "keep themselves aloof from women during their menstrual period."[47] Again, "As for those who have faith and do good works, We shall not deny them their reward."[48]

44. Qur'an 4:157–58.
45. George, *Father of Jesus*, 110.
46. Qur'an, 5:42.
47. Ibid., 2:222.
48. Ibid., 18:30.

Like orthodox Christians, Muslims believe that a "day of reckoning for mankind is drawing near."[49] While Christians can face that day with calm assurance and "approach the throne of grace with confidence,"[50] Muslims live with no such assurance because the outcome of that day is not settled. While Christians can humbly rest in the familiar words of Jesus from the cross, "It is finished," Muslims, relying on their own works, must strive until the end to earn a place in paradise. When the moment of judgment comes, Muslims understand that day as a weighing of their good works: "We shall set up just scales on the Day of Resurrection, so that no man shall in the least be wronged. Actions as small as a grain of mustard seed shall be weighed out."[51]

Good works for Muslims include the "five pillars of faith": belief, prayer, fasting, giving money to the poor, and at least one pilgrimage to a Muslim holy site. Unbelievers, those who reject Muhammad's teaching will "strive in vain to shield their faces and their backs from the fires of Hell."[52] Whereas biblical Christianity teaches that our only hope of eternal salvation is to trust in the good works of Jesus, Islam teaches that we are saved by trusting in our own good works as defined by the Qur'an. Like deists Benjamin Franklin and Thomas Jefferson, Muslims expect a final judgment when their good deeds are weighed to determine their destiny. God forgives, or not, based on the outcome of that weigh-in. Ironically, when it comes to the doctrine of salvation, Islam shares more similarities with deism than it does with biblical Christianity.

NOT BASICALLY THE SAME

Christianity and Islam do share some common ground. Both have a global vision, desiring the whole world to hear and heed their respective messages. Both are monotheistic (belief in one God) and both believe in moral absolutes, the proposition that God has given us universal laws that are standards by which we determine right and wrong. There is some overlap in the ethics of each of these religions, though compared to the New Testament, the Qur'an speaks little of love. And when it comes to the basics, these two religions are not "basically the same." Islam explic-

49. Ibid., 21:1.
50. Hebrews 4:16.
51. Qur'an 21:47.
52. Ibid., 21:39.

itly denies at least four of the core beliefs of Christianity. It is not fair, either to Muslims or Christians, to conclude that these two religions, the two largest religions in the world, are basically the same. To equate them misrepresents both Islam and Christianity. When it comes to Jesus, either Islam is right or Christianity is wrong; or Christianity is right and Islam is wrong; or they are both wrong. But they cannot both be right.

Thanks to the wisdom, compromise, and common sense of our founders, there is plenty of room in the United States for different religious ideas. Thanks in large part to thousands of men like Lieutenant Pressley O'Bannon and their "fight for right and freedom," America remains one of the safest places on the planet to practice any religion you choose. In the marketplace of religion, these ideas should be exchanged freely, and each allowed to compete according to some fundamental rules of civility.[53] Christians have no need to fear the truth, and in the diverse religious environment that is now America, we have an extraordinary opportunity to practice genuine Christian tolerance, that is, "to put up with error." Properly understood, tolerance has never meant that we should believe that everyone is right, even if they hold contradictory opinions. Biblical tolerance leads us to love people we do not agree with, while love for people leads us to enter into a gentle dialogue with them. It is our love for Jesus that compels us to engage in dialogue with a view to persuading people to agree with us. That kind of freedom is what the Bill of Rights is all about, and there is no place on earth where the dialogue between Christians and Muslims is freer than in the United States. But there remains at least one more important difference between the two religions, which is perhaps the most controversial of all.

53. As with all analogies, this one can be pressed too far. For example, churches committed to Jesus are not in competition with one another, trying to "steal each other's sheep." Also, businesses in the marketplace only survive if they change and revise their product to meet market demands. In making the customer sovereign (to get his or her money) they are willing to abandon their original mission and offer a new and improved product. The church, however, has a timeless mission and an eternal message that is not for sale. Neither the gospel nor Jesus should be revised in order to accommodate the changing tastes and latest trends of America's spiritual consumers. Some church growth advocates who might consider themselves conservative and orthodox may not realize how perilously close they come to the deist error of revising Jesus in their ambition to capture market share.

9

Growth: "By Such Weapons as These"

*Put your sword back in its place . . . for all who draw the sword
will die by the sword.*[1]

—Jesus

When you meet the unbelievers in the battlefield, strike off their heads.

—Qur'an 47:4

*If you are a Christian, you do not have to believe that all the other reli-
gions are simply wrong all through. . . . But, of course, being a Christian
does mean thinking that where Christianity differs from other religions,
Christianity is right and they are wrong."*

—C. S. Lewis[2]

To this day, United States Marines are told the story of Lieutenant
Pressley O'Bannon. Every time they hear the Marine Corps Hymn,
they are reminded how he fought his country's battle on "the shores of
Tripoli." That military intervention by the United States attempted a regime
change that would replace a Muslim leader in Tripoli (Yusef Karamanli)
who had declared war on the United States, with another Muslim leader
who would have maintained a more friendly policy (Hamet Karamanli,
Yusef's brother). After the Battle of Derne, Hamet presented O'Bannon
with his personal jeweled sword, the type used by his Muslim tribesman.

---

1. Matthew 26:52.
2. Lewis, *Mere Christianity*, 43.

To this day, Marine Corps officers carry the "Mameluke" sword, a representation of a Muslim leader's gift of gratitude to a United States Marine. When O'Bannon returned to the United States, he moved to Kentucky and like so many war heroes in American history, ran for office, and served in the state legislature from 1812 to 1820. Politics, religion, and war. All three have been messily intertwined from our founding.

"THE PROPAGATION OF MAHOMETANISM"

The deist use of Islam as a weapon to attack the orthodox Jesus did not go unnoticed by Jonathan Edwards. Sometime after 1747, he took up his pen and outlined a defense he probably intended to develop in greater detail in a season of life that never came. In recording his thoughts on Islam (unpublished until the nineteenth century), Edwards focuses on drawing the distinctions between Christianity and Islam. Along with the four crucial differences we have already examined (Gospels, God, Grave, and Grace), another feature that sets Christianity apart from Islam is the way the founder of each religion intended for the movement to grow. Edwards's seminal thoughts form a useful apologetic that I have gathered under six principles.

In the following pages, I realize I offer a view of Islam that is not politically correct. But it is not fair, either to Muslims or Christians, to swallow the uncritical assessment that these two religions are "basically the same." I do not intend to create more heat than light for the ongoing and necessary dialogue between Christians and Muslims, but it seems to me that one of the first steps in the dialogue is for Christians and Muslims to be honest about the past. My aim here is to gain more understanding as to why Edwards, in the eighteenth century, believed what he did about Islam and the deist attempts to use the Qur'an to dethrone Jesus.[3]

In essence, deists claimed that the only reason Christianity grew so expansively is not because the Bible was a revelation from God, or because Jesus performed authenticating miracles, or because credible eyewitnesses to his resurrection were willing to die for their testimony. Rather, Christianity grew because early Christians used violence to coerce conversions. In this way, said the deists, Christianity is just like Islam. At the outset, Edwards is clear that his objective is to show "in what re-

---

3. Gerald McDermott notes that in Edwards's day, deists were using Islam "as a weapon against Christian orthodoxy." McDermott, *Jonathan Edwards Confronts the Gods*, 9.

spect the propagation of Mahometanism is far from being worthy to be looked upon as parallel with the propagation of Christianity."[4] Inspired by Edwards, I'll try to summarize some of the principles that should guide any analysis regarding how these two religions were intended by their respective founders to grow.

1. *In the first century, the New Testament nullified the Old Testament sanctions of holy war, while in the seventh century, the Qur'an revived the Old Testament sanctions of holy war.* Skeptics often charge Christians with having no moral authority to condemn Islamic terrorism because the Bible is just as full of holy war as the Qur'an. At this point, they trot out Old Testament verses from the book of Joshua sanctioning holy war and ethnic cleansing. But here we may remind them that Christians re-fer to the Old Testament as "Old" for a reason. With the coming of the Messiah, predicted by Old Testament prophets, the old covenant has been superseded by a new and superior covenant. What were foreshadows in the Old Testament have become reality in the New Testament. While in the Old Testament, God worked mainly through a theocratic nation with defined borders, an equipped army, and vicious enemies on every side, Jesus declared that his coming marked the beginning of a new way.

"My kingdom is not of this world," Jesus told Pilate, "If it were, my servants would fight to prevent my arrest by the Jews. But now my king-dom is from another place."[5] As king of kings, Jesus would reign in the hearts of billions. "In your hearts," wrote Peter, "set apart Christ as Lord." This spiritual kingdom was not to be advanced or defended with political or military might. Rather, loyal subjects of King Jesus must "always be prepared to give an answer to everyone who asks you to give the reason for the hope that you have. But do this with gentleness and respect."[6] By the Spirit-empowered preaching of the gospel and credible testimony of genuine Christians, God intends to capture territory for his glory.

Yet the deists could not see their own inconsistencies. They conceded that the moral system taught by Jesus was superior to all others. Since Muhammad arrived on the scene six centuries after Jesus, his movement must necessarily represent a step backwards, toward the Old Testament and its use of holy war to advance a theocracy. How, then, can deists

4. Edwards, *Works*, 23:325.

5. John 18:36.

6. 1 Peter 3:15.

claim that Islam and Christianity are basically the same when, as Edwards notes, "the new Mahometan religion, only tended exceedingly to debase, debauch, and corrupt the minds of such as received it"?[7] In other words, Edwards might say, if you want to compare Islam to Judaism, then compare the Qur'an to the Old Testament. But if you want to compare Islam to Christianity, then compare the Qur'an to the New Testament.

2. *Muhammad taught his followers to kill for their faith while Jesus taught his followers to die for their faith.* Jesus prepared his disciples for difficult days ahead. "If anyone would come after me," he told them, "he must deny himself and take up his cross daily and follow me."[8] The cross was an instrument of death, and though most Christians would not die for bearing witness to the faith, many would, and all must be willing.

We have already seen the clear sanctions in the Qur'an for the use of violence in the spread of Islam. The history of Islam is replete with obedience to the command to slay unbelievers. Upon Muhammad's death, his first successor (caliph), Abu Bakr recruited Arabs to fight in the Islamic conquest by promising them the wealth of those they intended to conquer. The spoils of war would make Muhammad's successors and closest friends wealthy men.[9]

Abu Bakr was succeeded by Umar ibn al-Khattab who led Muslim armies to capture Syria, Damascus, and Jerusalem where he built a small mosque on Mt. Moriah. But from the earliest days of Islam, the neighbors of Muslim tribes were not the only ones who feared Qur'an-inspired aggression. Muslims had good reason to fear one another in this culture of violence. Choosing to live by the sword, Muslim leaders also died by the sword. Umar was murdered by a slave in 634, while the third and fourth caliphs were killed by political opponents competing to rule the Muslim world.

A mere century after Muhammad's death, Muslim armies had conquered Egypt, North Africa, and southern Spain, continually expanding until Charles Martel defeated them at the Battle of Tours in 732. In 1451, the Ottoman Turks made another run at Europe, capturing Constantinople in 1453 and then the Balkan Peninsula (Serbia in 1459; Bosnia in 1463; Herzegovina in 1483). They were finally checked at Vienna in 1683, the

7. Edwards, *Works,* 23:329.

8. Luke 9:23.

9. Karsh, *Islamic Imperialism,* 25.

high-water mark of the Turkish Ottoman Empire. By Jonathan Edwards's day, Islam could claim a broad territory from India to North Africa. While the rapid growth and expansion of Islam is indeed a remarkable human accomplishment, it was not accomplished merely through friendly persuasion and force of argument, but also through violence and war. Consequently, Edwards was of the opinion that Islam "was propagated by the power of the sword, by potent sultans, absolute tyrants, and mighty armies."[10]

On the other hand, in Edwards's view, Christianity conquered the Roman Empire through non-violent means. The gospel was spread, he wrote, "by the weakest of men, unarmed with anything but meekness, humility, love, miracles, clear evidence, a most virtuous, holy and amiable example, and the power and fervor of eminent virtue joined with assured belief of the truth, with self-denial and suffering for truth and holiness. And by such weapons as these," concludes Edwards, "it was propagated against the power, authority, wealth, and armor of the world."[11] The violence option was certainly available to the earliest Christians in the first century, as the armed defiance of Jewish zealots against Roman rulers demonstrates. But the early Christians, following the example of Jesus, did not take up the sword in the cause of the gospel.

In fact, the early Christians did not take up the sword in any cause. There is no evidence of Christians serving in the military prior to AD 170. Taking Jesus's commands seriously, they were pacifists who refused military service. After 170, some Christians began serving in the Roman military, realizing that they were enjoying the benefits of Roman peace without bearing the burden of defending Roman borders. Even then, when church was clearly separate from state, the church did not employ violence in these early centuries as a means of propagating the gospel.[12]

Did early Muslims respond peacefully to violent opposition as the early Christians had done? Islam faced initial resistance from the residents of Mecca when Muhammad first claimed to receive revelations from Allah, and this opposition might be characterized as persecution. But within ten years, as soon as he consolidated several tribes and attracted enough followers, Muhammad established the use of violent force as an inseparable feature of Islam. In the early years following Muhammad's death,

---

10. Edwards, *Works*, 23:331.

11. Ibid.

12. Swartley, "War," 1172–73.

Islam faced no organized persecution to speak of, while after the death of Jesus, Christianity faced the state-sanctioned persecution of mighty Rome. The claims of Islam were not tested in the crucible of persecution as the claims of Christianity had been. While Jesus and the eyewitnesses to his resurrection had no apparent motive to lie about what they had seen, Muhammad and his inner circle would have had numerous motives, including the accumulation of enormous political power and material wealth. While Christianity was "propagated against all the strength of the strongest empire that ever was in the world,"[13] wrote Edwards, Islam "endured no persecutions and hardships of various kinds; but wherever their weapons go, that religion follows."[14]

3. *The earliest generations after the founder's death are better reflections of the founder's teachings.* Edwards makes another distinction between Christianity and Islam. The earliest followers of Jesus spread a message that was built "on certain, great, and wonderful visible facts; such as Christ's resurrection from the dead." Because these facts were "extensively propagated in and near the places and time when the facts" occurred, anyone could have confirmed them. This is "everlasting evidence of the truth of the facts." Yet the witnesses bore a non-violent testimony to these facts at all times. Islam has no such extraordinary and distinguishing public facts as a foundation, only Muhammad's claim of private contact with heaven and his success in "murder and violence."[15]

Edwards's words may seem harsh and over-generalizing to us today. After all, Christians cannot deny there is "murder and violence" in our own past. After the Roman Emperor Constantine gave official protection to the Christian church early in the fourth century, the church began to change. The authenticity of Constantine's conversion experience in AD 312 remains a debated subject, but there is no question that he found Christianity to be a useful political tool in uniting the empire, even issuing edicts to his soldiers to worship the Christian God on the first day of the week. By 439, in a stunning reversal, *only* Christians were permitted to serve in the military. Yet even then, Christians tried to apply the teachings of Jesus to the practice of warfare. The best-known effort is Augustine's theory of just war developed in the fifth century. War happens. It is always

13. Edwards, *Works*, 23:331.

14. Ibid., n 9.

15. Edwards, *Works*, 23:332.

awful, but no culture has been able to escape it. It should be avoided as long as possible, used as a last resort to restrain evil, and even when it happens, Jesus's commandments to love God and neighbor must be rigorously and wisely applied at all times. However, Augustine's theory did not allow the advance of the gospel message as a just cause for war and it never advocated force to coerce professed conversions.[16]

With the removal of systematic persecution, the purity of the church began to diminish. In general terms, before Constantine, the church influenced the culture; after Constantine, the culture influenced the church. The subsequent corrupting alliance between the church and state bred an aberrant form of Christianity that the original disciples would not have recognized. For reasons too complicated to discuss in this small space, the church reverted to an Old Testament theocratic mindset that employed the use of force—the power of the sword—in the spread of the gospel. And somewhere along the way, even the gospel was eclipsed. This is the unholy alliance that deists like Paine and Jefferson came to abhor.

In 1099, Christian armies defeated Muslim armies in Jerusalem and held the Holy City long enough to convert the mosque (by then, the Dome of the Rock) into a church. The army had been raised and sent after Alexius Comnenus, the Byzantine Emperor, asked Pope Urban II for help in fighting the invading Turks. This belated response to the earlier Muslim invasions was the first of at least eight Crusades in which Christianized Europe sent armies to liberate the holy lands previously conquered by Muslims. Regrettably, the atrocities committed by both sides continue to adversely influence Muslim-Christian relations.

Yet as wrong and sinful as these "Christian" armies may have been, a solid historical fact remains: In the first three hundred years after the death of Jesus, his followers consistently refused violence as a means to spread their message, while in the first three hundred years after the death of Muhammad, his followers consistently used violence as a means of propagating the new religion.[17]

16. Swartly, "War," 1173.

17. While Augustine may have built on the idea of a just war from Cicero, he sharpened and expanded the concept for Christ-followers. Augustine's Just War Theory is a considered attempt to reconcile the tension of living in two worlds, the City of God and the City of Man. In this dual citizenship, Christians might engage in war as a last resort, in self-defense, and defense of their country, fighting alongside unbelievers against a common aggressor. I recognize that after Constantine, other Christians argued the notion of a holy war, a kind of Christian *jihad*, to advance Christianity and gain converts (i.e., the Crusades)

Sadly, skeptics in Edwards's day and ours point to the Crusades to discredit the message of Jesus by equating Muslim violence with the violence perpetrated in the Crusades. True, we must acknowledge and condemn sins committed by the church a thousand years ago. But it is crucial in this ongoing discussion to distinguish not so much what the followers of Jesus and Muhammad throughout history have done, but what their respective religions say they *should* have done. What did Jesus and Muhammad actually teach? And would it not give us a better idea of their actual teaching if we look at what happened to their movements in the first three centuries after their deaths?

4. *Obedient Muslims are like disobedient Christians.* It is common to hear something like this from the opponents of the orthodox Jesus who want to equate Islam and Christianity: "What's the difference between Timothy McVeigh, a professing Christian, and the Muslims who slammed jets into the Twin Towers?" The difference is actually quite clear. Timothy McVeigh, who killed hundreds of Americans in the Oklahoma City bombing, was categorically disobedient to the commands of the New Testament while the terrorists of 9/11 who killed thousands of Americans in New York were arguably obedient to the commands of the Qur'an by attacking the economy and taking the lives of unbelievers in a holy war.

When Christians take the Bible seriously, interpreting the text with a view to the original intent of the author and following the example of Jesus, good things happen. They will love their neighbors, and even their enemies. They will speak the truth, honor their parents, be faithful to their spouses, conduct business with honesty, and respect the private property of others. They will honor the sanctity of human life, from the youngest to the oldest. They will care for the sick, feed the poor, respect authority, cultivate a strong work ethic to avoid becoming an economic burden on others and share with those who cannot work. They will aspire to be peacemakers, working for justice and reconciliation. They will speak of their faith, seeking to persuade others, in gentle, respectful, and winsome ways. They will show a courteous tolerance for those who disagree with them, seeking to be servants rather than controlling tyrants. Tragically, these kinds of things do not happen nearly enough among professing Christians. When they don't, it is because Christians are disobeying Jesus.

---

in which Christians fought alongside only Christians against unbelievers. However, in so doing, these professing followers of Jesus were explicitly disobeying Jesus.

When Muslims take the Qur'an seriously, seeking to apply the verses as they were intended in the seventh century, following the example of Muhammad, tragic things happen. Four years before the attacks in New York and Washington, Harvard professor Samuel Huntington famously warned of "Islam's bloody borders." Huntington observed that "Wherever one looks along the perimeter of Islam, Muslims have problems living peaceably with their neighbors."[18]

Islam has a universal vision which seeks a global submission to Allah and his will revealed in the Qur'an. Faithful, orthodox Muslims see the world as two houses, or domains: the House of Islam (peace) and the House of War. Where people have come under the rule of Islam, living by the Qur'an, there is peace. Where they have not, there is war. For all male, adult Muslims, participation in *jihad* is a duty until everyone in the world has either converted to Islam or lives as tribute-paying subjects to Muslim rulers.[19]

What about the objection that Muslim aggression is merely an on-going and understandable response to the Crusades and later European colonial imperialism? Here it is helpful to examine Islamic teaching about war before Christian armies invaded lands previously conquered by Muslims. *Jihad*, the struggle of holy war, is not an event in Islam, but an institution. Islamic theologian and jurist, Al-Mawardi, who died in 1058, forty years *before* the first crusade, was a recognized expert on Islamic law from Baghdad. Al-Mawardi reminded his fellow Muslims to invite non-Muslims to submit to Allah and convert to Islam, the Muslim version of evangelism. The initial invitation should be non-violent, and Muslims were forbidden to attack non-Muslims before the invitation is explained to them. Non-Muslims had three options at this point. First, they could surrender and convert, renouncing their religion, but keeping their lives and their property. Second, they could submit to Islamic law (*sharia*) and not convert, living under Muslim rule as second-class citizens who paid an annual poll tax levied on unbelievers (infidels). Third, they could resist by neither converting nor agreeing to pay the tax.

If they chose the third option and resisted, Muslims were obligated to fight the non-Muslims in a holy war or *jihad*. Muslims had two options in prosecuting the *jihad*. First, they could harass and terrorize unbeliev-

18. Huntington, *Clash of Civilizations*, 256.
19. Karsh, *Islamic Imperialism*, 66.

ers by burning their houses, making night raids, cutting down their date palms and trees, ruining their crops, cutting off their water supply, and otherwise sabotaging their economy and threatening their lives. Second, if Muslims believed they had a superior force, they could declare war and fight non-Muslims in military ranks by conventional means. In the course of battle, any non-Muslim man who was captured may be put to death, even if he were a non-combatant. Women and children should not be killed, unless they had become combatants. If women and children were used as shields by non-Muslims, Muslims were to be careful to avoid killing them and only kill non-Muslim men, unless they judged it impossible to kill the men without killing the women or children.

The *jihad* was pursued until one of four things occurred. First, the non-Muslims converted to Islam. Second, all non-Muslims were killed, captured, or enslaved, and their wealth seized. Third, the non-Muslims agreed to stop fighting and pay the tribute poll tax for the rest of their unbelieving lives. Or fourth, if the non-Muslim resistance was strong enough, and the Muslim force believed it could not win, Muslims armies were allowed by the Qur'an to agree to a truce, ceasing the *jihad* until they gathered more strength. Each step outlined in Al-Mawardi's work is replete with references to the Qur'an, which was delivered to the world by Muhammad four hundred years of bloodshed earlier.[20]

Bat Ye'or points out that *jihad* could be waged by military means such as burning villages, taking hostages, pillage, massacre, and anything else to destabilize the political structure and economy of non-Muslim cultures. Or *jihad* could be waged by peaceful means such as proselytism, propaganda, or bribes. But the strategic objective of the *jihad* is always the same: "to subjugate the peoples of the world to the law of Allah, decreed by his prophet Muhammad."[21]

In making the point that Jesus and Muhammad taught two divergent means for the growth of their movements, I have been careful to avoid citing evangelical Christians, who can be inclined to misrepresent and oversimplify the diverse and complicated belief system that is Islam. For that reason, my sources have been either Muslim or otherwise non-evangelical authorities in this field. Another example is Anthony Pagden, distinguished professor of political science and history at the University of California. In

20. Al-Mawardi, "The Laws of Islamic Governance," 190–95.

21. Bat Ye'or, *Decline of Eastern Christianity Under Islam*, 40.

his writings, he has not always had kind things to say about Christianity, and he is certainly not viewed as a champion of Christian orthodoxy. In fact, he would align himself with Dawkins, Harris, and Hitchens in believing that "the myths perpetrated by all monotheistic religions—all religions indeed—have caused more lasting harm to the human race than any other single set of beliefs."[22]

Still, even Pagden has to admit that the early Christian church was the victim of state-sponsored persecution, and that "despite persecution" the church kept adding converts in those first three hundred years. "Why is still something of a mystery," he writes. "As a religion of an empire, Christianity, with its insistence on turning the other cheek, on renunciation and forgiveness, on the final triumph of the weak and the poor over the powerful and the successful, would not have seemed to have had very much going for it."[23] Pagden sees "one major distinction between Christianity and Islam" in that from the beginning the church "could claim no social or political authority as such"[24] and Jesus "had explicitly recognized a distinction between Church and state."[25]

On the other hand, states Pagden, in Islam, "there can be no separation between religion and politics."[26] Muhammad's life set the example: if you offer the message of the Qur'an to an infidel and he "does not forsake his idols, he must be compelled by force."[27] For this, and other reasons, "the overwhelming majority of jurists have, therefore, interpreted *jihad* as a military obligation."[28] Professor Anthony Pagden might be surprised to find himself in agreement with an eighteenth century Puritan pastor from Massachusetts.

Thankfully, the majority of Muslims today are friendly, hospitable, peace-loving people who do not interpret or conform to the Qur'an as closely as Muhammad might have hoped. This has been my personal experience with Muslim people. Like many Christians, many Muslims are nominal in their faith, Muslim in name, but not fully committed to the

22. Pagden, *Worlds at War*, xix.
23. Ibid., 130, 131.
24. Ibid., 165.
25. Ibid., 167.
26. Ibid., 165.
27. Ibid., 171.
28. Ibid., 172.

cause. Others, more devout, choose to "spiritualize" the text, and see the references to war as metaphorical. Islam means "peace," many of them tell us, "submission" to the will of Allah. It is an inner peace that comes after a spiritual *jihad*, a spiritual struggle, in which one finally bends to the will of God. It has nothing to do with taking up arms to physically force others to bend to that will.

This revised version of Islam is something we can all live with, I suppose, but it would have been difficult to find it in Edwards's day while the Barbary states extorted tribute money from the nations of the world in exchange for not attacking their ships and stealing their stuff. Over two hundred years later, it is the dangerous, but not tiny, minority of Muslims seeking to emulate Muhammad that raises the most concern.

5. *A founder's actions are the best interpreters of the founder's words.* I would like to say that there is nothing in the New Testament that could even possibly be construed to mean that Jesus implored his followers to use violence to establish and expand his kingdom. I cannot say that. There is one troublesome verse in Matthew 10:34: "Do not suppose that I have come to bring peace to the earth. I did not come to bring peace, but a sword." Ripped from its context, someone might argue that this sounds an awful lot like Muhammad.

There are only two ways to take this statement: literally or figuratively. If literally, Jesus is telling his disciples to arm themselves and start severing heads until people believe in him. If figuratively, Jesus is telling his disciples that if they follow him, they can expect conflict (a metaphorical understanding of "sword"), even with family and friends. As a sword divides an arm from the body, following Christ may result in the Christian being severed, ostracized, from family, friends, and community. How do we decide what Jesus means?

First, we look at the context. He is sending out his twelve disciples to preach the message that the kingdom of heaven is near. As they preach this kingdom, and Jesus as king, they can expect to be mistreated, arrested, and hated by those who reject Jesus, including their own family members. They will be tempted to disown Jesus, but he commands them not to fear "those who kill the body but cannot kill the soul."[29] Though he prepares them to die for their faith, he never prepares them to kill for it. Never.

---

29. Matthew 10:1–33.

While the context supports a figurative understanding of the sword, what does the example of Jesus tell us? At no time did Jesus use violence in the expansion of his kingdom. On those occasions where there was an opportunity to use violence against his enemies, he clearly refrained and instructed his disciples to do likewise. So the example of Jesus himself also argues for a figurative understanding of sword in Matthew.

In contrast, Muhammad's advocacy for the use of force in the spread of Islam is virtually uncontested. Even Muslims agree that he was a religious prophet *and* a military leader, attacking towns and caravans of non-Muslims, often enslaving those he did not kill, and taking their possessions. After one such attack, the decisive Battle of Badr, Muhammad conveniently received a revelation explaining how the spoils of war are to be divided. One fifth of the spoils seized by Muslim soldiers "belong to God, the Apostle, the Apostle's kinfolk, the orphans, the destitute, and the traveler in need."[30] The Apostle in Muhammad's day was Muhammad.

Gerald McDermott laments that Jonathan Edwards failed to see that "Islam deserved appreciation as a living faith." He detects in Edwards's analysis an unreasonable "hostility toward Islam," a "visceral hostility," that Edwards's critique of Islam is "snarled," and that Edwards "slavishly followed his sources."[31] Of course, sources on Islam in colonial America were limited, and perhaps some personal contact and dialogue with Muslim people might have softened some of the rhetoric. Edwards's tone also might be explained in that he is not addressing Muslims in his writing, but deists who are using Islam to discredit Christianity. Furthermore, as we mentioned earlier, his private notes in the *Miscellanies* were not intended for publication and he would have made the pre-publication adjustments that all authors make when they consider their target audience, if he had lived long enough. But considering the way Islam demoted Jesus to a position lower than a Warrior Prophet who made a living by killing people and seizing their property in God's name, I'm finding it easier to forgive Jonathan Edwards for his eagerness in differentiating Christianity from Islam.

6. *Christians and Muslims can celebrate the common ground between them as the starting point for dialogue.* The reality that there are fundamental and irreconcilable differences between Christianity and Islam should

---

30. Qur'an, 8:41.

31. McDermott, *Jonathan Edwards Confronts the Gods*, 166–67, 174.

not eclipse the crucial points of agreement. Edwards points out that the Qur'an "owns Jesus to be a great prophet, the messenger of God."[32] Not only that, it does not escape Edwards's notice that the Qur'an agrees that Jesus worked miracles, raised the dead, was born of the virgin Mary, was without sin, was the Messiah predicted by the Old Testament prophets, and ascended into heaven. As C. S. Lewis said, "If you are a Christian, you do not have to believe that all the other religions are simply wrong all through."[33] Those words are wise counsel. But Lewis went on to write "But, of course, being a Christian does mean thinking that where Christianity differs from other religions, Christianity is right and they are wrong."[34] We might add that where Islam differs with Christianity, Muslims believe Islam is right and Christianity is wrong. That should not surprise Christians, or keep them from respectful and meaningful conversations with Muslims. While Edwards had no opportunities for personal evangelism among Muslim people, everything we know about Edwards tells us that if he had, he would have loved Muslim people deeply, having great concern for their souls, as he did for the Indians at Stockbridge, and no doubt would have used the common ground between Christianity and Islam as a starting point to share with them the majesty of Jesus.

THE BEAUTY OF COMPETITION

If you interpret my words so far as nostalgic longing for the good old days of Christian dominance of our state and federal governments, you would be wrong. I am not arguing for public prayer in public schools in Jesus's name. In that case, I am less worried about the schools than I am about Jesus's name. I am not petitioning for the Ten Commandments to be displayed in courtrooms. Nor am I arguing for a return to Edwards's New England where Quakers, Baptists, and Roman Catholics were treated unjustly and marginalized. The Puritan experiment in establishing a "city set on a hill," envisioned as an Old Testament kind of theocracy governed by ministers and magistrates, failed because it was not mandated by Jesus. Edwards lived in a day when many in New England were coming to see such a theocracy as not only unworkable, but unhealthy for the preaching

---

32. Edwards, *Works*, 23:333.
33. Lewis, *Mere Christianity*, 43.
34. Ibid.

of the gospel. Had Edwards lived longer, we might have the benefit of his thoughts on the subject.

Many Edwards Patriots—orthodox Christians among the Founding Fathers—eventually saw the wisdom of a separation of powers at every level. Informed by a biblically pessimistic view of human nature, they understood no one could be trusted with much power, and that included the ministers and magistrates. Lord Acton had famously said that "Power tends to corrupt and absolute power corrupts absolutely." Jonathan Edwards might have said, "We are already corrupt and absolute power only provides the occasion for that corruption to be displayed in more catastrophic ways."

If the message of Christianity is true, it does not need extraordinary aid from the state in order to prosper. If God is for us, who can be against us? God owns every government in the world and the role of every government is to restrain evil. Government officials "do not bear the sword for nothing."[35] That means that the church should be protected by the state, given freedom to bear witness to the remarkable life of Jesus with a view to non-coercively persuading others to follow him. And that protection should also be extended to the mosque and synagogue and temple and atheists who write bestsellers. Frankly, if my Muslim friends ever try to persuade me to become a Muslim, I will consider it a sign of their concern for me. There are few places on the planet where so many religions can so peaceably co-exist, and religious freedom in America has not seemed to hinder the vitality of the church. Competition in the religious marketplace, as in the economic arena, has contributed to its vibrancy. And since Christianity got its start in a culture marked by religious pluralism, we have much encouraging precedent.

As it turns out, those nations where the dominant religion is Christianity have proven to be among the most receptive to the kind of religious freedom envisioned by our founders. That is due, in large part, to the discovery and re-discovery of the words of Jesus that distinguish two kingdoms and forbid his followers to use the power of the sword to advance his cause. It is after all, a rather practical application of Jesus's well-known rule: "do to others what you would have them do to you."[36] In the twentieth century, the atheistic presuppositions of communism pre-

---

35. Romans 13:4.
36. Matthew 7:12.

sented the greatest global obstacle to religious freedom. But in the early years of the twenty-first century, the most daunting threat to religious freedom appears to be a militant form of Islam.

Whatever else we might say about the subject, those nations where Islam is the dominant religion have proven to be the least receptive to religious freedom and the free exchange of religious ideas. The government of Saudi Arabia currently pours millions of dollars into the construction of mosques and Muslim schools in the United States[37] while Christians in Saudi Arabia who attempt to persuade Muslims to become Christians not only break the law, but can face the death penalty. There are not many "Ben Franklins" in that Islamic nation calling in print for the construction of a meeting hall in Mecca where Christian missionaries are free to preach Jesus and seek converts. If one were to arise, he probably would not live as long as Franklin did. Perhaps that is because the words of Muhammad on this topic are so dissimilar to the words of Jesus.

"THE EXACTION OF TRIBUTE"

Lieutenant Pressley O'Bannon returned to a country that did not fully appreciate his efforts. His tombstone in a Frankfort, Kentucky, cemetery errs in listing his rank and simply reads: "As Captain of United States Marines, he was the First to Plant the American Flag on Foreign Soil."[38] He would not be the last. The United States would eventually become the mightiest military superpower in the history of the world. The combined brilliance and character of both Edwards Patriots and Franklin Patriots, orthodox and deist, formed a government that kept the sword of the state out of the church's hand *and* off of its neck. Our national conscience has been informed—if not always heeded—by the ethics of Jesus who praised the faith of a Roman soldier, never telling him to quit his job, but who also commanded his followers to love their enemies.[39]

America's past and present bear stains of dishonor, and good intentions have often led to unintended and deadly consequences. American foreign policy has too frequently been naïve, self-serving, and misguided, not always adhering to the highest ideals of our nation's founders. Yet, on the whole, it is difficult to think of a nation that has a better record than

37. Jacoby, "The Boston Mosque's Saudi Connections."

38. Zacks, *Pirate Coast*, 378–79.

39. Matthew 8:10; 5:44.

the United States of conquering nations that have threatened us only to rebuild them and give them back, freer than they were before. The present war in Iraq, like America's first war on foreign soil, was an attempt at regime change by replacing one Muslim leader with another who might promote more peaceful policies. Future historians will know if American intervention in Iraq is a turning point for peace and stability in a war-torn region or a debacle of the highest order.

Many have argued that no nation has possessed so much military power and yet shown such great restraint as the United States. That is largely due to the complicated partnership and ingenious separation of church and state. Intentionally, the First Amendment protects the two institutions best suited to hold government accountable: a free church and a free press, charged with speaking truth to power and the people. It remains to be seen how rising Islamic aggression will alter the delicate balance of freedom we have enjoyed for over two centuries, as the very real threat of terrorism forces our government to impinge on civil liberties in order to "provide for the common defense."

Those Americans who believe that Christianity and Islam are "basically the same" might profit from studying the past and noting with Jonathan Edwards how they are fundamentally different. And finally, those who think the days of Muslim nations receiving tribute money from the United States have ended, may want to consider the characterization by Mordechai Nisan of the 1973 oil crisis as "the exaction of tribute from a deflated and faltering enemy civilization."[40] Thirty-five years later, the tribute is higher than ever.

40. Bostom, *Legacy of Jihad*, 102.

10

Conclusion

Man is naturally exceeding prone to exalt himself
and depend on his own power or goodness;
as though from himself he must expect happiness.

—Jonathan Edwards[1]

If we take only a part of Christianity, and leave out a part that is essential
to it, what we take is not Christianity; because something that is of the
essence of it is wanting. So if we profess only a part, and leave out a part
that is essential, that which we profess is not Christianity.

—Jonathan Edwards[2]

IF YOU HAVE MADE it this far, you have discovered that reading Jonathan Edwards is not for people who are unwilling to engage their minds. You can't breeze through Jonathan Edwards's works like Poor Richard's Almanac. Likewise, the Bible is a treasure that God has opened up to all his people, and Edwards believed that if we remain ignorant of the great doctrines of Scripture, it is only "because we are too lazy to gather it in."[3] Discourses on complex theological issues, you may be thinking, are for seminary professors and pastors, but this is where Jonathan Edwards would disagree with you. In 1739, Edwards, concerned about the level of biblical literacy in his own congregation, wrote that "Every Christian should make a business of endeavoring to grow in knowledge in divinity."[4] Does Edwards really mean every Christian should aspire to be a good theologian?

1. Edwards, *Works*, 17:214.
2. Ibid., 2:413.
3. Ibid., 22:95.
4. Ibid., 22:85.

This must be the case, reasoned Edwards, because the author of Hebrews complains that "though by this time you ought to be teachers, you need someone to teach you the elementary truths of God's word all over again. You need milk, not solid food!"[5] If God really intended for the study of doctrine to be limited to pastors and professors, "he would never have blamed the Christian Hebrews for not having acquired knowledge enough to be teachers."[6] Therefore, laypeople cannot say "'Let us leave these matters to ministers and divines; let them dispute them out among themselves as they can; they concern not us,' for they are of infinite importance to every man."[7]

Benjamin Franklin preferred the route that Edwards denounced. The theological disputes of the day seemed infinitely unimportant to Franklin. It was fine to think about Jesus, but not about his deity. It was helpful to consider the ethics of Jesus, but not his grace. Theologians and philosophers had argued about these matters for centuries, and Franklin might have said with some in Edwards's congregation, "they concern us not." Better to study lightning than the God who made it. Better to enrich life now, than prepare for life after death. Better to improve the woodstove, than to investigate the evidence for the resurrection of Christ. Better to revise Jesus for this generation, than to point this generation to the original Jesus. It is not surprising that Franklin's approach has become the way of American culture. Sadly, in many quarters, it has become the way of the American church. Professing Christians by the millions are obsessed with life-easing technology, but settle for an inactive theological mind.

LET'S MAKE IT EASIER TO USE THIS BOOK

Few Christians will achieve the level of theological knowledge that Edwards did. Frankly, reading Edwards makes my head hurt. Yet all Christians can master a working knowledge of basic Christian doctrine that is built on the framework presented in this book. Here, I want to offer a practical working model for a way to talk to your friends about Jesus. When someone says to you "All the religions are basically the same," you can continue a meaningful conversation with a few basic talking points if you can remember the five G's: Gospels, God, Grave, Grace, and Growth.

5. Hebrews 5:12.
6. Edwards, *Works*, 22:85.
7. Ibid., 22:92.

"Actually," you might respond, "Christianity is distinguished from all other religions in at least five ways."

Since the heart of the Christian message is the good news that Jesus died in the place of sinners, was buried to prove he really died, and was raised again to prove his payment was accepted by the Father, I suggest you start with the middle three: God, Grave, and Grace. Leave the other two (Gospels and Growth) in reserve in case you need them. How is Christianity different from all other religions?

1. Only Jesus claimed to be **God**. Neither Moses, nor Muhammad, for example, claimed to be God, the Creator of heaven and earth. This is an audacious claim with enormous implications. Go to chapter 5 for more support on this point.

2. Only Jesus was raised from the **Grave**. No other world religion claims this for its founder. Christians believe Jesus is God, not because he claimed to be, but because he was raised from the dead to prove his claim. There is more historical evidence for the resurrection of Jesus than there is for the proposition that Julius Caesar ever lived. Chapter 6 presents a line of evidence you can use with honest inquirers.

3. Only Jesus taught that we are saved by **Grace** alone, not by our own works or effort. We are justified (declared righteous) in the sight of God when we trust in the death of Jesus on the cross to pay the penalty for our sins. Every other religion in the world is spelled D-O, but biblical Christianity is spelled D-O-N-E.[8] "It is finished,"[9] and we can add nothing to his work. Jesus did not teach that works were superfluous, but rather than a *condition*, they are a *consequence* of salvation. Jesus had little patience for religious hypocrites who professed to be right with God, but did not live righteous lives. Chapter 7 gives more detail on the essential Christian doctrine of grace.

4. The **Gospels** are historically reliable accounts of the life of Jesus. No other ancient document has stronger evidence for its veracity. If you reject the Gospels as historically unreliable, then, consistency demands that you reject every other ancient document. Now, if you don't have to go into this topic, then don't. It can be confusing to follow and may distract from the real issue, which is the good news of Jesus

---

8. I heard this statement, or something like it, from Bill Hybels, Senior Pastor, Willow Creek Community Church in South Barrington, Illinois.

9. John 19:30.

and what he has done for us. Keep in mind that the gospel—the good news—is not that the Bible is reliable. That is good news, but not *the* good news. However, you will be using many of the Bible verses that Jonathan Edwards used and eventually, someone may say, "We can't trust the Bible." That's where chapters 3 and 4 can help you out.

5. The **Growth** of Christianity depends on Spirit-empowered love and logic. Somewhere along the way, especially in our generation, someone will try to discredit Christianity by associating it with the terrorism of radical Islam. This is an intellectually lazy accusation, but it will need to be addressed. At this point, we can inform them that Jesus commanded his followers to abstain from force or violence as a means of advancing his message. When professing Christians have used violence to frighten or force people into becoming Christians, they have disobeyed the clear commands of Jesus, casting doubt on the authenticity of their own conversion. Go to chapters 8 and 9 to review the fundamental differences between Christianity and Islam.

While you are discussing this topic, the subject of faith and politics might come up. In particular, many of our unbelieving friends have grown suspicious and weary of the involvement of professing Christians in power politics. Because they are more aware of Muslim nations that have welded together mosque and state, they are genuinely frightened of the United States doing the same with church and state. They have an understandable aversion to theocracies.

Many Christians have diminished their credibility because of their naïve grasp of American history. Mindless talk of a "Christian Nation" and claims that all the founders were orthodox Christians will cause unbelievers to lose confidence in you as an authoritative source. Furthermore, they will be suspicious of your political agenda. In this book, I have tried to demonstrate that some of the founders were orthodox Christians who held to the historic, apostolic faith, and some of them were not. The genius of America is that we have a system of government that encourages competition not only in the marketplace of business, but also in the marketplace of religion. Biblical Christianity needs no special treatment from the state. Just give us an even playing field. Because we have confidence in the substance of our message and the church Jesus built, we feel no need for assistance from the government. Just let us compete!

At the same time, the founders were in agreement that the moral system taught by Jesus and safeguarded by the church is essential for our government to work. Therefore, the church in general, and Christians in particular, are just as free to persuade, protest, and influence government as anyone else. That is one of the oldest of American traditions.

Finally, your conversation may lead your skeptical friend to grasp the implications of Jesus's message. What about people in other religions? What about people who have never even heard about the real, historic Jesus? What happens to them? Of course, the logical end of our message is missions. If Jesus is God's only provision for reconciling people to himself, love demands a sense of urgency in telling the world about him. For those who want to dig deeper on this difficult topic, I have written about Jonathan Edwards's thoughts on the matter in the Appendix.

HUMBLE CONFIDENCE?

I have focused on only five central characteristics of the real Jesus. While Jesus is not less than these, he is certainly more. I spoke in general terms about Jesus's ethical system, but I did not discuss many of the particulars. Today, there is much interest about how Jesus's ethics apply to racism, social justice, poverty, the environment, materialism, abortion, gender specific roles, gay marriage, and a host of other relevant issues that are worthy of meaningful discussion. But unless these five features (Gospels, God, Grave, Grace, Growth) are accepted, then Jesus's ethical system has no greater authority than anyone else's. If Jesus is not supreme, his moral imperatives will be trumped at the earliest convenient moment.

The sustained attacks against the supremacy of Jesus Christ will elicit three main responses from various churches and denominations. Many Christians, feeling intimidated by what they view to be a superior force in the culture, longing to be loved and adored by the world, become embarrassed of Jesus, ashamed of his gospel, and simply keep their mouths shut. They may still attend church services, but during the week, they try to fly under the radar, avoiding conflict as they silently surrender to the majority. Other Christians, feeling threatened, respond in anger and arrogance, defending orthodoxy by publicly ridiculing or misrepresenting the views of their opponents. The damage they do is compounded when church leaders, such as pastors, become overtly involved in politics, such as in endorsing particular candidates. Their self-righteous and smug attitude is often interpreted as the insecurity that it is, and it does not add to the credibility of the gospel.

There is, of course, another way, the way of Jesus, and the way that Jonathan Edwards tried to go. It is the way of humble and informed confidence.

Humble confidence is a trust in God that is so solid, that we do not fear people, and are therefore free to love them, even when suffering at their hands. Because we do not need their approval, we are in a position to help them. Paul asked the Galatians, "Am I now trying to win the approval of men, or of God? Or am I trying to please men?"[10] He answers these rhetorical questions with resistless logic: "If I were still trying to please men, I would not be a servant of Christ." And as a servant of Christ, he preached the gospel to the Galatians. Humble confidence may seem like an oxymoron, but when our confidence is in God and not ourselves, humility thrives.

There is a direct link between humility before God and humility before people. When we begin to understand the unspeakable mercy God has shown us, it becomes more reasonable to show mercy to others. We are commanded to "accept one another, then, just as Christ accepted"[11] us. Paul tells the Colossians to "forgive as the Lord forgave you."[12] It is as if to say, "How dare you receive grace from God and not extend it to others?" It only makes sense that we "in humility consider others better than ourselves."[13] Yes, we are "God's chosen people," but that is exactly why we should clothe ourselves with "compassion, kindness, humility, gentleness, and patience."[14]

John Jay certainly would have been familiar with these biblical instructions, but like all Christians, was inconsistent in their application. Once, during an exam, his physician began to ridicule the doctrine of the bodily resurrection. Jay stopped him immediately and curtly informed him, "'Sir, I pay you for your medical knowledge, and not for your distorted views of the Christian religion!'"[15] This is a positive example in that it supports one of the theses of this book: there were many orthodox Christians among the founders who were willing to speak up. It is, how-

10. Galatians 1:10, 11.
11. Romans 15:7.
12. Colossians 3:13.
13. Philippians 2:3.
14. Colossians 3:12.
15. Monaghan, *John Jay*, 218.

ever, a negative example in that John Jay missed an opportunity to help another person come to know the real Jesus. We can imagine how this conversation on spiritual matters came to an abrupt and awkward end.

The doctrine of the supremacy of Jesus Christ is a dangerous doctrine. Like a scalpel, it can be used to either incite healing or inflict wounds. In the hands of the proud, it harms. In the hands of the humble, it heals. We must be careful, gentle, and precise when we declare it. The Bible often reminds us to show respect and honor to unbelievers, and to live our lives so as to "win the respect of outsiders."[16] Peter exhorts his readers to "always be prepared to give an answer to everyone who asks you to give the reason for the hope that you have. But do this with gentleness and respect."[17]

Christians who wield this doctrine with arrogance, speaking to and about unbelievers roughly and disrespectfully, have done immeasurable harm to the advance of the gospel. There are ugly blemishes on the history of the church, as some professing Christians have used hateful words, political power, or even deadly violence to promote their unbiblical spin on what it means for Jesus to be supreme. How odd that we would use a doctrine that should make us the most humble as a weapon to exalt ourselves above others. Never forget that it was this brand of Christianity, fraught with pride and hypocrisy, that turned Benjamin Franklin, Thomas Paine, Thomas Jefferson, and countless others, away from the church and the message it was supposed to guard.

Jesus did not use uncertain terms when he told us to love our enemies, "pray for them,"[18] and "do good"[19] to them even if they hate us. That means we love them enough to listen to their challenges, understand their questions, answer their objections, risk their rejection, and seek to persuade them to bow their knee to the King of Kings for their good and God's glory. That is what it means to have a humble confidence. Ask yourself, If Jesus Christ really is supreme, what is the most loving thing I can do for this person? Is it really loving to deny, dilute, or distort the supremacy of Jesus? But also ask, Is it loving to share this truth in an arrogant, angry, condescending, or patronizing way?

16. 1 Thessalonians 4:12.
17. 1 Peter 3:15.
18. Matthew 5:44.
19. Luke 6:27.

As Jonathan Edwards reviewed the history of the church, he noticed a pattern in the strategy of the devil—whom he believed to be very real. First, the devil tries to prevent a revival, that work of God where the church comes alive, wakes up to God, returns to the Bible and sound doctrine, repents of sin, grows in love, and bears much fruit as people come to the real Jesus. Second, if the devil fails to prevent the reviving and reforming work of God, he focuses on driving Christians "to excesses and extravagances."[20] That is, if he cannot stop the church from moving in the right direction, he does what he can to push it in the right direction too far, to take it, in pendulum fashion, to an unhealthy extreme. This is a great danger in this doctrine. Christians who find in the supremacy of Jesus a reason to nurse pride have missed the point. Those who rudely confront unbelievers with arrogant triumphalism, angry words, or a "my-god-can-beat-up-your-god" attitude will do more harm than good.

Edwards was keenly aware of the ever-present temptation of spiritual pride. He saw it as the "main door [by which] the devil comes into the hearts of those who are zealous for the advancement" of the gospel.[21] This is a warning for those who love the doctrine of the supremacy of Christ. Do not forget that "nothing sets a person so much out of the devil's reach as humility."[22] Even the Bible's directives to "contend for the faith" can be misunderstood and abused. The early Christians, Edwards reminds us, "defended the truth with arguments and a holy conversation, but yet gave their reasons with meekness and fear. [They] resisted unto blood striving against sin, but the blood that was shed was their own blood, and not the blood of their enemies."[23] Some Christians may give the appearance of humility, but "pure Christian humility," wrote Edwards, "has no such thing as roughness, or contempt, or fierceness, or bitterness in its nature; it makes a person like a little child, harmless and innocent, and that none need to be afraid of."[24]

As you read Edwards, it may appear that he was not always gentle. Just keep in mind that he was often dealing with people inside the church who called themselves followers of Christ and leaders of Christians, people

20. Edwards, *Works,* 4:410.
21. Ibid., 4:414.
22. Ibid.
23. Ibid., 4:425.
24. Ibid., 4:422.

who enjoyed the privileges of the community of faith without meeting the responsibilities. Paul had warned that "savage wolves" would come into the church and "not spare the flock."[25] Before that, Jesus told his disciples to "Watch out for false prophets. They come to you in sheep's clothing, but inwardly they are ferocious wolves."[26] It is hard to gently handle wolves.

Jesus himself reserved his harshest criticism for religious leaders who claimed to represent God, but twisted God's word and led many astray. Consider the words of the humblest man who ever lived to the religious leaders of his day: "You snakes! You brood of vipers! How will you escape being condemned in hell?"[27] The problem with so many of the deists is that they claimed to be real followers of Jesus even as they fabricated a Jesus the apostles would not recognize. If Jonathan Edwards seems hard-edged when he crushes the arguments of other ministers, college professors, theologians, and deist authors, it is likely because he was being a good shepherd.

When we are communicating with those outside of the church, with those making no claim to belong to Jesus, the tone changes. The same people that Jesus excoriated often criticized him for the respect he showed for outsiders. "But the Pharisees and the teachers of the law muttered, 'This man welcomes sinners, and eats with them.'"[28] And Paul's interaction with unbelievers throughout the book of Acts is the model of tact while declaring the supremacy of Christ to those who do not claim him. In Athens, Paul is gracious and deferential, even favorably citing one of their poets.[29] To King Agrippa, Paul exhibits exemplary diplomacy when he tells him "I consider myself fortunate to stand before you today as I make my defense."[30] In this he follows his own counsel to the Colossian church: "Be wise in the way you act towards outsiders; make the most of every opportunity. Let your conversation be always full of grace, seasoned with salt, so that you may know how to answer everyone."[31]

25. Acts 20:29.
26. Matthew 7:15.
27. Matthew 23:33.
28. Luke 15:2.
29. Acts 17:28.
30. Acts 26:2.
31. Colossians 4:5.

HUMBLE, NOT IGNORANT

To be humble is not the same as remaining ignorant. To be sure, Christians who fail to grow in their knowledge of doctrine have a lot to be humble about. Paul does warn the Corinthians that "knowledge puffs up,"[32] but he also commends them for excelling in knowledge.[33] He prays that the Philippians will "abound more and more in knowledge and depth of insight."[34] He tells Timothy to instruct those in the church so that they will come to "a knowledge of the truth."[35] And Peter tells his readers to "grow in the grace and knowledge of our Lord and Savior Jesus Christ."[36] So there must be a way to walk with humility and grow in our understanding of theology.

HUMBLE, NOT UNSURE

To be humble is not the same as being uncertain about the core essentials of the Christian faith. "Faith," says the writer of Hebrews, "is being sure of what we hope for and certain of what we do not see."[37] We are told to be sure that Christ was crucified and raised from the dead and that those who reject this will not spend eternity in his kingdom.[38] Though it may appear to the world as humility, doubting the truth of God's Word is a breathtaking distrust in God. Being unsure is unbelief. So there must be a way to be both humble and sure.

HUMBLE, NOT SILENT

It is not necessarily godly to avoid controversy. That is a common misperception. If men or women are quiet, behind-the-scenes, never at the center of controversy, they are often assumed to be humble, not drawing attention to themselves. By that definition, Jesus was the most arrogant human to walk on the planet. Sometimes people are quiet because they are humble. Sometimes they are quiet because they are proud. Overly

32. 1 Corinthians 8:1.
33. 2 Corinthians 8:7.
34. Philippians 1:9.
35. 2 Timothy 2:25.
36. 2 Peter 3:18.
37. Hebrews 11:1.
38. 2 Corinthians 3:4 and Ephesians 5:5.

concerned with their image or what people might think of them, longing to be loved and applauded by the world, they keep their mouths shut. Rather than being humble, they are merely cowards, ashamed of the gospel and the foolishness of the cross.[39] Yet, church leaders must be humble people who can "encourage others by sound doctrine and refute those who oppose"[40] the teaching of the apostles. When Peter was ordered by the governing authorities to stop teaching about Jesus, he told them, "We must obey God rather than men!"[41] Jude urges all Christians to "contend for the faith that was once for all entrusted to the saints."[42] So there must be a way to be humble and to speak up.

And that is what this book has been about. I wanted to speak up. There are many things being said about Jesus today that are not true. There is nothing new about that. He was falsely accused at his trial and he is falsely accused in our times. He was ridiculed on the cross and he is ridiculed in our culture. Contemporary religious leaders pretend to be his friend by stripping him of his deity, yet this is not the first time he has been betrayed by insiders. The result in America is often a salad-bar Jesus, whose traits have been personally selected by an indulged American public that is used to getting its way. Jesus—the real Jesus—makes some demands on us we do not want to accept and says some things we do not want to hear. Not surprisingly, each generation seeks some way to demote, misquote, and revise him. Jonathan Edwards was having none of it in his generation, and neither should we in ours.

---

39. Romans 1:16 and 1 Corinthians 1:18.
40. Titus 1:9.
41. Acts 5:29.
42. Jude 3.

Appendix

Missions and Those Who Have Never Heard of Jesus

Christ did, as it were, make a Great feast and set the door wide open and bid all nations come to that feast and He still continues to Invite all. He makes no difference between English and Indians, white or black. All are alike welcome.

—Jonathan Edwards[1]

So there are none saved but only those that hear the Calls of the Gospel. That is God's way and his only way of bringing men to salvation, by the Gospel . . . Men can't believe on him of whom they have not heard.

—Jonathan Edwards[2]

He prefer'd the Doers of the Word to the meer Hearers . . . &c. tho' they never heard of his Name, he declares shall in the last Day be accepted, when those who cry Lord, Lord; who value themselves on their Faith tho' great enough to perform Miracles but have neglected good Works shall be rejected.

—Benjamin Franklin[3]

I'm not necessarily explaining deep, theological questions and doctrine and stuff like that; I'm talking about how you can live your everyday life.

—Joel Osteen[4]

1. Edwards, MS "Speech to the Mohawks," 3.
2. Edwards, MS Sermon on Matthew 22:14 (1732), 3, 5.
3. Franklin, Papers, 4:505–6.
4. Butler, "Sermon With a Smile," 57.

O N JUNE 20, 2002, Joel Osteen, the pastor of the largest church in America, was handed a rare opportunity to speak to his nation of the supremacy of Jesus Christ. Larry King asked him the ultimate question on CNN, point blank. A portion of the transcript as it appears on CNN's website reads:

> KING: What if you're Jewish or Muslim, you don't accept Christ at all?
>
> OSTEEN: You know, I'm very careful about saying who would and wouldn't go to heaven. I don't know . . .
>
> KING: If you believe you have to believe in Christ? They're wrong, aren't they?
>
> OSTEEN: Well, I don't know if I believe they're wrong. I believe here's what the Bible teaches and from the Christian faith this is what I believe. But I just think that only God will judge a person's heart. I spent a lot of time in India with my father. I don't know all about their religion. But I know they love God. And I don't know. I've seen their sincerity. So I don't know. I know for me, and what the Bible teaches, I want to have a relationship with Jesus.[5]

On this point, the pastor of the largest church in America seems to be in agreement with Benjamin Franklin, who believed that many sincere, religious people would go to heaven regardless of their opinion of Jesus or even if "they never heard of his Name."[6]

This would be news to William Carey. In 1793, when Carey left the relative comfort of England to take the gospel to India, there was even less of the gospel there than Joel Osteen finds today. Currently, less than three percent of India's population call themselves Christians and the nation is still dominated by a religious caste system that keeps millions of Indians locked in cycles of poverty. William Carey saw their religious sincerity and concluded that sincerity was not nearly enough.

When Carey, the "Father of Modern Missions," moved his family to India, it was not a matter of enduring a few hours on a plane. It required five months at sea. When he arrived in Calcutta, he wrote to a friend that he felt what Paul felt "when he beheld Athens and 'his spirit was stirred within him.'"[7] Of course, what stirred Paul's spirit and caused him great

---

5. Osteen, "Interview."
6. Franklin, Papers, 4:505–6.
7. George, *Faithful Witness*, 92, 186.

distress was that "the city was full of idols."[8] Imagine Paul observing that idolatry and saying, "I don't know. They seem so sincere. I know they love God." But he did not say that because he did not believe that. Instead, he confidently proclaimed to the men of Athens the supremacy of Jesus Christ, validated by his resurrection. That's what Carey spent the rest of his life doing in India.

William Carey was a cobbler turned missionary who chose to live in the midst of disease, poverty, and filth. He labored for forty years to translate the Scriptures into thirty-five languages and dialects. He buried two wives in India and left a widow. If Christ is not supreme, William Carey was a fool.

But if Christ is supreme, William Carey was wise. He is also in good company. The message of the church from its beginning has been the supremacy of Jesus Christ. This is the position of the apostles, the church fathers, Augustine, Athanasius, Wycliffe, Hus, Luther, Calvin, Zwingli, the Pilgrims on the Mayflower, and the Puritans who settled New England. And this was the position of Jonathan Edwards. William Carey knew what Edwards believed because Carey read Edwards's books. In fact, Timothy George observes that "the writings of Jonathan Edwards were the single most important theological influence" on William Carey.[9] If William Carey is the Father of Modern Missions, then, it might be argued, Jonathan Edwards is the Grandfather of Modern Missions.[10]

ARE MISSIONARIES FOOLS?

Because Christianity was birthed in the diverse culture of the Roman Empire, the challenge of religious pluralism is nothing new. In the face of that challenge, Jesus and his followers proclaimed that explicit faith in Jesus Christ was the only hope for people to be reconciled to God. If this is true, the majority of people have died without hearing of that hope. Can so many people be so wrong? What about the millions of adherents to other religions who sincerely believe in the supremacy of their own religious tenets? What about those who have never heard of Christ? As thoughtful people are confronted with the teaching of Jesus and the

---

8. Acts 17:16.

9. George, *Faithful Witness*, 49.

10. My observation here is not original.

apostles, they find themselves drawn into one of three main categories: pluralism, inclusivism, or exclusivism.[11]

PLURALISM: JESUS IS ONE OF MANY SAVIORS, BUT THE ONLY SAVIOR FOR CHRISTIANS

Religious pluralism asserts that all the major world religions, and probably some minor ones, provide direct access to God/gods as they understand him/her/it/them. No religion can claim exclusive rights to the "divine reality." All the world religions share a great deal of common truth and no single religion can claim to be unique or superior to others.

This view requires the unvarnished rejection of the Bible as a reliable authority and of Jesus as the Savior of the world. British theologian John Hick, a well-known pluralist, following the well-worn path of eighteenth century deists, denies that Jesus ever claimed to be God and asserts that in the years following his death "Jesus was gradually deified in the minds of Christians."[12] Only in the succeeding centuries, the church made the deity of Christ a fixed doctrine, something that the real, historical Jesus (in Hick's opinion) would have abhorred. While exclusivism proclaims that Christ is the only way, pluralism asserts that Christ is the only way for Christians. Other religious people have their "only way." This is unrecognizable as the historic, apostolic, Christian faith.

INCLUSIVISM: JESUS IS THE ONLY SAVIOR, BUT PEOPLE DON'T HAVE TO HEAR ABOUT HIM TO BE SAVED

Inclusivism is the position taken by many liberal Protestant theologians and most Catholic theologians after Vatican II. Inclusivism has grown in popularity in recent decades among evangelicals and provides a way to retain a good portion of Christian orthodoxy while adopting a more optimistic view of the scope of salvation. It also has the effect of offending fewer

11. Some theologians take views that do not seem to fit any three of these categories. Okholm and Philipps acknowledge that in recent years, participants in this ongoing debate have used three categories: pluralism, inclusivism, and exclusivism. However, in their judgment "exclusivism" is a word that in our politically correct environment is fraught with enough negative baggage that it precludes a fair hearing. In place of exclusivism, the editors elect to use the word "particularism." However, within particularism, there seems to be room for subcategories. Consequently, they present four views on salvation in a pluralistic world (16).

12. Hick, "A Pluralist View," 36.

people. In this view, salvation is offered in Jesus Christ alone, but is available to all, even if they never hear the name of Jesus. As Gerald McDermott observes, inclusivists "believe 'good' Buddhists can be saved by Jesus if they recognize their inability to save themselves and cry out for mercy."[13]

A growing number of evangelicals would rather avoid the issue altogether. As an example, I offer Brian McLaren, leader in the emergent movement, who advises us that the message of Jesus and his apostles does not mean that "making disciples must equal making adherents to the Christian religion. [Because it] may be advisable in many circumstances to help people become followers of Jesus and remain within their Buddhist, Hindu, or Jewish contexts."[14] Additionally, the "Christian faith . . . should become (in the name of Jesus Christ) a welcome friend to other religions of the world, not a threat."[15] I'm not quite sure what to do with McLaren's statements, which is exactly what he wants. He warns his readers from the outset that "people who try to label me an exclusivist, inclusivist, or universalist on the issue of hell will find here only more reason for frustration."[16] I understand that McLaren's burden is to move Christians to address the hypocrisy in their own ranks before critiquing the faith of others, and I wish him well. Jonathan Edwards, as we have seen, was willing to suffer great loss to rid the church of some hypocrisy himself.

However, in the name of humility, those in McLaren's sphere of influence might conclude that they should remain silent when Jesus wants them to speak. After all, it is hard to imagine the Apostle Paul presenting the gospel in such a way that the religious leaders in Jerusalem or Athens would not see it as a threat. As someone with insight has said, "If it doesn't get you kicked out of a synagogue or a mosque, then whatever you are preaching is probably not the gospel." That would apply, I think, even to a "generous orthodoxy." Christians are not entitled to be brusque and insensitive to people of other religions, but the message of the gospel has always been offensive and, well, threatening. It tends to turn worlds upside down. If the gospel is right, then Hinduism, Buddhism, and Islam are wrong about who God is and how to be connected to him. Oh, how I wish sometimes I could be an inclusivist, so I didn't have to say that.

13. McDermott, *God's Rivals*, 23.

14. McLaren, *Generous Orthodoxy*, 260.

15. Ibid., 254.

16. Ibid., 37.

There are several variations of inclusivism, but the form advocated by Clark Pinnock has attracted the most attention in the evangelical world. Pinnock attempts to maintain a high view of Scripture, holding that Jesus is the only mediator of salvation, but he believes that many will receive salvation without explicit knowledge of that mediator. They may remain practicing Hindus, Muslims, or Buddhists, but still experience the Holy Spirit in a way that leads them to faith in God and consequent good works, even if they do not have knowledge of God's Son. In the end, when they get to heaven, they will discover, like Old Testament saints, that they have been saved by Christ.[17]

Pinnock acknowledges his "debt to the Catholic church for its leadership"[18] in developing the inclusivist position. Significantly, he points out that though inclusivism, in terms of church history, is "relatively new," it "has become widely accepted and may even be called the mainline model."[19]

In answer to the charge that the inclusivist position diminishes the motivation for world missions, Pinnock argues that these believers who don't yet know Christ still need to hear the gospel so they can experience the "fullness of salvation in the fellowship of the body of Christ"[20] so we should still send missionaries. In other words, it is better to be a Christian and know it, than to be a Christian and not know it. But this raises two important questions.

First, if the inclusivist view is correct, is it really worth risking life and limb to take the gospel to unevangelized people? Historically, have missionaries left the families, language, and food of their home nations to inform people in distant lands that they really are Christians even if they don't know it yet? Does this not diminish the sense of urgency in the Great Commission?

---

17. John Piper addresses the question of salvation prior to the resurrection of Christ and argues that inclusivists like Pinnock do not "reckon seriously enough with the tremendous significance that the New Testament sees in the historical turning point of the incarnation." Piper adds that "the coming of Christ was a decisive turn in redemptive history that henceforth makes him the focus of all saving faith." (Piper, *Let the Nations Be Glad*, 134.) Piper's conclusion: "Therefore, it accords with this purpose that Christ be the sole and necessary focus of saving faith. Apart from a knowledge of him, none who has the physical ability to know him will be saved" (133). Piper makes a strong case for the traditional view of exclusivism.

18. Clark Pinnock, "Inclusivist View," 109.

19. Ibid., 101.

20. Ibid., 120.

Second, if the inclusivist view is correct, does proclaiming the gospel to the unreached of the world not place them in greater jeopardy? While the question of those who have never heard may not be as directly addressed in Scripture as we would like, the question of those who hear the gospel and reject Jesus could not be clearer: they will perish. Would it not be better to leave them without the gospel in this life rather than risk their rejection of it? Would missions at this point become a death sentence for millions who otherwise might be saved? Pinnock's reply is telling: "My instinct is to leave this matter with the grace of God, who knows the factors that go into such a decision and makes valid judgments."[21]

This leaves us to wonder why Clark Pinnock's instinct, which led him to be so bold in declaring that evangelicals can be "open and generous to other religious traditions,"[22] has now led him to be so cautious on a point which, if conceded, would be harmful to his position.

EXCLUSIVISM: JESUS IS THE ONLY SAVIOR, AND PEOPLE MUST HEAR ABOUT HIM TO BE SAVED

Exclusivism[23] insists that God's special revelation is necessary for salvation. Human reason cannot discern from general revelation (in creation and conscience) the way of salvation. As J. I. Packer notes, "God's general revelation of himself, though genuinely given to all, is correctly received by none."[24] Exclusivists operate on the rule that "people are not saved

---

21. Clark Pinnock, "Inclusivist View," 120.

22. Furthermore, Pinnock seems to practice what he condemned in others in 1992. Because some exclusivists like J. I. Packer and Lesslie Newbigin are unwilling to make dogmatic assertions where there is no specific biblical teaching on the eternal destiny of those who have not heard the gospel, he accuses them of playing it safe: "They will opt for reverent agnosticism on this subject . . . Many try to duck the issue in this manner. But this sudden attack of modesty does not seem quite right. Isn't theology supposed to face tough questions as well as easy ones?" (Pinnock, *A Wideness in God's Mercy*, 150–51). Pinnock continues: "But such an attitude is a cop out to avoid answering a fair and urgent question in a responsible way." Theologians choosing to be agnostic concerning the salvation of those who have not heard "should find easier work" (152). A few pages later, Pinnock, not one to duck an issue, admits that "it may even be that there is a greater danger for nominal Christians to be condemned rather than those who have not heard of Jesus" (175). However, by 1995, Pinnock was more inclined to become "agnostic" about the way inclusivism likely decreases the motive for missions. Likely, Pinnock would not consider this a case of trying to "duck the issue" (Pinnock, "An Inclusivist View," 110).

23. Sometimes called restrictivism or particularism.

24. Packer, "Evangelicals and the Way of Salvation," 109.

apart from explicit faith in Jesus Christ." This view enjoys the longest history, being "the oldest enduring tradition in Christian theology."[25]

However, there are various views even within the exclusivist camp, some being more optimistic than others. Many consider themselves exclusivists but admit the possibility of exceptions to the rule that "people are not saved apart from explicit faith in Jesus Christ." Since it seems to them that Scripture does not directly address this question, they choose not to speculate where God is silent.[26] "Living by the Bible," says J. I. Packer, "means assuming that no one will be saved apart from faith in Christ, and acting accordingly."[27] While we can hope that God will save some of those who have never heard, we cannot know that he will, so we press on as if he will not.[28] Other exclusivists have even greater confidence that when Paul posed the questions in Romans 10:13–15, God was not so silent on the fate of those who never hear the gospel.

> "Everyone who calls on the name of the Lord will be saved." How, then, can they call on the one they have not believed in? And how can they believe in the one of whom they have not heard? And how can they hear without someone preaching to them? And how can they preach unless they are sent?

Arguing for "the supremacy of Christ as the conscious focus of all saving faith," John Piper draws the following conclusion:

> But when Christ came, all faith narrowed in its focus to him alone as the one who purchased and guaranteed all the hopes of the people of God. From the time of Christ onward, God wills to honor

25. Okholm and Phillips, *Four Views on Salvation*, 19.

26. Some believe that John Calvin's maxim would apply here: "We should not investigate what the Lord has left hidden in secret, nor neglect what he has brought out into the open so that we may not be convicted of excessive curiosity on the one hand, or of excessive ingratitude on the other (Calvin, Institutes, 3.21.4).

27. Packer, "Evangelicals and the Way of Salvation," 123 (italics mine).

28. For several years now, we have been hearing reports from Muslim nations, which have been closed to the gospel, that Muslims are indeed coming to Christ. They do not have the Scripture (written revelation) in their possession and they have not been contacted by missionaries. However, they report that Jesus is appearing to them in dreams and visions. If these accounts are accurate, Jonathan Edwards's position (exclusivism) remains intact. While God is certainly able to call people to saving faith apart from Scripture or missionaries, it is still not apart from explicit knowledge of Jesus Christ. Edwards would still argue that salvation has come through special revelation (dreams and visions) and not human reason (contra the deists).

Christ by making him the sole focus of saving faith. Therefore, people must call on him and believe in him and hear him and be sent as messengers with the Word of Christ.[29]

DID JONATHAN EDWARDS CHANGE HIS MIND?

No one suggests that Jonathan Edwards was a pluralist, and no pluralist would claim him. Our options are limited to two: Was Edwards an inclusivist or an exclusivist? As we saw in chapter 7, Edwards clearly affirmed the historical exclusivism of the Westminster Confession which is closer to John Piper's view mentioned above. In his sermons and all of his published writings, Edwards leaves no room for doubt as to where he stands on this issue.[30]

But Edwards wrote more than was preached or published. In his private correspondence and personal notebooks, Edwards scholars have a treasure trove of Edwards's thought put on paper. In the past, these manuscripts, housed in the Beineke Rare Book and Manuscript Library at Yale University, have only been accessible to professional scholars who made the trip to Yale. Recently, more of them have been made available to the public online.[31] Are these private writings consistent with Edwards's public ministry?

WHAT IF EDWARDS HAD LIVED AS LONG
AS BENJAMIN FRANKLIN?

As we saw in chapter 2, Jonathan Edwards died of a smallpox inoculation gone awry at the age of fifty-four in 1758. He died, like everyone else, with an unfinished to-do list. It is tempting to play the game of historical "what

---

29. John Piper, *Let the Nations Be Glad*, 147.

30. Edwards's position is so clear that Clark Pinnock wisely does not attempt to enlist Edwards for his cause in *A Wideness in God's Mercy*. The only reference by name to Edwards is to link him with Augustine as examples of not being "sensitive persons" in their views of eternal punishment (157). Pinnock, advocating annihilationism, does not count Edwards or Augustine as friends. The only other reference to Edwards is veiled, but obvious: "Sinners are not in the hands of an angry God. Our mission is not to urge [sinners] to turn to Jesus because God hates them and delights in sending them to hell" (177). Though Edwards clearly taught that sinners were indeed in the hands of an angry God, it is not so clear that Edwards taught that God delighted in sending them to hell. Edwards's actual sermon on the subject suggests otherwise.

31. See http://www.edwards.yale.edu.

if." What if the Spanish Armada had encountered no storms off the coast of Scotland? What if Robert E. Lee had not lost "Stonewall" Jackson at Chancelorsville? What if the 101st Airborne had not held Bastogne in the Battle of the Bulge? How would the course of history been redirected?

What if Jonathan Edwards had not been inoculated with a smallpox vaccine? What if he had lived as long as Benjamin Franklin? We know his plans were to write a great work entitled "History of the Work of Redemption." George Marsden observes that Edwards "envisioned it as the culmination of his life's work."[32] It is worth noting that Marsden, the most authoritative biographer of Edwards in the twenty-first century, asserts that "fundamentally," Edwards "viewed other religions, such as Islam, as false and pernicious."[33] In this *magnus opus* (great work), Edwards would have surely clarified and expanded on the thoughts he recorded in his private notebooks. But Edwards did not live long enough to complete this writing project.

STOP HERE TO REST

You are about to enter the most tedious part of this book, which is why I put it in the appendix. This is a perilous point for me as an author, because I am running the risk of losing your interest. You may get a few minutes into the next section and decide to skip it and go to the end. I wouldn't blame you. But if you have heard some things lately about Jonathan Edwards that make you think he was won over on some points by deist arguments in his later years, I recommend you press on.

GERALD MCDERMOTT'S "STRANGE, NEW EDWARDS"

Gerald McDermott believes he has found evidence in the private notebooks of Jonathan Edwards (called *Miscellanies*) to support the theory that near the end of his life, Edwards changed his mind about those who have no explicit knowledge of Jesus Christ. McDermott seeks to introduce a "strange, new Edwards"[34] based on his study of Edwards's private musings, which were not intended for publication. In these notebooks, Edwards wrote his

---

32. Marsden, *Jonathan Edwards*, 481.

33. Ibid., 486.

34. McDermott, *Jonathan Edwards Confronts the Gods*, 3.

thoughts, shaped his arguments, and prepared for future writing projects. But we do not have in them the benefit of a finished product.[35]

McDermott has invested much research in his argument, raised some excellent questions, and come to some controversial conclusions. In particular, he insists that Jonathan Edwards "reflected late in his career, tentatively, but positively, on the possibility of salvation for the heathen"[36] without the gospel, or explicit knowledge of Jesus Christ. McDermott repeatedly concedes that Edwards did not state this plainly or dogmatically. McDermott admits that in the *Miscellanies*, Edwards is "hesitant and tentative"[37] and that his remarks are "cryptic."[38] Nevertheless, McDermott believes he is able to discern that Edwards "made a series of important theological moves that *could have* opened the door for a more hopeful view of salvation of the heathen."[39] Because the evidence is absent, McDermott must confess that Edwards never walked through the door himself.

McDermott makes a significant contribution to our understanding that many of Edwards's writings are a rejoinder to deist arguments that were gaining traction in his lifetime. As we have seen, deists believed human reason was sufficient to discern a right view of God. By observing creation, man can discover the "the laws of Nature" and "Nature's God."[40] Salvation, then, was equally accessible to all people, because all people can reason. God does not need to reveal himself in special ways, through prophets, miracles, or an incarnation. Besides, argued the deists, if we can only know God through special revelation, then that would be supremely unfair, since the vast majority of the world is cut off from what

35. Douglas Sweeney writes in the introduction to Miscellanies 1153–1360 that the Miscellanies represent Edwards's "serious efforts to rough out his theological reflections" (Edwards, *Works*, 23:1). It is prudent to keep in mind that what we have in the Miscellanies is just that: roughed-out theological reflections. Sweeney goes on to add: "In the tradition of Perry Miller, many scholars continue to suggest that JE intended at the end of his life to publish a 'Rational Account of the Main Doctrines of the Christian Religion.' As the story usually goes, this crowning achievement of JE's career was to be a systematic presentation of his previously 'hidden' religious views. That this was not JE's intention has been clear to specialists for some time, but the force of Miller's interpretation of JE's mind continues to be felt" (Edwards, *Works*, 23:9, 10). It seems to be felt rather strongly by Gerald McDermott.

36. McDermott, *Jonathan Edwards Confronts the Gods*, 140.

37. Ibid., 141.

38. Ibid., 140.

39. Ibid., 143 (italics mine).

40. The Declaration of Independence.

Christianity claims to be the written record of God's revelation. They have no access to the Bible. Therefore, insisted the deists, it must be possible to know God through human reason apart from revelation.

A significant element of McDermott's case is Edwards's use of the *prisca theologia* (ancient theology) in refuting the deist arguments of his day. Edwards agreed there were relatively virtuous people in other cultures dominated by non-Christian religions because in all the nations of the earth, there exists the remnants of the original revelation to Adam and then to Noah and distributed throughout the world through Noah's sons.[41] This is the ancient theology from which world religions borrow. Consequently, these "heathen" may have many right notions of God.

However, in his published works, Edwards never clearly expresses hope that there was enough revelation remaining in the *prisca theologia* to lead the heathen to salvation. Somewhere between Moses and David, the *prisca theologia* had been so corrupted that "all the nations in the world, except the Israelites, and those who embodied themselves with them were given up to idolatry; and so continued till Christ came."[42] In this lost state, "all of the heathen philosophers could not deliver them from their darkness." At this point, Edwards reminds us that the only one who can deliver them is Jesus Christ "by his glorious gospel" and he does it by "the foolishness of preaching to save them that believe."[43] There is not a hint here that salvation would come to the heathen world apart from preaching the gospel of Jesus Christ. Nonetheless, by citing remarks in the *Miscellanies*, McDermott insists that near the end of his life, Edwards changed his mind.

41. Edwards, *The Works of Jonathan Edwards*, 1:548. "The written word of God is the main instrument employed by Christ, in order to carry on this work of redemption in all ages. There was a necessity now of the word of God being committed to writing, for a steady rule to God's church. Before this, the church had the word by tradition, either by immediate tradition by eminent men inspired, that were living, or else by tradition from former generations, which might be had with tolerable certainty in ages preceding this, by reason of men's long lives. Noah might converse with Adam, and receive traditions from him . . ."

42. Ibid., 1:547. See also Edwards, MS "Controversies" Notebook, 551. While deists like Jefferson would argue that the story of Christ's death and resurrection is derived from ancient myths, Edwards argued that the ancient myths are derived from the early promises in the Scripture of a coming Messiah who would suffer and rise from the dead. For example, he speaks of "the first prophecy of the serpent's bruising the heel of the Messiah from whence probably came the Egyptian Fables of Orus's conflict with the serpent Python and Hercules's conflict with monsters" (554).

43. Edwards, *The Works of Jonathan Edwards*, 1:547.

Perhaps McDermott has misunderstood Edwards. Greg Gilbert suggests that as more people adopt an inclusivist view, they will seek "some historical figure to carry the flame and serve as a spokesman for the idea. Despite the arguments by some to hand that torch to Jonathan Edwards, it seems impossible from looking at the evidence to conclude that one can justly conscript America's greatest theologian into that service."[44] Jonathan Edwards, concludes Gilbert, believed that "salvation would come only through explicit knowledge of the gospel resulting in conscious faith in Jesus Christ as the only Redeemer."[45]

In McDermott's rebuttal to Gilbert,[46] he predictably denies the charge that he has misunderstood Edwards, and then refers to one quote from Edwards that he had cited in his book, but which Gilbert fails to address. This is an important text for McDermott's theory, so since Gilbert did not specifically address it, I will take some time to do so here.

MISCELLANY 1338

Because Gilbert is using a journal article to respond to a book of over two hundred pages, it is understandable that he is limited on what he can address. Nevertheless, McDermott informs his readers that Gilbert "does not mention" *Miscellany* 1338[47] in which Edwards writes that the heathen world

> . . . are not so entirely and absolutely cast off, but that there is a possibility of their being reconciled; and God has so ordered the case, that there is an equal possibility of their receiving the benefit of divine revelation.[48]

This is all of *Miscellany* 1338 that McDermott quotes in his article. He allows that "Edwards is not dogmatic about heathen being saved" without explicit knowledge of Christ, but here again he believes Edwards "opens the door to that possibility."[49] McDermott does emphasize that if they are

44. Gilbert, "Nations Will Worship," 75.

45. Ibid., 53.

46. McDermott, "Response to Gilbert," 77–80.

47. *Miscellany* 1338 was written about 1757.

48. Edwards, *Works*, 23:354–55. "Miscellanies 1153–60." This is the extent of the quote that McDermott offers of *Miscellany* 1338 in his journal response to Gilbert, while offering even less in his book *Jonathan Edwards Confronts the Gods* on page 141.

49. Edwards, *Works*, 23:354–55.

saved apart from explicit knowledge of Christ, they are saved by grace alone, not by works, and their mediator is Christ, even if they do not yet know him or what he has done for them. In other words, McDermott seems to be arguing that Edwards, at the end of his life, was deliberately heading toward an inclusivist position.

"THE BENEFIT OF DIVINE REVELATION"

But maybe there is another way of understanding this perplexing quote. Edwards is answering the deist claim that special revelation is not necessary to accurately know God as redeemer.[50] All people, maintained the deists, can observe the natural world by their own reason, and, therefore, all people have equal access to God. Many will come to saving conclusions about God, said the deists, for the truths about him in nature are self-evident. In *Miscellany* 1338, Edwards is making the case, against the deists, that human reason is insufficient and that special revelation is absolutely necessary. Surprisingly, he meets the deist challenge with the affirmation that this revelation is available to nearly every person in the world (through the *prisca theologia*), even if they do not have the Bible.

Edwards begins by affirming "God's moral government of a kingdom or society";[51] that is, God reigns over the nations of the earth, giving and enforcing laws, "threatening the just punishments and promising the most suitable and wise rewards."[52] And how do these societies know God's laws and the consequences of obedience and disobedience? It is through God's revelation, the Word of God. Likely, he is thinking of nations like England and America when he says that there should be "conversation" between these societies and God. By conversation, Edwards means that communication "is maintained by God's word on his part and prayer on ours."[53] God speaks to mankind and mankind speaks to God. By revela-

---

50. Calvin makes the distinction that through general revelation we might come to know about God as Creator, but only through special revelation (Scripture) will we come to know God as Redeemer, and thus be saved. While it is true that God's creation bears witness to his character, "it is needful that another and better help be added to direct us aright to the very Creator of the universe. It was not in vain, then, that he added the light of his Word by which to become known unto salvation" (Calvin, *Institutes*, 1:69, 70).

51. Edwards, *Works*, 23:345.

52. Ibid., 23:346.

53. Edwards, *Works*, 23:350.

tion, man is shown what he "is to aim at with respect to God, who stands in no need of us and can't be in the least dependent on us."[54]

As God is the ruler and we are the ruled, he governs us. "If we have offended and deserved judgment," writes Edwards, "it must be known on what terms we may be forgiven and restored to favor, and how far we may be restored to favor, and what benefits of favor we shall receive if we are reconciled."[55] But there would be no hope of ever knowing these things without special revelation from God. "Men would undoubtedly forever be at a loss what God expects from us and what we may expect from him."[56] Simply put, unaided human reason is unable to discover these things about God through general revelation.

The deists would agree that God is the "Head of society" and the "supreme governor," but they believed they would be judged by "the laws of nature" not the laws allegedly revealed in Scripture.[57] Consequently, many deists looked forward to heaven, "a most perfect and happy union with God their Head."[58] But Edwards contested the deist notion of a God who created the world as "some piece of his workmanship" and then withdrew forever so that "no word ever should pass, or anything of that nature and no word left behind in writing, nor any word ever spoken left in the memory."[59] The deists were confident that they were on friendly terms with God. Edwards was confident they were not.

At this point in the notebook entry, Edwards anticipates the first deist objection. The deists agree that God "does maintain a moral government over all mankind," but most of the world has no revelation. Therefore, they concluded, revelation is not necessary for his moral government. But Edwards clarifies that what he has said so far in *Miscellany* 1338 about revelation concerns a society "where the union between king and subjects is not broken or dissolved."[60] He has not been speaking of a "country of rebels who have forsaken their lawful sovereign" and "cast off his government."[61] That is a different case.

54. Edwards, *Works*, 347.
55. Ibid.
56. Ibid.
57. Ibid., 349.
58. Ibid., 350.
59. Ibid., 351.
60. Ibid., 353.
61. Ibid., 354.

A country of rebels, though they cast off his government, and defy him, are "still under the king's power and moral dominion in some sense,"[62] for he is able to "conquer, subdue, judge and punish them for their rebellion." However, because they have broken off from their king, the king is not required to maintain conversation (including special revelation) with them any longer. In this case, "the union ceases between God and man by which they should be of one society."[63] As long as they remain "obstinate in their rebellion," justice does not demand God "to publish among them ways and terms of reconciliation."[64] The only thing that justice requires of the king at this point is condemnation. This explains the state of much of the heathen world. They once had revelation (through the *prisca theologia*),[65] they rebelled against it, and God is not obligated to give them more.

It is important to note here that Edwards divided the world into the "heathen" and "those under the gospel,"[66] which would be "Christian nations" like England or America. In other words, Edwards often spoke, as he does here, of heathens at a national level, as well as on an individual level.

Now comes the pivotal quote. It is at this point that Edwards speaks of the "union between God and the heathen world."[67] There is still hope for many of them. Though the union is broken, it may not be, in some

62. Edwards, *Works*, 354.

63. Ibid., 354.

64. Ibid.

65. I am not necessarily arguing here to prove Edwards's understanding of the *prisca theologia*. I am only arguing that Edward's understanding of it is key to interpreting *Miscellany* 1338.

66. Consider the following excerpts from Edwards's sermon on Revelation 3:15, delivered in 1729: "We can't fairly draw such a consequence from the words of [our] text, as that the best, the most sober and civilized of natural men that live under the gospel are worse and more abominable to God than the worst of the heathen . . . Therefore those that have a heart of unbelief, they have the hearts of heathen. Those that live under the gospel and profess to be Christians, that yet do not really believe the great truths of Christianity, that are not heartily convinced that Jesus Christ is the Son of God and the Savior of the world, ben't really persuaded of that future state and those invisible things the gospel speaks of: such as [these] never truly embrace Jesus Christ . . . The heathen very commonly lived in a very great degree of indulgence of their lusts, as we learn by many passages of the New Testament. And we are particularly informed in the latter part of the first chapter of Romans [that] the heathen, they walk in the vanity of their mind . . . And it is no wonder that they are so, for they are destitute of those restraints that those that live under the gospel have." (Edwards, "A Man Had Better Be a Heathen." Italics mine.)

67. Edwards, *Works*, 23:354.

nations, "utterly broken."[68] There are degrees of severed relationships. As I read Edwards at this point, I think of damaged limbs in an orchard after a severe storm.[69] Though mangled, hanging from the tree, they remain connected by enough fibers so as to be reparable and fruitful once again. They are not "utterly broken." There is still hope, "a possibility of their being reconciled."[70] The current flow of sap is not sufficient to save the limb if left unattended, but there is a possibility of the limb being braced, mended, secured to the life-giving tree, and eventually, fruitful. In some parts of the heathen world, the rebellion was more egregious than others, and thus, some unions were more "broken" than others. But for many heathen nations, "there is a possibility of being reconciled" and "receiving the benefit of divine revelation."[71]

The question is this: What does Edwards mean by reconciliation? Is he speaking of individual sinners being reconciled to God through faith, led to salvation by the remnants of revelation in the *prisca theologia*, thus proving that explicit knowledge of Christ is unnecessary for salvation? That would be the inclusivist view.

Or is he saying that if these obstinate rebels seek reconciliation with him and "inquire after his will,"[72] God, the benevolent King, will cease his policy of non-communication with them and release his revelation. If they seek reconciliation, will he not "publish among them the ways and terms of reconciliation"[73] by sending his messengers, preachers and missionaries, with the gospel to their dark land? If so, then when they explic-

---

68. Edwards, *Works*, 23:354.

69. I cannot prove Edwards has an orchard in mind here, but I am certain that Edwards had used an apple orchard as a metaphor in a sermon to the Indians at Stockbridge in June 1751 on Luke 13:7. "The people that live under the Gospel are as it were God's orchard . . . the teaching advice and warnings . . . are like the Husbandman's taking Care of his orchard . . . the fruit that God expects is the Fruit [of a] Good heart and a holy Life." Some trees do not bear good fruit. Sometimes God "takes much Pains; waits a great while—many years. But when He sees—then he cuts it down." (MS Sermon on Luke 13:7 (1751), 1–3. Edwards is specifically referring here to people who have heard the Gospel, but the broader principle might be this: If people do not positively respond to the revelation of God, who owns and tends the orchard, God's patience will eventually run out. On the other hand, a positive response to the revelation (regardless of the extent of the revelation) might be met with a positive response from God in the form of more revelation.

70. Edwards, *Works* 23:355.

71. Ibid.

72. Ibid., 23:354.

73. Ibid.

itly hear the gospel and receive it, having been prepared by the remnants of revelation in their culture, they will be reconciled to their king forever. That would be the exclusivist view.

Edwards's main point, which is easy to lose in this discussion, is that the heathen world is not full of people "destitute of all benefit of divine revelation"[74] as the deists claimed. From the descendants of Noah, revelation was handed down by tradition and much was borrowed from the Jews. Creation also bears witness to the Creator's magnificence. These are God's merciful gifts "to convince them that there was a divine revelation extant, sufficient to induce 'em to seek after it . . . to draw men's attention to it."[75]

However, for those "nations that are separated from the true God and live in open and obstinate and full rejection of him as their supreme moral governor,"[76] though they may have a remnant of revelation available to them, that revelation becomes the grounds of their condemnation in judgment. Theirs was a willful rebellion. They knew what they should do, and they did not do it. Edwards concludes that in those "parts of the world which have been destitute of revelation," there is a "blindness and delusion"[77] which is evidence that revelation is indeed necessary for good moral order. That is the point, I think, which Edwards is trying to make in this entry. Not that people can be saved outside of explicit knowledge of Jesus Christ, but rather societies can respond to the King in such a way that induces him to graciously communicate with them so they might know how to be reconciled to him. But in the end, it is still necessary that the gospel be preached in these lands if people are to be saved.

GOD'S COMMON GRACE AND JUDGMENT IN HEATHEN NATIONS

Edwards says there is a "benefit of divine revelation."[78] McDermott understands this benefit to mean eternal salvation itself.[79] But divine revelation

74. Edwards, *Works*, 23:354.

75. Ibid., 23:355.

76. Ibid.

77. Ibid.

78. Ibid.

79. When McDermott comments on Edwards's reference to the "great benefits" of revelation to the heathen in *Miscellany* 1162, he flatly concludes that this "notion is incoherent unless it means they can be saved" (McDermott, *Jonathan Edwards Confronts the Gods*, 140, 141). I am attempting here to show the coherence of this notion if it does not

can have other benefits, such as the preparation to receive the gospel message that can in fact lead to salvation. Divine revelation can also benefit an entire culture. When a nation adheres to biblical principles in family life, social justice, sexual relationships, business, and government, there are many benefits that even unbelievers can enjoy. This is God's common grace which he extends even to the heathen nations.[80]

In *Miscellany* 1338, Edwards has asserted God's kingship over all the nations of the earth.[81] In common grace, God maintains order and restrains evil in these societies, even though they may have no saving knowledge of him. Some societies are relatively submissive to his rule, ordering their nation's laws roughly according to the moral laws of God revealed in Scripture. In other places Edwards has written about this undeserved kindness in relation to moral government. In *Miscellany* 864, he notes that God maintains moral government over all mankind (in both Christian and heathen lands) and that

> ... there should be some moral government maintained amongst
> men; because, without any, either in nations, provinces, towns, or
> families, and also without any divine government over the whole,
> the world of mankind would not subsist, but would destroy itself
> ... Often the wicked prosper ... They are mounted on thrones;
> while the righteous remain in cottages.[82]

The point seems to be this: God governs all people, even those who do not and will not have eternal life. He graciously gives their society order, restraining evil in their nation, granting peace to their borders and rain to their fields, as they submit to his moral order, which is summarized in the Ten Commandments. He continues to show great patience, granting undeserved extensions before he pours out his wrath.[83] Submitting to God's moral order results in a more just and prosperous society, even if it does

---

mean they can be saved without explicit knowledge of the gospel.

80. Even Clark Pinnock, an advocate of the inclusivist view, acknowledges the doctrine of common grace that makes for a more decent life: "Calvinists use the idea of common grace to account for goodness and justice in sinners, while Wesleyans prefer to speak of prevenient grace. Either way, it means that the grace of God mitigates the effects of sin in human life and preserves the creature from self-destruction" (Pinnock, *A Wideness in God's Mercy*, 103, 121).

81. Edwards, *Works*, 23:355. God, says Edwards, is the "supreme moral governor."

82. Ibid., 20:105.

83. 2 Peter 3:9.

not result in eternal salvation. Recognizing the good sense of the laws can be beneficial, even if one does not come to love the Lawgiver.

However, a society can defy and rebel against the moral government of God to the extent that they "cast off his government."[84] Their rebellion against his moral order reaches such a degree that God, as King of the nations, visits them with punishment and judgment. They are "broken off from their king," and "in that case, society ceases."[85] God can and will destroy whole nations, as the sovereign ruler over his creation. Though Edwards mentions no Scripture references in *Miscellany* 1338, the description of the devolution of culture in the first chapter of Romans might fit here. As a culture moves farther away from God's moral order, God, in judgment, gives them up to the next level of immorality, loosening his restraining hand on depraved mankind, until finally, they go too far, and he removes them from the face of the earth. Their "society ceases." In the words of Paul, "God gave them over to a depraved mind, to do what ought not to be done,"[86] and the result is a culture in a downward moral spiral, marked by self-destruction. Recorded history is a catalogue of such nations who dared to challenge God's moral reign.[87]

A DIFFICULT QUOTE IN A NEW LIGHT

The one thing we might all agree on is that *Miscellany* 1338 is not as clear as we would like it to be. It is, after all, an entry in a private journal that is unpolished and unfinished. Edwards could not have envisioned some of the best minds in Ivy League schools hanging on his every scribbled word almost three hundred years later. He did not intend it for publication, but

---

84. Edwards, *Works*, 23:354.

85. Ibid.

86. Romans 1:28.

87. Edwards shows this in *History of Redemption* by reference to the heathen nations of Babylon, Persia, Greece, and Rome. "The strength and glory of Satan's kingdom in these four mighty monarchies, appeared in it greatest height; for, being the monarchies of the heathen world, the strength of them was the strength of Satan's kingdom" (Edwards, *The Works of Jonathan Edwards*, 1:562). Also, "The heathen very commonly lived in a very great degree of indulgence of their lusts, as we learn by many passages of the New Testament. And we are particularly informed in the latter part of the first chapter of Romans [that] the heathen, they walk in the vanity of their mind . . . And it is no wonder that they are so, for they are destitute of those restraints that those that live under the gospel have" (Edwards, "A Man Had Better Be a Heathen").

rather intended to record his thoughts on an important topic, likely with a view to using them in a later treatise.

With these things in mind, now look at Edwards's words in *Miscellany* 1338 in a larger immediate context than McDermott affords his readers (in both his book and his response to Gilbert) and see if it means something different to you than it does to him:

> So far as the union between God and the heathen world has not been utterly broken, so far they have not been left utterly destitute of all benefit of divine revelation. They are not so entirely and absolutely cast off but that there is a possibility of their being reconciled. And God has so ordered the case that there is an equal possibility of their receiving the benefit of divine revelation.[88]

The benefit of divine revelation can include a morally ordered society where evil is restrained and justice is done. No society is perfect, but some protect the innocent and punish the guilty better than others. Some observe God's standards for sexuality more closely than others. The union between God and the heathen world, like the union of a King to his subjects or a head to a body, will be strained almost to the point of severance, but as long as there is not yet an "utter breach of the union,"[89] there is still hope that God might be merciful and spare that society long enough for the gospel to come to them through obedient Christians (especially missionaries) preaching the gospel. In the end, McDermott is forced to admit that "Edwards is not dogmatic about the heathen being saved through truth they receive in the *prisca theologia.*"[90]

To summarize, in *Miscellany* 1338, when Edwards refers to a "possibility of their being reconciled," perhaps he means that the cultures in many non-Christian nations are not so far gone, so far in rebellion, as to be without any hope. Maybe Edwards is saying that God has not totally "cast off" these people so that they are beyond all reach. If only the church would obey the Great Commission, if only the gospel could be preached to them, if only they could hear of Jesus, if only missionaries could go to them, many would see the supremacy of Jesus Christ and receive him as Savior. The revelation that they had received through the *prisca theologia* serves to prepare them to receive Jesus as their mediator if the gospel

---

88. Edwards, *Works*, 23:354–55.
89. Ibid., 354.
90. McDermott, "Response to Gilbert," 80.

comes to them. This is an interpretation of Edwards's words that is far more consistent with his entire body of work than the novel interpretation McDermott advances. If this is the case, there is nothing here about Edwards that is either "strange" or "new."[91]

A MISSIONARY'S PERSPECTIVE

It is often overlooked that Jonathan Edwards was a missionary. When he took the gospel to the Indians of western Massachusetts in 1751, here is what he told them:

> You have a better opportunity than many poor Indians. You have the Gospel preached to you and the way of salvation by Christ when they know nothing about it. They live in darkness and you live in the light. God gives you an opportunity by bringing you here to this Place. Therefore, Improve this opportunity . . . . Tis from the Great kindness of God to you that you have not died before now in your sins and gone to Hell.[92]

That sounds like Edwards had harbored no hope for the salvation of those Indians in Massachusetts who had not heard of Jesus in 1751. It also sounds like something William Carey might have said to the Indians of India in 1793. And finally, it sounds like we have a lot of work to do if we are to reach the nations of the earth with the message of hope in Jesus Christ. May God bless our missionaries.

---

91. I do not pretend to deal with McDermott's entire proposal here. McDermott has made a positive contribution to Edwards studies and offers a great deal of careful scholarship in his works. Yet, there are commendable responses to his conclusions about Edwards's alleged change of mind concerning the salvation of those who have never heard the gospel. In addition to Greg Gilbert, several scholars have identified some of the weaknesses in McDermott's arguments. Oliver Crisp notes that the Edwards presented by McDermott "is certainly a stalwart defender of orthodoxy against deism. He is clearly an apologist for the particularity of Christianity. But he is not an inclusivist . . . And McDermott is unable to demonstrate otherwise" (Crisp, "Reviews," 83). John Bambaro is also unconvinced. After a critique of McDermott's thesis, he concludes that Edwards did not believe in a "larger hope" outside of the gospel proclamation. Instead, he was part of an "earlier orthodox tradition not embarrassed about the confessional doctrines that say that those who die unevangelized or unconverted are destined to eternal damnation. He did not attempt to lay out a new paradigm to suggest anything otherwise" (Bombaro, "Dispositional," 157).

92. Edwards, MS Sermon on Hebrews 9:27 (January 1751), 31.

Bibliography

Adams, John. *The Diary and Autobiography of John Adams*. 4 vols. Edited by L. H. Butterfield. Cambridge: Harvard University Press, 1961.

Adams, John. "Letter to Benjamin Rush, January 21, 1810." In *John Adams*, 2 vols., by Page Smith. Garden City: Doubleday and Company, 1962. 2:2078.

Adams, Samuel. *The Writings of Samuel Adams*. 4 vols. Edited by Harry Alonzo Cushing. N.p: Putnam and Sons, 1908. Reprint, New York: Octagon Books, 1968.

Al-Mawardi. "The Laws of Islamic Governance." In *The Legacy of Jihad: Islamic Holy War and the Fate of Non-Muslims*, edited by Andrew Bostom, 190–95. Amherst, NY: Prometheus Books, 2005.

Argetsinger, Amy and Roxanne Roberts. "But It's Thomas Jefferson's Koran!" *Washington Post*, January 3, 2007. CO3. http://www.washingtonpost.com/wpdyn/ content/ article/2007/01/03/AR2007010300075.html (accessed February 2, 2008).

"The Barbary Treaties: Treaty of Peace and Friendship, Signed at Tripoli, November 4, 1796." Avalon Project at Yale Law School. http://www.yale.edu/ lawweb/avalon/ diplomacy/barbary/bar1796t.htm (accessed February 21, 2008).

Barna Group. "Americans' Bible Knowledge Is In the Ballpark, But Often Off Base." July 12, 2000.http://www.barna.org/FlexPage.aspx?Page=BarnaUpdate&BarnaUpdateID=66 (accessed April 14, 2008).

———. "Beliefs: Heaven and Hell." http://www.barna.org/FlexPage.aspx?Page =Topic &TopicID=3 (accessed April 14, 2008).

Bat Ye'or. *The Decline of Eastern Christianity under Islam: From Jihad to Dhimmitude*. Translated from the French by Miriam Kochan and David Littman. Cranbury, NJ: Fairleigh Dickinson University Press, 1996.

Bauckham, Richard. *Jesus and the Eyewitnesses: The Gospels as Eyewitness Testimony*. Grand Rapids: William B. Eerdman's Publishing Company, 2006.

Blomberg, Craig. *The Historical Reliability of the Gospels*. Downers Grove, IL: InterVarsity Press Academic, 1987.

Bock, Darrell. *The Missing Gospels: Unearthing the Truth Behind Alternative Christianities*. Nashville: Thomas Nelson Publishers, 2006.

———. *Studying the Historical Jesus: A Guide to Sources and Methods*. Grand Rapids: Baker Academic, 2002.

Bombaro, John. "Dispositional Peculiarity, History, and Edwards's Evangelistic Appeal to Self Love." *Westminster Theological Journal* 66 (2004): 121–57.

Borg, Marcus and N. T. Wright. "The Resurrection of Jesus: Interview of Marcus Borg and N. T. Wright, March 26, 1999." By Bob Abernethy. *Religion and Ethics Newsweekly*. Episode No. 230. http://www.pbs.org/wnet/religionandethics/ week230/cover.html (accessed January 18, 2008).

Bostom, Andrew G. *The Legacy of Jihad: Islamic Holy War and the Fate of Non-Muslims.* New York: Prometheus Books, 2005.

Boudinot, Elias. *The Age of Revelation Or the Age of Reason Shewen to Be an Age of Infidelity.* Philadelphia: Asbury Dickins, 1801. http://olivercowdery.com/texts/boud1790.htm (accessed April 3, 2008).

———. *Elias Boudinot's Journey to Boston.* Edited by Milton Halsey Thomas. Princeton, NJ: Princeton University Press, 1955.

Breitenbach, William. "Religious Affections and Religious Affectations." In *Benjamin Franklin, Jonathan Edwards, and the Representation of American Culture,* edited by Barbara B. Oberg and Harry S. Stout, 13–26. New York: Oxford University Press, 1993.

Brookhiser, Richard. *What Would the Founders Do?* New York: Basic Books, 2006.

Bruce, F. F. *Are the New Testament Documents Reliable?* Grand Rapids: Eerdman's Publishing Co., 1954.

Butler, Carolyn Kleiner. "Sermon With a Smile." *U.S. News & World Report,* October 3, 2005, 57–58.

Calvin, John. *Institutes of the Christian Religion.* 2 vols. Edited by John T. McNeill. Translated by Ford Lewis Battles. Philadelphia: Westminster Press, 1960.

Car, Harold. "User Friendly Faith." *Christian History* 16.3 (1997): 20–22.

Craig, William Lane. *The Historical Argument For the Resurrection of Jesus During the Deist Controversy.* Vol. 23, *Texts and Studies in Religion.* Lewiston, NY: Edwin Mellen Press, 1985.

Cranfield, C. E. B. *A Critical and Exegetical Commentary on the Epistle to the Romans.* Edinburgh: T&T Clark Limited, 1975.

Crossan, John Dominic. "Opening Statement." In *Will the Real Jesus Please Stand Up?* edited by Paul Copan, 33–39. Grand Rapids: Baker Books, 1998.

———. *Historical Jesus: The Life of a Mediterranean Jewish Peasant.* New York: Harper Collins, 1991.

Crisp, Oliver. "Reviews." *International Journal of Systematic Theology* 4.1 (March 2002): 82–83.

Dawkins, Richard. *The God Delusion.* Boston: Houghton Mifflin Company, 2006.

Eddy, Paul Rhodes and Gregory A. Boyd. *The Jesus Legend: A Case for the Historical Reliability of the Synoptic Jesus Tradition.* Grand Rapids: Baker Academic, 2007.

Edwards, Jonathan. "A Man Had Better Be a Heathen: Lukewarm Christians." 1729. Sermon on Revelation 3:15. http://edwards.yale.edu/archive/documents/page?document_id=5541&search_id=&source_type=edited&pagenumber=1 (accessed May 20, 2008).

———. "It Concerns All To Determine Who Jesus Was." 1749. Sermon on Matthew 16:15. http://edwards.yale.edu/archive/documents/page?document_id =8304&search_id=7155121&source_type=edited&pagenumber=1 (accessed January 18, 2008).

———. "Jesus Christ Full of Grace and Truth." 1730. Sermon on John 1:14. http://edwards.yale.edu/archive/documents/page?source_type=edited&pagenumber=18&document_id=5995&body_id=148181&search_id=8188102 (accessed April 15, 2008).

———. "None Are Saved By Their Own Righteousness." 1729. Sermon on Titus 3:5. http://edwards.yale.edu/archive/documents/page?document_id =5470&search_id=8188102&source_type=edited&pagenumber=6 (accessed April 18, 2008).

———. Sermon notes. Jonathan Edwards Center, Yale University.

MS Sermon on 2 Peter 1:16 (1729).

MS Sermon on Matthew 22:14 (1732).

MS Sermon on Luke 13:7 (1751).

MS Sermon on Hebrews 9:27 (1750/51 and March 1752).

MS "Controversies" Notebook.

MS "Speech to the Mohawks" (1751) [Copy at Yale; Original at Andover Newton Theological Seminary]

———. *The Works of Jonathan Edwards.* 2 vols. Edited by Edward Hickman. London, 1834. Reprint, Edinburgh: Banner of Truth Trust, 1988.

———. *The Works of Jonathan Edwards.* John E. Smith, general editor. New Haven: Yale University Press, 1957–.

Vol. 1: *Freedom of the Will.* Edited by Paul Ramsey. 1957.

Vol. 2: *Religious Affections.* Edited by John E. Smith. 1959.

Vol. 3: *Original Sin.* Edited by Clyde A. Holbrook. 1970.

Vol. 10: *Sermons and Discourses 1720–1728.* Edited by Wilson H. Kimnach. 1992.

Vol. 13: *The Miscellanies, a-500.* Edited by Thomas A. Schafer. 1994.

Vol. 14: *Sermons and Discourses 1723–1729.* Edited by Kenneth P. Minkema. 1997.

Vol. 15: *Notes on Scripture.* Edited by Stephen J. Stein. 1998.

Vol. 16: *Letters and Personal Writings.* Edited by George S. Claghorn. 1998.

Vol. 18: *The Miscellanies 501–832.* Edited by Ava Chamberlain. 2000.

Vol. 19: *Sermons and Discourses 1734–1738.* Edited by M.X. Lesser. 2001.

Vol. 20: *The Miscellanies 833–1152.* Edited by Amy Plantinga Pauw. 2002.

Vol. 22: *Sermons and Discourses 1739—1742.* Edited by Harry S. Stout and Nathan Hatch. 2003.

Vol. 23: *The Miscellanies 1153–1360.* Edited by Douglas A. Sweeney. 2004.

Vol. 24: *The Blank Bible.* Two Parts. Edited by Stephen J. Stein. 2006.

Eusebius. *Ecclesiastical History.* Translated by C. F. Cruse. Peabody, MA: Hendrickson Publishers, 1998.

Ferling, John. *Adams vs. Jefferson: The Tumultuous Election of 1800.* New York: Oxford University Press, 2004.

Franklin, Benjamin. *The Autobiography of Benjamin Franklin.* Edited by Leonard W. Labaree, Ralph L. Ketcham, Helen C. Boatfield, and Helene H. Fineman. New Haven: Yale University Press, 1964.

———. *The Papers of Benjamin Franklin.* 38 vols. Edited by Leonard W. Labaree. New Haven: Yale University Press, 1959–.

———. *The Works of Benjamin Franklin.* 8 vols. Edited by Jared Sparks. Boston: Billiard, Gray, and Company, 1837.

———. *Writings.* Edited by J. A. Leo. New York: Library of America, 1987.

Funk, Robert W., Roy W. Hoover and the Jesus Seminar. *The Five Gospels: What Did Jesus Really Say? The Search for the Authentic Word of Jesus.* New York: Polebridge Press, 1993.

Gallup Research. "Americans Remain Very Religious, But Not Necessarily in Conventional Ways." December 24, 1999. http://www.gallup.com/poll/3385/ Americans-Remain-Very-Religious-Necessarily-Conventional-Ways.aspx (accessed, April 15, 2008).

George, Timothy. *Faithful Witness: The Life and Witness of William Carey.* N.p.: New Hope Publishers, 1992.

———. *Is the Father of Jesus the God of Muhammad?* Grand Rapids: Zondervan, 2002.

Bibliography

Gilbert, Greg D. "The Nations Will Worship: Jonathan Edwards and the Salvation of the Heathen." *Trinity Journal* 23.11 (2002): 53–76.

Grudem, Wayne. *Systematic Theology: An Introduction to Biblical Doctrine*. Grand Rapids: Zondervan, 1994.

Gottschalk, Louis. *Understanding History: A Primer of Historical Method*. New York: Knopf, 1963.

Habermas, Gary R. and Michael R. Licona. *The Case for the Resurrection of Jesus*. Grand Rapids: Kregel, 2004.

Harris, Sam. *The End of Faith: Religion, Terror, and the Future of Reason*. New York: Norton and Company, 2004.

———. *Letter to a Christian Nation*. New York: Alfred A. Knopf, 2006.

Hick, John. "A Pluralist View." In *Four Views on Salvation in a Pluralistic World*, edited by Dennis L. Okholm and Timothy R. Phillips, 27–92. Grand Rapids: Zondervan, 1995.

Hitchens, Christopher. *God is Not Great: How Religion Poisons Everything*. New York: Twelve, Hatchette Book Group, 2007.

Hodgson, Godfrey. *A Great and Godly Adventure: The Pilgrims and the Myth of the First Thanksgiving*. New York: Public Affairs, 2006.

Holmes, David. *The Faiths of the Founding Fathers*. New York: Oxford University Press, 2006.

Huntington, Samuel P. *The Clash of Civilizations and the Remaking of World Order*. New York: Touchstone, 1996.

Isaacson, Walter. *Benjamin Franklin: An American Life*. New York: Simon and Schuster, 2003.

Jacoby, Jeff. "The Boston Mosque's Saudi Connection." *Boston Globe*, January 10, 2007. http://www.boston.com/news/globe/editorial_opinion/oped/articles/2007/ 01/10/ the_boston_mosques_saudi_connection?mode=PF (accessed May 12, 2008).

Jefferson, Thomas. "Letter to Joseph Priestly." In *The Jefferson Bible*, edited by Forrest Church, 9–10. Boston: Beacon Press, 1989.

———. "Letter to the Danbury Baptists." *Library of Congress Information Bulletin* 57.6 (June 1998). http://www.loc.gov/loc/lcib/9806/danpre.html (accessed May 20, 2008).

———. "The Life and Morals of Jesus of Nazareth." In *The Jefferson Bible*, edited by Forrest Church, 32–147. Boston: Beacon Press, 1989.

———. *The Papers of Thomas Jefferson*. 34 vols. Edited by Julian P. Boyd. Princeton, NJ: Princeton University Press, 1950–.

Josephus, Flavius. *Complete Works of Flavius Josephus*. Translated by William Whiston. Edinburgh, Scotland: 1867. Re-published, Grand Rapids: Kregel Publications, 1985.

Karsh, Efraim. *Islamic Imperialism: A History*. New Haven: Yale University Press, 2007.

Komoszewski, J. Ed, M. James Sawyer, and Daniel B. Wallace. *Reinventing Jesus: How Contemporary Skeptics Miss the Real Jesus and Mislead Popular Culture*. Grand Rapids: Kregel Publications, 2006.

The Koran. 5th rev. ed. Translated by N. J. Daewood. New York: Penguin Classics, 1999.

Levin, David. "Reason, Rhythm, and Style." In *Benjamin Franklin, Jonathan Edwards, and the Representation of American Culture*, edited by Barbara B. Oberg and Harry S. Stout, 171–85. New York: Oxford University Press, 1993.

Lewis, C. S. *Mere Christianity*. New York: MacMillan Publishing Company, 1952.

Lutzer, Edwin. *Ten Lies About God: And How You May Already Be Deceived*. Nashville: Word, 2000.

Marsden, George. *Jonathan Edwards: A Life*. New Haven: Yale University Press, 2003.

———. *The Soul of the American University: From Protestant Establishment to Established Non-Belief.* New York: Oxford University Press, 1994.

May, Henry. *The Enlightenment in America.* New York: Oxford University Press, 1976.

Mayer, Henry. *A Son of Thunder: Patrick Henry and the American Republic.* Charlottesville: University Press of Virginia, 1991.

McBeth, H. Leon. *The Baptist Heritage: Four Centuries of Baptist Witness.* Nashville: Broadman Press, 1987.

McCullough, John. *John Adams.* New York: Simon and Schuster Paperbacks, 2001.

McDermott, Gerald. *God's Rivals: Why Has God Allowed Different Religions? Insights From the Bible and the Early Church.* Downers Grove, IL: IVP Academic, 2007.

———. *Jonathan Edwards Confronts the Gods: Christian Theology, Enlightenment Religion, and Non-Christian Faiths.* New York: Oxford University Press, 2000.

———. "Response to Gilbert: 'The Nations Will Worship: Jonathan Edwards and the Salvation of the Heathen.'" *Trinity Journal* 23.11 (2002): 77-80.

McDowell, Josh. *Evidence that Demands a Verdict: Historical Evidences for the Christian Faith.* N.p.: Campus Crusade for Christ, 1973.

McGirk, Tim. "Jesus 'Tomb' Controversy Reopened." *Time Magazine* January 16, 2008. http://www.time.com/time/world/article/0,8599,1704299,00.html?cnn=yes (accessed: May 5, 2008).

McLaren, Brian D. *A Generous Orthodoxy.* Grand Rapids: Zondervan, 2004.

Meyer, Donald. "Religious Concerns." *Critical Essays on Benjamin Franklin*, edited by Melvin H. Buxbaum. Boston: G. K. Hall and Co., 1987.

Monaghan, Frank. *John Jay: Defender of Liberty.* New York: Bobbs-Merrill Company, 1935.

Neuhaus, Richard John. *The Naked Public Square: Religion and Democracy in America.* 2nd ed. Grand Rapids: Eerdman's Publishing Co., 1984.

———. "While We're At It." *First Things* 171 (March 2007): 65.

New England's First Fruits (1640). *Collections of the Massachusetts Historical Society, 1792*, 242–248. http://www.constitution.org/primarysources/firstfruits.html (accessed: May 18, 2008).

Noll, Mark. *America's God: From Jonathan Edwards to Abraham Lincoln.* New York: Oxford University Press, 2002.

———. *Christians in the American Revolution.* Washington, D.C.: Christian University Press, 1977.

Novak, Michael and Jane Novak. *Washington's God: Religion, Liberty, and the Founding of Our Country.* New York: Basic Books, 2006.

Oberg, Barbara B. and Harry S. Stout, editors. *Benjamin Franklin, Jonathan Edwards, and the Representation of American Culture.* New York: Oxford University Press, 1993.

Okholm, Dennis L. and Timothy R. Phillips, editors. *Four Views on Salvation in a Pluralistic World.* Grand Rapids: Zondervan, 1995.

Oren, Dan. "Stamp of Approval," *Yale Alumni Magazine* March 2001. http://www.yalealumnimagazine.com/issues/01_03/seal.html (accessed May 17, 2008).

Osteen, Joel. "Interview with Joel Osteen." *Larry King Live.* June 20, 2002. transcripts.cnn.com/TRANSCRIPTS/0506/20/lkl.01.html (accessed April 18, 2008).

Ostling, Richard. "Heaven and Hell." *Decatur* (AL) *Daily*, June 17, 2006.

Packer, J. I. "Evangelicals and the Way of Salvation: New Challenges to the Gospel—Universalism, and Justification by Faith." In *Evangelical Affirmations*, edited by Kenneth Kantzer and Carl F. H. Henry, 107–36. Grand Rapids: Zondervan, 1990.

Pagden, Anthony. *Worlds at War: The 2,500-Year Struggle Between East and West*. New York: Random House, 2008.

Paine, Thomas. *The Writings of Thomas Paine*. 4 vols. Edited by Moncure Daniel Conway. New York: AMS Press, 1967. Reprinted from the edition of 1894–1896.

———. *The Age of Reason: Being an Investigation of True and Fabulous Theology*. New York: The Truth Seeker Company, 1898.

Pinnock, Clark. "An Inclusivist View." In *Four Views on Salvation in a Pluralistic World*, edited by Dennis L. Okholm and Timothy R. Phillips, 93–148. Grand Rapids: Zondervan, 1995.

———. *A Wideness in God's Mercy: The Finality of Jesus Christ in A World of Religions*. Grand Rapids: Zondervan, 1992.

Piper, John. *Let the Nations Be Glad: The Supremacy of God in Missions*. 2nd ed. Grand Rapids: Baker Academic, 2003.

Puls, Mark. *Samuel Adams: Father of the American Revolution*. New York: Palgrave MacMillan, 2006.

Rand, Edward Kennard. "Liberal Education in Seventeenth-Century Harvard." *The New England Quarterly* 6.3 (1933): 525–51.

Roberts, Mark. *Can We Trust the Gospels? Investigating the Reliability of Matthew, Mark, Luke, and John*. Wheaton: Crossway Books, 2007.

Strobel, Lee. *The Case for the Real Jesus: A Journalist Investigates Current Attacks on the Identity of Christ*. Grand Rapids: Zondervan, 2007.

Swartley, Willard M. "War." In *Encyclopedia of Early Christianity*. 2nd ed. Edited by Everett Ferguson, 1171–73. New York: Garland Publishing, 1998.

Sweet, Leonard. "The Laughter of One: Sweetness and Light in Franklin and Edwards." In *Benjamin Franklin, Jonathan Edwards, and the Representation of American Culture*, edited by Barbara B. Oberg and Harry S. Stout, 114–33. New York: Oxford University Press, 1993.

Tacitus. *The Complete Works of Tacitus*. Translated by Alfred John Church and William Jackson Brodribb. New York: The Modern Library, 1942.

Thirty-Nine Articles of Religion. http://anglicansonline.org/basics/thirty-nine _articles. html (accessed April 14, 2008).

Tobin, Gary A. and Aryeh K. Weinberg. "Religious Beliefs and Behavior of College Faculty." *Institute for Jewish and Community Research*, 2007. http://jewishresearch.org/PDFs2/ FacultyReligion07.pdf (accessed May 18, 2008).

Van Doren, Carl. *Benjamin Franklin*. New York: Viking, 1980 (original text, 1938).

———. *Jane Mecom: The Favorite Sister of Benjamin Franklin—Her Life Here First Fully Narrated from Their Entire Surviving Correspondence*. New York: Viking Press, 1950.

Waldman, Steven. *Founding Faith: Providence, Politics, and the Birth of Religious Freedom in America*. New York: Random House, 2008.

Wesley, John. *A Calm Address to Our American Colonies*. 1775. Reprinted in *Christian History*, 15.2 (1996): 39.

Westminster Confession of Faith, Together with The Larger Catechism and the Shorter Catechism with Scripture Proofs. 3rd ed. Atlanta: The Committee for Christian Education and Publications, 1990.

Weststar Institute, "Mission." http://www.westarinstitute.org/Mission/mission.html (accessed March 18, 2008).

"Who Goes to Heaven?" Newsweek/Beliefnet poll. http://www.beliefnet.com/ story/173/ story_17353_1.html (accessed April 15, 2008).

Witherington, Ben. *What Have They Done With Jesus? Beyond Strange Theories and Bad History—Why We Can Trust the Bible.* San Francisco: Harper Collins, 2006.

Witherspoon, John. *The Works of John Witherspoon: Late President of the College at Princeton, New Jersey.* Harrisonburg, VA: Sprinkle Publications, 2006.

Wright, N. T. *The Resurrection of the Son of God.* Minneapolis: Fortress Press, 2003.

Zacks, Richard. *The Pirate Coast: Thomas Jefferson, the First Marines, and the Secret Mission of 1805.* New York: Hyperion, 2005.